A SOLDIER'S LIFE

General Sir Ian Hamilton

1853–1947

John Lee is an Executive Officer of the British Commission for Military History and has an MA in War Studies from King's College, London. He is widely known as a writer, lecturer and tour guide specializing in the operational history of the First World War. He lives in London with his wife, Celia, also a historian and biographer.

John Lee

A SOLDIER'S LIFE
General Sir Ian Hamilton
1853–1947

PAN BOOKS

First published 2000 by Macmillan

This edition published 2001 by Pan Books
an imprint of Macmillan Publishers Ltd
25 Eccleston Place, London SW1W 9NF
Basingstoke and Oxford
Associated companies throughout the world
www.macmillan.com

ISBN 0 330 48400 1

1 3 5 7 9 8 6 4 2

A CIP catalogue record for this book is available from
the British Library.

Typeset by SetSystems Ltd, Saffron Walden, Essex
Printed and bound in Great Britain by
Mackays of Chatham plc, Chatham, Kent

To my friend and mentor, Brian Bond,
Professor of Military History, King's College, London

And to a practitioner of amphibious warfare
who understands Ian Hamilton better than most others,
Major-General Julian Thompson, Royal Marines

Contents

Acknowledgements

This book would never have been begun without the help and encouragement of Professor Brian Bond, who introduced me to Ian Hamilton's life and times when I studied under him for an MA in War Studies at King's College, London. My subsequent inclusion in a seminar group looking at the historiography of the First World War made me see that a new biography of this highly misunderstood general was needed.

Though they might not realize it, two Royal Marines also helped me a great deal to clarify my ideas and more fully understand the problems posed by amphibious warfare – Major-General Julian Thompson and Captain Jim Beach.

The massive Ian Hamilton archives are kept at the Liddell Hart Centre for Military Archives, King's College, London, and my warmest thanks go to Patricia Methven and her staff for the several years of unfailingly good-natured help they have given me. Quotations from the Hamilton archives are made with the kind permission of The Trustees of the Liddell Hart Centre for Military Archives. Nigel Steel, then at the Department of Documents, Imperial War Museum, himself a 'Gallipoli' author of no mean repute, has also been a good friend. In a less personal but equally efficient way, the staff of the Public Records Office, Kew, are also to be thanked.

For keeping alive the memory of our military history, and for all the invitations to lecture and write for them, I thank the Gallipoli Association, the Western Front Association and the British Commission for Military History.

As news of my interests spread through the military history community, many friends came up with references and ideas to help the work along. They include, in alphabetical order, Jim Beach, Richard

Brooks, Brad King, Morris Le Fleming, Kate Mazur, Laurie Milner, Chris Page, Gary Sheffield, Keith Simpson, Nigel Steel and Julian Thompson.

And I was goaded along by some other friends who deplore Hamilton and his wasteful side-show; they too have had their part to play. Thank you Ian, Tony and Chris!

In the later stages of my research I received great help and encouragement from the grandchildren of Ian Hamilton's brother, Vereker – Helen, Alexander (and Sarah), and Ian (and Barbara).

The book has benefited enormously from two careful readings by Professor Brian Bond and Tony Cowan. J. R. Macleod spotted an error that has been corrected in this edition.

Any errors or infelicities of judgement are, of course, entirely the responsibility of the author.

Finally, I thank my dear wife, Celia. She began offering to help me 'translate' the handwriting of Lady Jean Hamilton, discovered her diaries and has now produced a magnificent companion biography, which is indispensable to all those who would really understand Sir Ian Hamilton.

List of Illustrations

Acknowledgements

Imperial War Museum, London: 7, 8, 9, 10, 11, 12, 13, 14, 15, 16, 17

Liddell Hart Centre for Military Archives, King's College, London: 1, 2, 3, 4, 5, 6, 18, 19, 20

List of Abbreviations

AG	Adjutant-General
AAG	Assistant Adjutant-General
ADC	Aide-de-camp
ANZAC	Australian and New Zealand Army Corps
BEF	British Expeditionary Force
CID	Committee of Imperial Defence
CIGS	Chief of the Imperial General Staff
C-in-C	Commander-in-Chief
CRA	Chief of Royal Artillery
DMO	Director of Military Operations
DMS	Director of Medical Services
DSO	Distinguished Service Order
GHQ	General Head Quarters
GOC	General Officer, Commanding
IG	Inspector General
ILH	Imperial Light Horse
KOSB	King's Own Scottish Borderers

MEF	Mediterranean Expeditionary Force
NCO	Non-Commissioned Officer
NPA	Newspaper Proprietors' Association
OTC	Officer Training Corps
PM	Prime Minister
PSC	Passed Staff College
QMG	Quartermaster-General
RHA	Royal Horse Artillery
RMA	Royal Military Academy
RN	Royal Navy
RND	Royal Naval Division
RSM	Regimental Sergeant-Major
TF	Territorial Force
VC	Victoria Cross

Maps

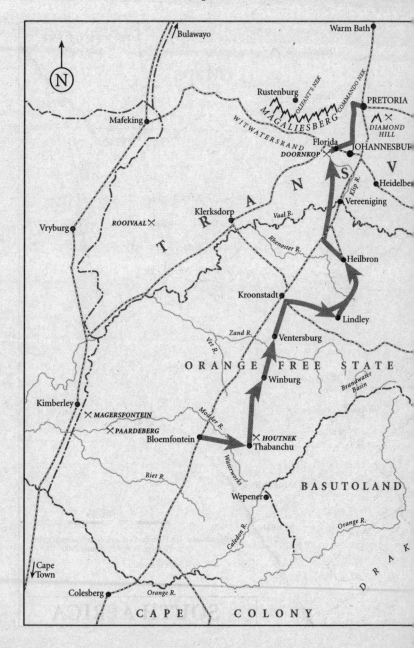

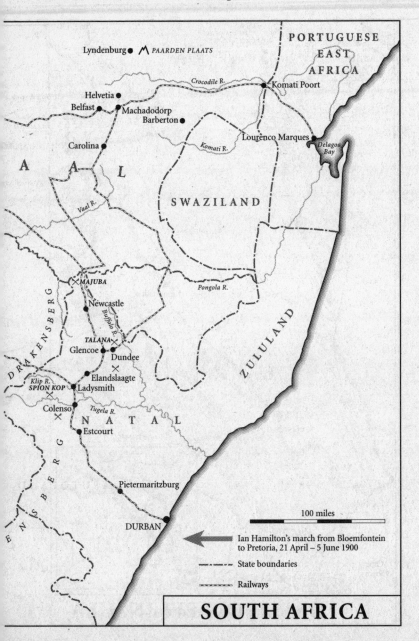

100 miles

Ian Hamilton's march from Bloemfontein
to Pretoria, 21 April – 5 June 1900

State boundaries

Railways

SOUTH AFRICA

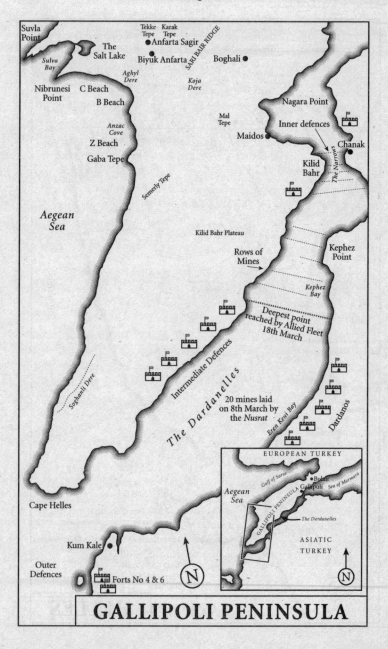

Suvla
Point

The
Salt Lake

*Sulva
Bay*

Tekke
Tepe

Karak
Tepe

●Anfarta Sagir

Biyuk Anfarta

SARI BAIR RIDGE

Boghali ●

Nibrunesi
Point

C Beach

B Beach

*Aghyl
Dere*

*Koja
Dere*

Nagara Point

Inner defences

Chanak ●

Mal
Tepe

Maidos ●

Kilid
Bahr

The Narrows

*Anzac
Cove*

Z Beach

Gaba Tepe

Semetly Tepe

*Aegean
Sea*

Kilid Bahr Plateau

Rows of
Mines

Kephez
Point

*Kephez
Bay*

Deepest point
reached by Allied Fleet
18th March

Soghanli Dere

Intermediate Defences

The Dardanelles

20 mines laid
on 8th March by
the *Nusrat*

Eren Keui Bay

Dardanos

Cape Helles

EUROPEAN TURKEY

Gulf of Saros

● Bulair

*Aegean
Sea*

Gallipoli

Sea of Marmara

GALLIPOLI PENINSULA

The Dardanelles

ASIATIC
TURKEY

Kum Kale ●

Outer
Defences

Forts No 4 & 6

N

N

GALLIPOLI PENINSULA

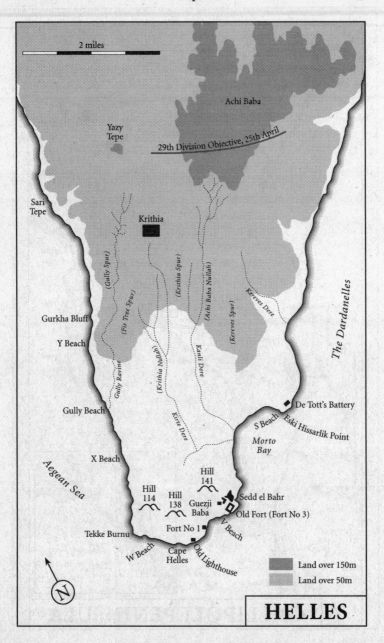

Achi Baba

Yazy
Tepe

29th Division Objective, 25th April

Sari
Tepe

Krithia

(Gully Spur)

(Fir Tree Spur)

(Krithia Spur)

(Achi Baba Nullah)

(Kereves Spur)

Kereves Dere

Gully Ravine

(Krithia Nullah)

Gurkha Bluff

Y Beach

Kanli Dere

The Dardanelles

Gully Beach

Kirte Dere

De Tott's Battery

S Beach Eski Hissarlik Point

*Morto
Bay*

X Beach

Aegean Sea

Hill
141

Hill
114

Hill
138

Guezji
Baba

Sedd el Bahr

Old Fort (Fort No 3)

Fort No 1

V Beach

Tekke Burnu

W Beach Cape
Helles Old Lighthouse

Land over 150m

Land over 50m

N

HELLES

2 miles

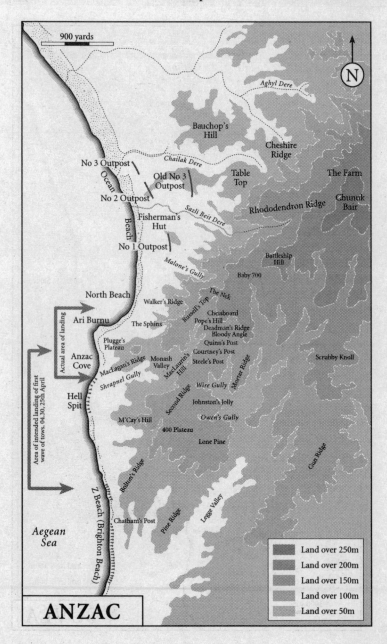

900 yards

Aghyl Dere

Bauchop's
Hill

Cheshire
Ridge

Chailak Dere

No 3 Outpost

Old No 3
Outpost

Table
Top

The Farm

Ocean

No 2 Outpost

Chunuk
Bair

Sazli Beit Dere

Rhododendron Ridge

Fisherman's
Hut

Beach

No 1 Outpost

Malone's Gully

Battleship
Hill

Baby 700

North Beach

Walker's Ridge

The Nick

Ari Burnu

The Sphinx

Russell's Top

Chessboard
Pope's Hill
Deadman's Ridge
Bloody Angle
Quinn's Post

Actual area of landing

Plugge's
Plateau

Courtney's Post

Scrubby Knoll

Anzac
Cove

MacLagan's Ridge

Monash
Valley

MacLaurin's
Hill

Steele's Post

Murray Ridge

Shrapnel Gully

Hell
Spit

Wire Gully

Second Ridge

Johnston's Jolly

M'Cay's Hill

Owen's Gully

400 Plateau

Lone Pine

Gun Ridge

Area of intended landing of first
wave of tows, 04.30, 25th April

Bolton's Ridge

Chatham's Post

Pine Ridge

Legge Valley

Aegean
Sea

Z Beach
(Brighton Beach)

Land over 250m
Land over 200m
Land over 150m
Land over 100m
Land over 50m

ANZAC

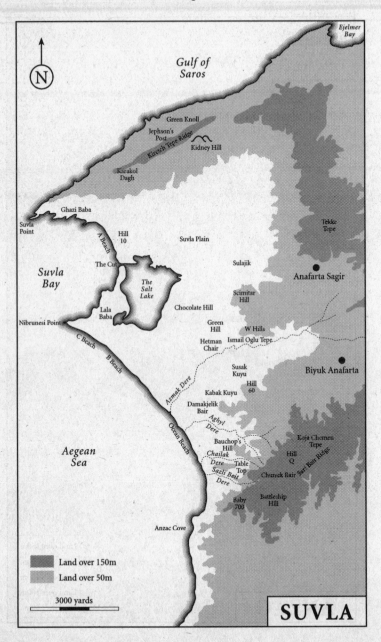

Ejelmer Bay

Gulf of Saros

N

Green Knoll

Jephson's Post

Kireçh Tepe Ridge

Kidney Hill

Karakol Dagh

Ghazi Baba

Suvla Point

Hill 10

Suvla Plain

Tekke Tepe

A Beach

The Cut

The Salt Lake

Sulajik

Anafarta Sagir

Suvla Bay

Scimitar Hill

Lala Baba

Chocolate Hill

Nibrunesi Point

C Beach

Green Hill

W Hills

Hetman Chair

Ismail Oglu Tepe

B Beach

Azmak Dere

Susak Kuyu

Hill 60

Biyuk Anafarta

Kabak Kuyu

Damakjelik Bair

Aghyl Dere

Ocean Beach

Bauchop's Hill

Chailak Dere

Koja Chemen Tepe

Hill Q

Table Top

Aegean Sea

Sazli Beit Dere

Chunuk Bair

Sari Bair Ridge

Baby 700

Battleship Hill

Anzac Cove

Land over 150m

Land over 50m

3000 yards

SUVLA

Foreword by Brian Bond

General Sir Ian Hamilton's long and brilliantly successful career as a soldier of empire ended in failure at Gallipoli in 1915 and ever since his reputation has been inextricably associated with that campaign. Was this hazardous, extremely difficult amphibious operation foredoomed by indecision and lack of commitment in London, or did Hamilton, as Commander-in-Chief, throw away fleeting chances of victory by inept generalship?

In the 1920s and 1930s there was a good deal of sympathetic writing about the campaign and its commander, in part as a tantalizing alternative to the attrition and heavy casualties on the Western Front. As Hamilton's own *Gallipoli Diary* (1920) suggested, his had been a romantic enterprise in a classical setting redolent with echoes from the ancient world. More prosaically, Liddell Hart defended Hamilton as a reformer who had vainly striven to render the army fit for modern war: 'He, almost alone, had pointed out its defects almost a dozen years before, with no result except his own injury.' Hamilton also emerged well from C. F. Aspinall-Oglander's elegant two-volume official history and from John North's elegiac evocation of what might have been in *Gallipoli: The Fading Vision* (1936).

After the Second World War, however, historical verdicts on the campaign and its commander became more critical. Alan Moorehead's *Gallipoli* (1956) set the tone that was taken further by Robert Rhodes James's more scholarly account nine years later. Popular opinion has been widely influenced by more-or-less bitter accusatory Anzac publications and films which show little understanding of Hamilton's political and military problems. The general's nephew, Ian B. M. Hamilton, had only moderate success in attempting to counter this critical trend with his biography *The Happy Warrior* (1965). Hamilton,

xxiv   **Foreword by Brian Bond**

in short, has badly lacked the equivalent of a John Terraine, who has stoutly defended the reputation of Sir Douglas Haig for more than thirty years.

If John Lee has not quite aspired to that role, he has nonetheless presented a concise and masterly case for the defence which is given additional weight by his widely recognized expertise on the First World War operations and his unrivalled knowledge of the Hamilton Papers. As the title makes clear, this is a military biography that concentrates single-mindedly on Hamilton's professional career, fully discussing his pre-1914 achievements – notably in the Boer War – but culminating in a thorough analysis of Gallipoli: its origins, conduct and aftermath. Little space is devoted to Hamilton's non-military or leisure interests, such as his numerous publications, or to his domestic life, though the latter should be fully covered by Celia Lee's biography of his wife, Jean.

John Lee's important achievement is to demonstrate that Ian Hamilton had proved himself as an outstanding staff officer, commander and military reformer long before 1914. His belated opportunity to hold an independent command in 1915 was fatally handicapped by the circumstances of his appointment by his revered former chief, Lord Kitchener. Lee depicts this initial stage as crucial, and shows that Hamilton never subsequently received the degree of political understanding and material support that any field commander might reasonably have expected. Lee's robust and thoroughly documented defence takes the reader dispassionately through the successive scenes of the unfolding tragedy, culminating in Hamilton's recall to London and failure to obtain another active command. John Lee's sturdy case for the defence may not convert Ian Hamilton's sharper critics, but it should persuade readers with an open mind that he was far more 'sinned against than sinning'.

Introduction

> However, our story is a true tragedy and
> therefore needs no villains. It needs only men
> whose ideals and actions give us the luxury of
> passing superior judgements at a safe distance.
> (Rayne Kruger, *Goodbye Dolly Gray*)

At a First World War conference in Leeds in September, 1994, I gave a
paper on Ian Hamilton's reflections on the Great War, which became
a crusade for reconciliation with Germany and against war in general.
As I rose to speak and began with a quotation from one of his speeches
at the opening of yet another war memorial, I suddenly felt my voice
thicken and my eyes begin to fill with tears, and I had to pause for
a second or two to compose myself. I am assured by friends in the
audience that my temporary lapse from academic rigour went
unnoticed but it occurred to me later that, steeped as I was in the
documents and speeches of Ian Hamilton, it wasn't until I had to
declaim one of his speeches in public that I fully realized the power of
his words and how they must have moved audiences in his day. It gave
me a much better understanding of this remarkable soldier/intellectual,
whose physical courage was unquestioned by anyone, but whose moral
courage was every bit as important in the making of his character.

Ian Hamilton forms an extraordinary link between the Victorian
army at the time of the much needed Cardwell reforms and the age
of the atomic bomb. He sat the first entrance examination for Sandhurst just as the purchase of commissions was abolished, and he
maintained a keen and perceptive interest in military affairs until his
death, aged ninety-four, in 1947. He was a powerful reforming force in

the army, always embracing the modern and often way ahead of his time.

In 1914 he was one of the most famous soldiers in the world and was a genuinely popular figure in the country. If a print-maker or a biscuit-tin designer wanted to portray the three most distinguished soldiers of the day, they would probably have chosen Lord Roberts, Lord Kitchener and Sir Ian Hamilton. In 1915 he was given command of the expedition to assist the Royal Navy in forcing the Dardanelles and seeking to put Turkey out of the war. If he failed in this, his big test, I hope the narrative, which is based carefully on the contemporary evidence and tries to let the story unfold as it was known at the time, will show that his task was one of extraordinary difficulty. The government of the day, acting through its principal military adviser, Lord Kitchener, failed to understand that in 1915 Britain could not afford to run two major military efforts simultaneously. The fighting at Gallipoli never received the backing it required or deserved and defeat there should come as no surprise. It is hard to understate the extent to which the original assault landings themselves were fraught with potential disaster, being the first time that men had ever attacked a coastline defended by the weapons of warfare of the industrial age. Many distinguished practitioners of war feared the worst and consider the lodgements that were gained a wonderful achievement in their own right.

Defeat at Gallipoli inevitably marred the image of Sir Ian Hamilton, though he retained the admiration of most of the active participants of the campaign itself, who knew better than most what had been achieved and almost achieved there. Between the wars, as something of a reaction set in against the terrible casualties on the Western Front, the Gallipoli campaign was seen again as one of the real alternatives to attritional warfare that might have brought great strategic success at much less cost if it had received the proper support it needed. The subsequent Bolshevik Revolution and the loss of Russia as an ally has somewhat anachronistically led to speculation about what might have happened if the Western allies had done more to succour Tsarist Russia with a more determined prosecution of the campaign.

Today, when amphibious warfare seems so much more 'normal' – though its practice always was and still is hazardous in the extreme – one senses that Hamilton is again being considered with the wisdom of hindsight and is judged harshly for his failure in 1915. It is my hope that this biography will allow us to assess his whole career and see how he was ideally suited in temperament and experience for this command. Indeed this book suggests that he was still better suited to the very highest military positions, where his reforming zeal and theoretical knowledge would have been put to good use.

The reader will, of course, pass a private verdict on Sir Ian Hamilton. But we should always bear in mind the stresses to which commanders in war are subjected. In a phrase of such poetic beauty that it could only have come from this Highland warrior, Hamilton once referred to sharing Kitchener's 'arctic loneliness'. The army of today is more aware of such problems and has instituted a psychological study of the pressures facing commanders.[1] The first factor it recognizes is that military men prefer not to think of stress as a problem; the task of the general is to achieve the objective set for him and it might seem 'unmanly' to look for personal factors to explain a reduced performance or outright failure. How much more true that must have seemed in the army of 1914. Working with personal staffs and the wholly new experience of co-ordinating activities with other armed services and allied forces added greatly to stress. It is now recognized that 'mission drift' – getting drawn into activity that was not originally planned for – is a major problem. Hamilton faced the biggest 'mission drift' of all time as he went in a few days from commander of an auxiliary force helping the Royal Navy to the task of a major amphibious assault to clear the Gallipoli peninsula. His force was not adequate in either numbers or equipment and it was wholly untrained for the task before it, while his political leaders were caught up in a crisis of their own when he needed them most. For a general with the highest regard for the popular press and its importance in keeping the nation enthusiastic in its support of the services, he was famously let down by two individuals whose jaundiced reports fatally wounded the expedition.

Though Hamilton was sixty-two in 1915, which some consider to be too old for active service, he was lean and wiry, with years of hard campaigning behind him. His headquarters at Imbros were much more Spartan than they need have been; he felt the need to share the common experience of his soldiers. Operating so far from the home base, at the end of supply lines constantly strained by other war demands, added to his difficulties. Unlike the commanders on the Western Front, he would always be denied the ability to return to the home country, to rest and recuperate amidst family, friends and colleagues, for the duration of the campaign. Physical danger held no terrors for him at all; he had been twice recommended for the Victoria Cross for acts of personal bravery.

There is no doubt that Hamilton found the 'small wars' of his earlier experience more congenial than the mass warfare that engulfed Europe in 1914. The huge staffs required to run modern war were anathema to him. When his command rose to over fifteen divisions, operating in four army corps, he was criticized for not being more in touch with the fighting troops and for failing to intervene enough in the decisions of his executive commanders. Giving orders that inevitably send some men to their deaths is not a prospect many of us have to contemplate. It is an added stress factor for military commanders, but Hamilton was a fighting general, as sanguine about these matters as one might expect. He quickly adapted his ideas at Gallipoli into encouraging the enemy to attack his lines as often as they wished, secure in the knowledge that they could be killed and wounded in prodigious numbers in the new conditions of war that prevailed.

In short, where Hamilton faced those constant factors that assail all commanders at all times, he had the experience and flexibility to cope with most difficulties. But in the magnitude of the task he was set and the inadequacy of the resources made available to him, he faced problems that would have overwhelmed any general of his day.

This is a military biography, of a man who loved the army and the empire he served. His intellectual prowess was every bit as important as his physical courage and his wide experience.

1

From Childhood to Army Commission, 1853–73

Ian Hamilton was born to be a soldier. His father, Christian 'Monti' Hamilton, was a career officer who, in 1853, was a captain in the 92nd Foot, the second battalion of the Gordon Highlanders then garrisoning the island of Corfu, and would rise to be the colonel of his battalion. An ancestor on his father's side had served as a colonel on the staff of the great Duke of Marlborough. Ian's mother, Maria Corinna, was from that Anglo-Irish military family, the Gorts, that would produce a commander of the British Expeditionary Force in the Second World War and the future Chief of the Imperial General Staff.

With comfortable properties in the home country and an assured place in society, these were not hugely wealthy people. Incomes from land were in relative decline in the latter half of the century; the army and imperial expansion provided a secure employment for this group. They supplied the army with something like 28 per cent of its colonels (and 33 per cent of its generals) and had a strong sense of duty to queen and empire. Scotland supplied officers to the British Army out of all proportion to its size. In the mid-nineteenth century it produced 12 per cent of the colonels and 13 per cent of the generals in the Army List.[1]

Ian Hamilton was born in Corfu on 16 January, 1853 and was christened Ian Standish Monteith. By May of that year the family was back in Scotland, at the home of his paternal grandfather in Argyllshire. While the battalion was in the Crimea, Monti was detained on home duty, which included a course at the School of Musketry at Hythe. During her second pregnancy, Maria Hamilton became ill and though a second son, Vereker, was safely delivered in February 1856, she lost strength steadily and died in July of that year. In his later autobiographical writings Hamilton expressed a deep sense of longing to have known his mother better. He clearly missed her influence and he wondered aloud how she might have guided a 'better being' in his path through war and peace.

Their father was away in India for some thirteen years, so the boys were raised in a household dominated by their aunts. An important influence was their Swiss maid, Henriette, who was encouraged by the rest of the family to make the boys thoroughly fluent in French. On one side of their development was the stiff Victorian protocol: having the children dressed and brought down to the drawing room after dinner to be returned to the charge of their nurse post haste, together with the imbibing of firm Presbyterian beliefs and strictly observed sabbaths (one of their uncles was chaplain to Queen Victoria in Scotland). By contrast they were left largely in the hands of the servants and were permitted to run wild, often kilted, in the hills of Argyll. They grew up fit and imbued with a love of the Scottish landscape and people. They were so much in the company of indoor servants and estate workers that through all his life Ian would have a special deep regard for the common people that would influence greatly his understanding of the soldiers he would command.

Hamilton later listed the greatest influences on his life from the age of four to nine.[2] First came Henriette. Next 'the whole of the great army of servants indoors and out of doors, with their children'. His Aunt Camilla, practical head of the household at Hafton, was next; his father only figured fifth in the list of nine influences (the rest being grandparents, uncles and aunts). To this Hamilton attributes his complete lack of any sort of class consciousness. Where he lived, he said, was that 'debatable ground between the Highlands and the Lowlands that produced an atmosphere in which the servants were minor partners (and not so very minor either) in running the show'.[3] He always deplored people in high society who barely knew the names of their servants, let alone anything of their circumstances. Such ignorance would never have been tolerated in the newest platoon commander in the army. Hamilton admits that his ease and familiarity with the servant class was often shocking to the circles in which he later moved.

At the age of ten Ian was sent away to private school at Cheam, taking great pride in the way he managed the long journey alone. The place, of great pedigree and expense, was a tremendous shock to him. He was largely unfamiliar with trousers and found them uncomfortable; he had been plucked from a loving and largely female household and thrust into a boisterous company presided over by a ferocious disciplinarian, the Rev. Dr Tabor. According to Hamilton, 'Cheam did a lot of harm to my character, which until then had been frank and open.' In the face of relentless bullying he had to learn to use his fists, and he proved so good at fencing that he won his one and only school prize in that field. His unhappiness was so profound at one stage that, during a particularly happy break with an aunt, he seriously contemplated suicide rather than return to school. He had bad dreams about the place for the rest of his life: 'bear-baiting is poor sport for the bear, especially when it is a cub.' What did almost as much damage spiritually was that the sadistic beatings meted out by Tabor stopped completely when one of Hamilton's wealthiest aunts sent a magnificent carriage and footmen to collect him for a visit to London. It was his first glimpse of the power of serious money and it gave him his first doubts about his future. Perhaps a life in business might be better than his beloved army after all. Cheam, Eton, Oxford, marry an heiress, take a seat in Parliament? Although Hamilton worked without enthusiasm in this unhappy environment, he had the makings of a decent classical scholar by the end of his time there.

When Hamilton's grandfather died at Christmas 1867, it put in jeopardy the plan to send the boy to Eton the following year. Hamilton's father was soon to retire from the army and would have to raise two boys on an army pension. From India 'Monti' wrote offering to put Ian through either his old school, Rugby, or the newly opened Wellington. Ian expressed no preference so Dr Tabor put him down for the latter. (Ian later thought that Eton might have been the finish of him, bowing as it did to the false altars of Fashion and Form.)

The first master of Wellington College, Dr Benson (a future Archbishop of Canterbury) modelled the school on Arnold's Rugby, including the significant use of sixth-form prefects for the day-to-day running of the place. Hamilton was to draw important theoretical lessons from his time there. When he first went to Wellington in the autumn of 1867 he was initially placed too low in the school and found the work far too easy. Having been driven unmercifully at Cheam, he was now allowed to drift without any mental stimulation at all. This led to a disappointing showing as he was thought to be wasting his time. He amassed the astonishing total of one hundred canings for unpunctuality! In old age he was to remark: 'For complete futility I doubt whether it can be beaten by anything in the past.' The only other saving grace at the school (after its prefect system) was a fine history teacher, Mr Eve, who awoke his passion for that most vital of subjects.

Hamilton's father heard from friends in the War Office that the purchase of commissions was soon to be abolished and that the summer of 1870 would see one mass examination of candidates for direct commissions. Hamilton had already determined to follow his father's career and had transferred to the 'Modern' side of the school to prepare for the army entrance examination. With the expected flood of candidates for this special exam (there were over 1,000 applicants), few of Ian's tutors and acquaintances held very high hopes for his success. Under the firm admonition of his father to work very hard, Ian was quietly confident as he spent the summer with Captain Lendy, a 'crammer' whose special skill was preparing young men for the army's examinations.

Ian did spectacularly well in his French viva and passed 76th in a list of 404 successful candidates for a commission into the British army. Most of those passing above him were in fact bound for the Civil Service and had only sat the army examination as a fall-back position, so he really had done very well indeed. The first hundred were offered a choice of a one-year course at the Royal Military College, Sandhurst, which would absolve the need of any further exams until they were eligible for field rank: alternatively they could spend a year overseas studying useful subjects before joining their regiments directly. Hamilton chose the latter.

There followed six months in the Dresden household of General Dammers, who had commanded the Hanoverian army that had put the Prussians to flight at Langensalza in 1866 (victors until, that is, they found themselves completely out of ammunition and obliged to surrender). General Dammers had refused an offer of high command in the army of Prussia, so under the guidance of this hater of all things Prussian Hamilton studied German, tactics, army organization and those other topics known to all military cadets of the day: astronomy, surveying, drawing and watercolour painting. He developed a very considerable command of the German language, but the knowledge of the people and military organization he acquired at this time reinforced his inherent dislike of state militarism. He also had to suppress his pro-French sympathies during the war then in progress between France and Germany. But he did respect the German nation and army for the way they set order, punctuality and service above the love of money – a recurring theme in all his speeches and writings for the rest of his life.

Hamilton was then ordered to report as one of the second batch of the new Sandhurst cadets for a short course to round out his training before joining his regiment. He counted this loss of a year's seniority a very great blow to his career. Hamilton freely admitted that, though he greatly improved his horsemanship, it was sadly all to easy to shirk everything else, which he duly did! He could have towered above his fellow cadets intellectually, had he chosen to do so, but he preferred the company of the gallants of the drag hunt.

As there was no vacancy in the Gordon Highlanders at the time, his first commission was with the 12th Regiment, the Suffolks, then serving in Ireland, in and around Athlone. The Colonel Hamilton, commanding, a friend of his father, was no relation but was the father of two future generals, Bruce and Hubert Hamilton, with whom Ian would serve in days to come. Athlone was a sportsman's paradise and Ian took full advantage of its facilities. The landing of a record-sized salmon took priority over training recruits in the late Victorian army! Hamilton kept a cool head and conducted himself very well during his only 'active service' when his regiment broke up a potentially violent civil disturbance in the town of Athlone in August 1873.

Hamilton was with the Suffolks for less than a year. By November 1873, aged twenty, he was sailing to India to join the Gordons. It would be twenty-five years before he was posted back to England.

2

Service in India (With an African Interlude), 1873–84

Overjoyed to be back in his beloved kilt, Hamilton was soon aboard the HMS *Jumna* bound for India. The subalterns of various regiments, twenty or thirty of them, all had their hammocks slung together in the fetid bowels of the ship 'just like hams being smoked in a chimney'. The ship began to roll like a drunken sailor as it left Portsmouth, and like a dozen drunken sailors in the Bay of Biscay and all the way to Malta. During shore leave at Valletta, Hamilton and his friends indulged in that typically naughty behaviour that has disgraced his class for many a long day. He confessed his part in some particularly wanton damage to Maltese civilian property in a letter to Vereker, then studying with the Dammers family in Dresden.

Having landed at Bombay he was given his orders and a railway warrant to join his regiment at Mooltan in north-western India. In a very pleasant surprise his father had also arranged that he receive a gift of 500 rupees, which were to help him get started in his new home, provide a bungalow, furniture, and so on. The scene was set for another act of youthful folly. In his disarmingly frank autobiographical writings, Hamilton wonders 'who in their proper senses would care to waste time following the adventures of an idiot?'[1] His hotel manager had secured for his journey the services of a bearer, a 'jewel' with many good 'chits' as to his character and past service. It should come as no surprise that, at the first break in the journey at Allahabad, this green young subaltern found himself minus the bearer and the rupees! He was helped out with some cash by British officials living there and went on his way, much chastened, to Mooltan.

When he arrived at this hellish spot in the Indian desert, he was taken in by the officers of the 41st Welsh Regiment, as his own regiment, due to relieve them in the garrison, was still on the march towards Mooltan. Hamilton was introduced to the tedium of the life of a subaltern in India: keeping the most unusual hours to avoid the worst of the killing heat; endless games of cards (which he tended to avoid as he had promised his father never to play cards for money before his twenty-fifth birthday!); a good deal of drinking in the mess; punctuated with welcome breaks to go hunting.

When the Gordons arrived their officers organized a splendid dinner for the departing officers of the Welsh Regiment, which was to pass into legend in the Indian Army. After a good meal, plenty of claret and champagne and much bonhomie, Major George White of the Gordons rose to toast his opposite number. On an impulse he seized a great salt cellar, a prized piece of regimental silver, and had it filled with neat whisky (nearly a full pint) and quaffed it to the last drop. He staggered but kept his feet as the Welsh major had to return the compliment before crashing to the ground. The colonels diplomatically took their leave, 'leaving General Pandemonium in command'. The adjutants, the senior captains and everyone down the ranks followed the precedent until the mess was littered with empty whisky bottles and paralytic bodies, some of them very seriously ill by now. One kindly officer of the Gordons, out of fond memory for the young officer's father, prevented Hamilton from taking part, so he was the last officer on his feet before it was realized that the ambulances were urgently needed. Having performed this vital duty, Ian slept off the night's effects in the guardroom. Church Parade next day was but thinly attended; dinner that night was not much better. Dinner at the Gordons' mess was a dread prospect for many a regiment ever after, though Hamilton insisted that they were not a hard-drinking regiment and this particular piece of bravado that had got quite out of hand was never repeated.

Still, the mess bills remained high and it took all of his father's allowance of £200 per annum above his salary to keep young Ian up to the mark with the Gordons. It is important to stress just what a traditional regiment the 2nd Gordon Highlanders were. The battalion was everything; its traditions meant everything. Nothing could be done to disturb it. If its standard of musketry (the British

Army's quaint way of describing its rifle skills) was execrable, what of it? The regiment could be relied on to carry out any task set for it, at the point of the bayonet if necessary. No officer had ever applied for the Staff College, Camberley, or would dream of volunteering for active service away from the battalion.

After drifting along for some months in this comfortable new family, Hamilton was about to demonstrate in several ways how he was different from many of his brother officers. He had returned from a welcome break in the cool hill country of Simla to the sweltering heat of Mooltan. He fell, as young men sometimes do, to musing about life and death, and the struggle for most people of life against death. It occurred to him that for the soldier this should be reversed. 'To him the call of danger was the call of duty – he must behave as if he *wanted* to lose his life, even seeking out danger, putting himself into the hands of God and if he was to get through, get through he would.'[2] The struggle was not just for survival but for priority. If a man could push his canoe upstream faster than the rest of the flotilla, a slack tide might offer him a good opening. Ian Hamilton suddenly desired to get on in his chosen profession and began to behave, as far as his colleagues were concerned, in a very odd way.

An elderly Indian teacher offered to coach him for the Lower Standard examination in Hindustani for 100 rupees on a no-pass, no-pay basis and Hamilton threw his whole being into the studies. He said he worked harder than he did under his crammer, Captain Lendy; every spare moment was spent at his books. The regiment was horrified! Only the prestige of his father saved him from complete disgrace. Instead he had to endure a steady flow of bantering and leg-pulling. He acquired a working knowledge of the Hindustani language, and of Urdu, Nagri and Arabic script and duly passed the examination, which he admitted was not too demanding. He was now qualified as an 'Interpreter', which brought a very welcome supplement of 30 rupees a month to his pay. It was entirely typical of Hamilton that he perfected his command of the language by seeking out at every opportunity the Indian rank and file in the cantonments and engaging them in talk of their homes and families. He would go on to pass the more serious Higher Standard later.

Soon after came the annual inspection by the General Commanding, Lahore District, Sir Charles Reid, VC. Because his company commander was ill, Hamilton had the command of A Company, which the Gordons still fondly called the grenadier company. There was a march past, and much forming of squares to repel cavalry, and finally a demonstration of new attack regulations in which companies advanced in rushes of fifty paces and then lay down to provide covering fire for their comrades. In a unit as traditional as the Gordons, fifty paces meant fifty paces as measured by the RSM's pace stick. After a spirited series of these 'Indian rushes' Hamilton saw that his last advance would leave him about twenty yards short of a brick wall, so he used his tactical common sense and advanced his company up to the wall, firing over it and then resting his men behind its cover. The adjutant was speechless with rage; the colonel and two majors were bearing down on him, and the RSM, who was fond of the young subaltern, busied himself elsewhere. Before the storm broke over his head the inspecting general called an end to the parade. At the subsequent 'Officer's Call' Hamilton half expected to be roasted alive. Instead the general said he deplored unrealistic training exercises that pretended brick walls did not exist and wished to commend the soldierly common sense of the commander of the right-hand company. Hamilton said he was absolutely mortified to have received praise at the expense of his brother officers, which cost him weeks of humility and months of modest behaviour. This young man had marked himself as a thinking soldier; not entirely unknown in the Victorian army, but a rare enough breed to deserve notice.

Perhaps it was lucky for him that he had the chance to lead a half-company off to the most remote British post on the upper waters of the Indus, Dera Ishmail Khan, known to Tommy Atkins as 'Dismal Khan'. Young officers without great private means often welcomed these postings where there was no opportunity to spend their meagre pay. They also developed a high degree of independence in the making of quite complex logistical arrangements. And then, of course, there was the hunting. Army officers had prodigious amounts of leave – two months at a time was not unusual – and much of it was spent on long and complicated, even dangerous, shoots in the hills of northern India. These hunting expeditions developed a very keen eye for country along the frontiers, as well as some very good shots. Hamilton was to become famous in both respects. As he was preparing for one arduous expedition he was pleased to receive an invitation from General Sir Charles Keyes to accompany him for part of the route. The general, a hero of the Afghan Wars, was the father of Roger Keyes, a future admiral who would figure very greatly in Ian Hamilton's story in 1915. On this occasion he was to save Hamilton's life.

Riding alone along a mountain path, the general doing a great deal of listening, the eager young subaltern doing a great deal of talking, their cavalry escort a long way ahead with the baggage, the pair were suddenly surrounded by a band of ferocious-looking Waziris. The general stopped Hamilton reaching for his pistol, which would have meant their instant death. Instead his perfect command of their Pushtoo language and his intimate knowledge of their homeland enabled Keyes to defuse the immediate crisis and get the bandits, for that is undoubtedly what they were, into such a fit of laughter that the two horsemen were able to gallop to safety.

For nearly two years (1875–6) Hamilton's life was dominated by these hunting expeditions, the only relief from the tedium of the subaltern's daily rounds in garrison. Photographs of him at this period, bearded, turbaned, only distinguishable from his native guides and bearers by a slightly paler skin, show him setting new records for the number and size of his kills. Besides keeping lean and fit, during this time he absorbed a prodigiously detailed knowledge of northern India and the frontier territories and the people inhabiting the region. And Hamilton was willing to break another Gordon Highlander taboo to get on in his chosen profession. Writing to Vereker in August 1876 he said that if a planned expedition against the Afridi in 1877 came off, he would volunteer his services on the staff as an interpreter and get attached to a Sikh regiment that was bound to see active service. The extra pay for British officers serving with Indian regiments was no small consideration. With annual mess bills now running at £270 per annum, he was permanently strapped for cash. It should come as no surprise that when he did step forward to volunteer the colonel took him to one side and told him he was too young to go chasing savages through the hills. The Gordons fought as Gordons, not as individuals.

Instead Hamilton's career took another interesting turn. He was given his first six-month leave from January to June 1878, and was able to return to the home country. The War Office, no doubt keen to save itself the cost of the passage money, chose this time to order him to the School of Musketry at Hythe, something he would never have been permitted by his regiment to volunteer for. He loved the work and made a great impression on the course, passing with an 'Extra First' Certificate. On his return to the Gordons in India this success, together with his recent spectacular hunting achievements, led to his being appointed the battalion's musketry instructor.

He tackled his new duties with gusto. He faced a mountain of inertia; this regiment was famous for its bayonet work and the beauty of its squares and time spent at the ranges was time lost to the parade ground. In Hamilton's own words, 'I sweated; I lectured; I begged; I made bad jokes; I even filled the pouches of the battalion with ball cartridge for private practice out of my own slender purse.'³ The battalion's performance in musketry tests began to improve. As the adjutant and the RSM became more exasperated, the field officers watched in astonishment as their regiment became the best shooting battalion in all India, while the drill and parade marches also improved. These were soldiers filled with a new enthusiasm by this troublesome son of the regiment. Besides reinforcing his admiration for volunteer soldiers when they were treated with respect and proving that they were capable of great progress, Hamilton had made an important theoretical leap forward. In 1878 he had foreseen the absolute end of close order fighting and the new dominance of the battlefield by scattered sharp-shooters armed with modern rifles. He was soon to have his first real taste of war and the start of his service with Lord Roberts.

Tsarist Russia had so greatly increased its influence in Afghanistan by 1876 that the tribes had once again put the British out of their country. By autumn 1878 invading British columns were seeking to restore their control of the frontier region. After the initial fighting the 2nd Gordon Highlanders were ordered up to join the Kurram Field Force, commanded by Major-General Roberts. Although this brought Hamilton into the theatre of war, he was actually kept back by a severe bout of malaria and was sent to recuperate at the base headquarters at the mountain pass of Peiwar Kotal. While out riding with a brother officer, 'Polly' Forbes, they were startled by a scattering of shots and the unseemly sight of a group of young British soldiers in full flight down the mountain side. They turned out to be a signalling picquet of new, short-service soldiers not long out from the home country, who told the two young gentlemen they had been rushed by fifteen or twenty Afghans and that two of their friends were missing. Forbes and Hamilton gave their ponies to two of the men and sent them for help, then immediately set out on foot, pistols in hand, for the summit. Hamilton's personal courage can never be doubted for an instant. He was living out his private thoughts about the need to seek out danger and confront it with zeal. The only runaway who still carried a rifle followed at a discreet distance, thus avoiding the court martial that awaited his comrades. The two officers passed one wounded Indian soldier on the way up but otherwise found the redoubt in perfect order, rifles stacked, signalling equipment in place and no sign of the enemy. Clearly the young soldiers had been sniped at and had fled in a panic.

When a company of the King's (Liverpools) arrived on the scene it was agreed to go forward and seek out the raiders. Because he was still weak from his fever, Hamilton fell behind and blundered into the party of Shinwarri raiders missed by the company. He took cover and blazed away with his pistol, trading wildly inaccurate shots in his malaria-induced weakness until help came and the enemy fled, leaving him in possession of a blood-stained mullah's sword, handed down as a family heirloom ever after.

The important development for Hamilton was that Sir Frederick Roberts invited him to visit him in his tent and tell the whole exciting story. After a glass of sherry, and the promise to write to Hamilton's father, which he did at length in long-hand, demon-strating why he was so adored by his soldiers, Roberts let the lieutenant go but kept him in his thoughts thereafter. Almost immediately he was made aide-de-camp to Brigadier-General 'Redan' Massy, commanding the Cavalry Brigade, an unusual posting for an infantry officer but a useful rounding out of his experience. While the Gordons were engaged in the battle of

Charasia (6 October 1879), where Major George White won his VC and Colour Sergeant Hector Macdonald earned his commission, Hamilton was getting as close to the fighting as he could with the cavalry. In the pursuit after the victory he led a troop of 5th Punjab Cavalry in a charge, which served greatly to increase his belief that the days of cavalry armed with swords were numbered. It was the carbine rifle that despatched most of the enemy that day.

Soon after, Hamilton was so ill with malaria that he was ordered before a medical board at Rawalpindi. He had also contracted dysentery by then and was sent home on the first troopship leaving Karachi. He felt so fully recovered by the time he reached England that he immediately set off to return to India and strove desperately to get back to the Gordons in time for the closing stages of the campaign. He rejoined the battalion on the day of the victory at Kandahar (1 September 1880) and was just too late to qualify for the subsequent award of the Kandahar Star, a personal disappointment. He did end his first real active service with the campaign medal, two clasps and two mentions in despatches.

The Gordons were drawing to the end of a long stint in India and the battalion was marched to Cawnpore to prepare for its return to England. The news was out of fighting in South Africa between the British and the Boers, and it was going none too well for the former. Hamilton, by now the senior subaltern in the battalion, had discussed a bold plan with his brother junior officers. He cabled the following to Sir Evelyn Wood: 'Personal. From subalterns 92nd Highlanders. Splendid battalion eager service much nearer Natal than England do send.' There would have been an unholy row if the field officers had known of this. Instead Wood was delighted to reward the subaltern's impudence, and three days later (6 January 1881) the battalion was thrilled to be ordered to the seat of the war forthwith.

Thus they found themselves on 26 February 1881 encamped before a spur of the Drakensberg Mountains in Natal, with the mass of Majuba Hill dominating the western end, firmly checked by the Boers under Piet Joubert, who had inflicted two successive defeats on the proud Sir George Colley over the past few weeks. Burning with shame and anxious to settle matters before a wavering government in London settled with the Boers, Colley had devised a secret plan to lead a night march of infantry up to the summit of Majuba Hill and turn the Boers out of their strong position astride Laing's Nek. In order to allow all his regiments to share in his triumph, Colley took up a very disparate force (two companies of the 2nd Northamptons, two of the 60th Rifles, three of 2nd Gordons and one of sailors), which added greatly to his difficulties as the battle developed. It is also suggested that political considerations demanded that the post-Cardwell reform short-service soldiers of the Northamptons and Rifles were to be given their chance beside the long-service veterans of the Gordons.

Hamilton had just come in from picquet duty at 9 p.m. on 26 February when his company was ordered to fall in by 9.30 and begin the night march. By midnight they were clambering on their hands and knees up almost vertical cliff faces to finally, in an exhausted state, reach the summit of the tabletop hill. Three companies of infantry had been dropped off to guard the approach and the sailors manned the immediate point of access to the summit. Four companies of infantry (two each of Northamptons and Gordon Highlanders) were deployed around the hill, about 365 men in all. 'We could stay here forever,' Colley said to his chief of staff, Herbert Stewart. He then made the ultimately fatal decision to let them rest rather than begin to entrench themselves immediately. Hamilton found his men in a high state of excitement and was sure Colley could have achieved more. Based on his experience in India, Hamilton did get his soldiers to make small stone breastworks in their assigned position on the side of the hill nearest to the Boers. His initial deployment of one man to every six paces had to be thinned to one man to every twelve paces when dawn revealed just how much ground they needed to cover.

Soon after dawn a party of some thirty Boers in complete ignorance of the British presence rode close under the hill and were fired upon. No British officer was aware of Colley's intentions. Some ordered the firing to stop; others wished the men to fire only if they were sure of doing serious damage to the foe. Hamilton, posted well forward with eighteen of his men, saw Boers entering a ravine, which soon became dead ground. Soon his detachment was under heavy and accurate rifle fire, and he watched as some 100 Boers broke cover and got in below the summit where he was posted and where they were lost to view. At some personal risk from sniper fire, Hamilton dashed back to the peaceful centre of the position, sought out the general and reported what he had seen. He was politely thanked and returned to his post, passing men comfortably eating, sleeping or smoking. When he had seen anything up to 350 Boers come in below him he again ran back to Colley and asked for reinforcements to help him suppress the storm of fire lashing his position. He was given one officer and five men of the Northamptons. At noon, as the Boers continued to mass below him, he made his last report, this time finding Colley asleep and giving the facts to Major Hay of the Gordons in his stead.

Suddenly a storm of fire broke over his position; Hamilton's men began to fall. He also saw a British reserve force coming up to assist but it was shot to pieces and put to flight. Hamilton's party had to scamper back towards the British second line; few of them made it. All was confusion as the thoroughly mixed British force failed to respond quickly to shouted instructions from so many strange officers as the Boers poured forward keeping up a tempest of fire. Hamilton would have launched an immediate counter-charge but was prevented from doing so by Hay; the numbers really were too few. But Hamilton was right to think that now was the best chance to catch the Boers at their maximum disorder and throw them back by determined action. He again ran up to General Colley, saluted and said, 'I do hope, General, that you will let us have a charge, and that you will not think it presumption on my part to have come up to ask you.' Sir George replied, 'No presumption, Mr. Hamilton, but we will wait until the Boers advance on us, then give them a volley and charge.'[4] The moment had passed and the volume of enemy fire increased steadily and overwhelmingly. Hamilton, only some ten paces from Colley, had grabbed a rifle and was returning fire with his men. As he raised the rifle to his cheek a bullet smashed into his left wrist, ruining the use of it for the rest of his days. The British line broke; a handful of Gordons under their new subaltern, Hector Macdonald, made some effort to serve as a rearguard. Hamilton was running to the rear, clutching his broken wrist in his good right hand, his tunic and kilt ripped with many bullets, when a blow on the head, either from a spent bullet or a stone thrown up by a bullet, knocked him senseless.

When he came around, two young Boers were relieving him of his sword, belts and haversack. He offered money to them if they would let him keep the sword given to him by his father, but he was promptly relieved of both money and sword. He was saved from further mischief by being summoned by a Boer commander to come over and identify the body of his slain chief, Sir George Colley. Hamilton estimated that something like 1,200 Boer riflemen were roaming over the hilltop by then.

The Boers simply told Hamilton he was free to go; one said quite frankly that they did not expect him to survive his wound. Another took pity and made a rough splint from the top of a bully beef tin, packing the wounded wrist with grass and securing it tightly with a red bandanna. Hamilton even had an exchange with Joubert himself, asking him if he could have his sword returned. Joubert was amiable enough, saying that he would do what he could, though surely knowing that would be little enough. He even asked the humble lieutenant why Britain had forced this war upon his country. Hamilton rather lamely retorted that he had read in the newspapers that the Boers had started it, which produced a torrent of abuse from Joubert directed at the press. After a couple of hours fetching water for other wounded British soldiers, Hamilton wandered off the hill and sank to the ground exhausted. His own distraught fox terrier, Patch, found him at daybreak and he was collected by a patrol of the Northamptons who brought him safely into camp on 28 February.

Hamilton reflected how, in 1881, the army was still at the ideological juncture between traditional and truly modern warfare. The men might carry entrenching tools but some regiments still wore the red tunic and pipeclayed belts (the Gordons, having come from the North-West Frontier, were the first regiment to wear khaki on campaign in Africa); not enough of their officers understood the need to dig in to be sure of success. Large British reinforcements had arrived but the British government had had enough and rapidly made peace, conceding all the Boer demands. The bitterness this left made a second trial of strength almost inevitable.

Hamilton was placed in hospital at Newcastle, Natal, where he became so ill that he heard two doctors describe him as 'moribund', which so greatly alarmed him that he clung to life with all the more determination. Sir Evelyn Wood himself rode over to see him and promised him an honourable mention in the despatches going back to England. Most doctors wanted to amputate his arm, but one wanted to try a new technique of excision of the wrist pioneered by Lister. The arm could always come off if it failed. At first the operation was thought to have failed and preparations were under way for the final cut, but his regimental surgeon and an old friend of his father's, Sam Roe, detected an improvement in the use of the left hand, saving it and Hamilton's career.

Vereker came out to South Africa and escorted his brother home. By August they were back in England and Ian was soon being treated by none other than Lister himself, who in fairly robust style repeatedly broke down and reset the wrist. While staying with Uncle Gort on the Isle of Wight, Ian was 'commanded' to dine with the Royal Household at Osborne House, after which he was ushered into the presence of Queen Victoria and made to tell the whole story of the tragic defeat at Majuba Hill. He was asked to write an account of it, which was subsequently hailed as a masterpiece of graphic and exciting writing. He was, of course, recommended for the Victoria Cross, but the army decided he was too young; he would have plenty of other opportunities to distinguish himself.

The wounded hero was lionized by society and his fame spread far and wide, but by December he was studying very seriously for the Staff College entrance examination, enlisting the services of his old friend, Captain Lendy, as good a crammer for Camberley as he was for Sandhurst. A medical board inspected his wrist and pronounced itself pleasantly surprised by a 'miracle of conservative surgery'. His future in the army was safe.

It was just a few days before the examinations. Hamilton was sure to do very well; his natural intelligence, practical experience and earnest desire to do well in the service of his country had seen him prepare very thoroughly. If he had acquired the letters 'PSC' (Passed Staff College) he might have been drawn into the mainstream of the British military establishment in that crucial period 1900–14. As it was his career took another sudden turn which opened up new possibilities and new dangers.

He was cabled by Sir Martin Dillon, Assistant Military Secretary at the Horse Guards, to come to London. There he was told that Sir Frederick Roberts, Commander-in-Chief in the Madras Presidency, had personally asked for Ian Hamilton as his ADC. Though he later said he would have advised anyone else to say no, Hamilton decided he had had enough studying and replied in the affirmative. On 24 January 1882 he cabled his father in Scotland: 'Been offered in very flattering way A.D.C. to Roberts. I have most carefully thought it all over and accept tomorrow morning at ten unless you positively forbid me to go which I sincerely trust you will not.'[5]

On 25 February 1882, before he left, he was promoted to captain, an unexpected and very welcome step up. He literally burnt his books and set off for India for another sixteen years' service. From Camberley he would have passed almost inevitably into the circle of officers associated with Sir Garnet Wolseley and his campaigns, the 'Africans' of the 'Wolseley Ring'. Instead he was to become one of the officers most completely identified with the 'Indians' of the 'Roberts Ring'. He could reflect in later life on the tragedy of this division of the brightest and best in the army, but at the time these groups could hardly bear to be in the same room as each other. The 'Indians' in particular felt especially aggrieved that the 'Africans' dominated the War Office and made sure that their friends were given appointments and advancement ahead of Roberts's officers. As it happened, Hamilton was one of the few 'Indians' to serve again in Africa and claim a foot in both camps, but the very strong emotions aroused amongst these ambitious career officers ran very deeply.

In June Hamilton landed at Bombay and took the train for Bangalore, arriving at 5.30 a.m. He was met by a jovial Roberts, who told him he was just in time to get into uniform and join him for a major inspection of a grand parade. By 11.30 he was wonderfully turned out and swinging into the saddle of a charger borrowed from the 4th Hussars. The poor beast proceeded along the serried ranks mostly on its hind legs, snorting, kicking and plunging, and Hamilton was dying of embarrassment at the spectacle he was creating at the side of his chief for the first time and before the eyes of what must have seemed like the entire army of India!

What a relief to be detailed to escort Lady Roberts and the

family up to the hill country. The summer residence was at a house called Snowdon at Ootacamund ('Ooty' to the India hands). There Hamilton entered a household as charming and friendly as that he had known in his childhood. Lord and Lady Roberts and their daughters Aileen and Edwina (aged eleven and seven respectively) were to be his friends for life. The Military Secretary was at first Gerald Pretyman, and later Reginald Pole-Carew. Everyone acquired a nickname in the British Army and these two were, perhaps inevitably, 'Pretty Boy' and 'Polly'. It is here that Hamilton became known, then and forever, as 'Johnny'. The other ADC was Neville Chamberlain, the inventor of snooker and something of a versifier. It was not long before Hamilton's latent inclinations in this direction were bearing fruit. He and Chamberlain were soon exchanging verses, and he joined a local literary club called 'The Scribblers'. He had full access to the extensive library of Grant Duff, the Governor of the Presidency, who encouraged his reading of history and literature. Roberts was delighted to have this obviously talented writer on hand and Hamilton was soon writing speeches and preparing despatches as part of his official duties.

The principal role given him by Lord Roberts, and undoubtedly the reason he was chosen in the first place, was that of Assistant Adjutant-General of Musketry at army headquarters. Roberts had no authority over the British forces in India but he could do whatsoever he pleased with the native army under his command. In his own hand Hamilton rewrote the whole of the musketry regulations for the Indian regiments, and claimed that the ensuing revolution in musketry training was an entirely original concept in his brain, based on the vivid experience at Majuba Hill in particular, although the Afghan Wars also had their place in the evolution of his thinking. He was simultaneously working his ideas up into a book called *The Fighting of the Future*. The new manual had chapters on 'Celerity and Precision', 'Head and Shoulder Figures', the 'Running Deer'. Its originality lay in the stress on the improved marksmanship of the individual soldier; until then all the emphasis had been on the efficacy of the massed volley. The old manuals may have taught 'steady fire, independent fire, volley fire, rapid fire, group fire, direct, enfilade, oblique, and cross fire, but of straight (i.e. accurate) fire, not one word.' Hamilton detailed the training required on the rifle ranges – building the confidence of the individual from using the rifle like an unsighted shotgun at ranges up to 200 yards, through slower and more deliberate firing at longer ranges, to snap shooting at 'jumping-up' targets at different, unpredictable ranges. Gradually building both speed and precision, he finally had the men shooting at barrels rolling and bounding downhill towards the firer to overcome the instinct to shoot wild and high.

This new training was imposed on the Indian regiments immediately and comprehensively, and over the next two years their standard improved so dramatically that they were regularly humiliating British battalions in any comparison of shooting skills. The British army was seeking new ways to improve but had gravitated towards Mayne's 'Fire Tactics', which negated individual excellence by aiming for a lower standard which could be achieved by larger numbers. The Duke of Cambridge saw the rapid and demonstrable improvement of the Indian army and took steps to see that Hamilton's system should become the basis for musketry training throughout the British army as well.

The Fighting of the Future was completed by June 1884 and was published in London early in 1885. It marks the start of Hamilton's long record of writings and speeches in defence of the British military system based on volunteer enlistment and the importance of valuing the quality of the well-trained enthusiast over the conscript masses. In a brief survey of military history he acknowledged that the power of discipline from Alexander the Great to von Moltke often ensured victory over much larger forces of less-controlled adversaries. But as gunpowder weaponry developed and army types became more standardized, so the battlefield became dominated by firepower, and the extension of formations and the sheer din of modern battle reduced the personal command function of the general. The personal skill and prompt courage of the individual soldier was now decisive.

As he developed his argument for the new rifle training, so the really radical aspect of Hamilton's ideas also developed. 'The first great difficulty which arises is to be found in the spirit of the army itself: with all its traditions rooted in drill and pipe-clay, it cannot easily make a new departure.'[6] The men needed time to practise their essential skills, not on the barrack square but on the rifle ranges. He called for the abolition of many useless pieces of drill – the Present Arms, the forming of squares, the parade march (a mere aping of the Prussian goose-step after their victories over Austria and France). From an army that practised shooting for 10 days a year and drilled for the other 355 but still could not hit its nimble Afghan enemy at point-blank range, he called for a basic drill just once a week and for all the soldier's training to be directed towards the ranges, the gymnasium and the classroom to develop physique and intellect alongside the decisive shooting skills. In one short passage he fulminated against the new magazine rifles as a recipe for huge volumes of wild and inaccurate fire, which makes him sound rather reactionary until you realize that he wanted to make sure that every soldier was trained to load single shots and make every single bullet fired count for an enemy. Only then could they be trusted to use the magazine rifle to its full effect.

It comes as no surprise that this progressive infantry officer predicted the demise of any battlefield role for the cavalry, which he proposed should be converted to mounted infantry straight away. He also predicted the end of the forward deployment of field artillery, where the crews were vulnerable to accurate, long-range rifle fire. Fewer guns of a heavier calibre were his suggestion at this time. For the time being, 'the future of Indian civilisation will depend on how the English handle their rifles.'

Writing now became a very important part of Hamilton's life. Having won a poetry competition set by 'The Scribblers', Hamilton was invited by the editor of the *Madras Mail* to become his 'Correspondent from Army Headquarters'. Roberts gave his full permission for Hamilton to take up this paid appointment – a useful addition to the captain's funds – provided the Commander-in-Chief was allowed (in secret) to approve the text of any article before it was published. This, of course, became a useful additional outlet for Roberts's ideas, though these were days when officers were permitted to write on military affairs quite freely. Hamilton took to the journalist's life and by June 1883 he could write to his father:

I feel that I am independent – that if I were kicked out of the Service tomorrow I should not be a mere loafer the more

thrown onto Pall Mall and the clubs but that I could fight my
own way. You may think this rather a high estimate to be
grounded on the receipt of a few hundred rupees from the
Madras Mail, but I base it on more than that: viz., on the fact
that I have done vastly, immeasurably better work since, and
that I imagine that I have potential possibilities in the way of
improvement still lurking in me.[7]

His brother, Vereker, was now working on a coffee plantation in
Ceylon and developing considerable skill as a painter. Together they
took a sailing holiday along India's western coast, which they
subsequently wrote up and published, anonymously, as *A Jaunt in
a Junk*. The book was widely reviewed, both in Britain where
it received faint praise and in India where it was very severely
handled. Hamilton even tried to pretend to the editor of the *Madras
Mail*, which had savaged the book, that he was a friend of the
author and asked if he would give the book another look. Back
came the reply that the criticism was not too severe: the book
should never have been published. Far from being discouraged,
Hamilton developed his creative writing and published a novel,
Icarus, in 1886. Helped by Vereker's descriptions of the artist's life,
this fairly racy story of a man about town and his numerous
flirtations, which end with a pistol shot from an outraged husband,
was well received. Reviewers found it 'decidedly naughty and
decidedly amusing'; if 'not free from the taint of Bohemianism', it
was still 'a very powerful novel, with plenty of sparkling dialogue';
'distinctly entertaining, although the situations are here and there
far more risqué than is necessary or desirable'.[8]

While Hamilton could write in 1884 that 'I'd rather write one
really sweet and famous sonnet than be Q.M.G. in India, or even
C-in-C himself', he was still studying very hard for the stiff
examination for his promotion to major. These were very fulfilling
days as he made real progress as a writer and a soldier. For some
six months in 1884 he served as Assistant Military Secretary to Lord
Roberts, a post to which he was perfectly suited, given his experience in both peace and war. The War Office refused to confirm
him in the post and he had to revert to being an ADC. It is entirely
typical of this period that he blamed Sir Redvers Buller, a leading

member of the 'Wolseley Ring', for what was seen as a vindictive decision to keep back any officer associated with Roberts.

Hamilton was due for six months' home leave, and he had written to Vereker saying that he planned to do some really serious creative writing, away from the considerable burden of his military duties. But he discussed with his chief another possibility before he left. A new campaign was afoot in the Sudan and Hamilton was not going to miss the chance for more active service. Roberts wrote to Hamilton's father in October 1884:

> Ian sailed from Bombay in the *Malabar* on the 22nd inst. I saw him off from the Apollo Bundur, and I was, I can assure you, very sorry to part with him. He has been my constant companion for more than two years, and like everyone at Snowdon I have a great affection for him. Both socially and officially Ian has been a perfect success, he is a thorough gentleman and a first-rate soldier: he has afforded me every possible assistance, and I look forward with great delight to his being with me again. ... Ian proposes remaining a week in Cairo in the hope of getting employment in the Sudan, I urged him not to stay longer, and I warned him not to be too sanguine, for I hear that Cairo is full of disappointed men.[9]

3

Service in Africa, India, Burma
and England, 1884–99

Having crushed a nationalist uprising at the battle of Tel-el-Kebir and occupied Egypt in 1882, Britain was extremely reluctant to get involved in the occupation of the extensive hinterland of the Sudan to the south. As the armies of the militant Islamic prophet, the Mahdi, extended their grip on that country, destroying an Egyptian army led by the British Colonel Hicks (November 1883), the government decided to evacuate all British and Egyptian families forthwith. General Charles Gordon was despatched to Khartoum in January 1884 to organize an orderly withdrawal, but he proved unwilling to deliver the country up to the tender mercies of the Mahdi and allowed himself to be invested in the city by the insurgent army. It was popular pressure in Britain that forced a reluctant Gladstone to despatch a military expedition to rescue Gordon. Lord Wolseley came out to Cairo to prepare a very cautious and deliberate advance along the Nile, in conjunction with a camel-borne desert column. His scheme would allow for arrival at Khartoum by March or April 1885. In November 1884 Gordon suddenly announced the city could fall within forty days. The race was on.

Hamilton's steamer put into Suez at the end of October 1884 to find that half the officers travelling with him had written to various friends and connections in Egypt in the hope of finding a posting with the expedition. They were dealt with in the main as upstart glory-seekers and received dire threats that their importuning would be reported to London and that they could face disciplinary charges. The last thing Wolseley wanted was an invasion of 'Indians'. This quickly discouraged many of the applicants, but not Ian Hamilton. He got ashore in a small boat and, after a half-mile run across desert sand with his kit, just managed to catch the only train that day for Cairo. As he breezed into Shepheard's Hotel he had the astounding good luck to fall in with a subaltern of the 1st Gordon Highlanders, one of the British battalions assigned to the expedition. The colonel was only too happy to fill out his depleted complement of officers with this experienced man, but when the base commandant, Colonel Ardagh, heard that the new arrival served on Roberts's staff in India his courage failed him and he said he would not put his name forward to headquarters.

Hamilton pleaded with Ardagh to at least cable a request to headquarters that he might be allowed to serve with the Gordons. He was told that the request would go to the chief of staff, none other than the 'evil genius' of the Wolseley Ring, Redvers Buller. It is entirely to Buller's credit that, despite all the injunctions against 'medal-hunting' officers jumping ship, he recognized that the Gordons needed a company officer and that there on the spot was one of the most experienced they could possibly wish for. His wire read: 'You may attach Hamilton to Gordons.' Perhaps the popular conception of the mutually exclusive 'rings' needs to be re-assessed, especially as another 'African' general was about to rescue Hamilton from a very dreary posting indeed.

He commanded a company of 1st Gordons on the journey up the Nile to Wadi Halfa. He pushed the boat and the men along relentlessly, passing many other companies en route. His reason for wanting to arrive first was that it was almost inevitable that one company would be dropped off there as a depot/rearguard and he hoped it would be the last to arrive that got that dreary, if vital, duty. At Wadi Halfa the colonel took him to one side and explained that, having helped him thus far, he really felt obliged to his own battalion officers to give them the active duty and that Hamilton would have to stay behind. As he returned to his tent with heavy heart he met none other than Sir Evelyn Wood, who knew him very well from the days of Majuba Hill and exclaimed, 'Hullo. What are you doing here? I thought you were surely serving with Roberts in Madras.' 'Alas, and alas,' Hamilton replied and poured out his tale of woe to his old acquaintance.[1] Nothing more was said but soon afterwards the colonel and the adjutant of the 1st Gordon Highlanders went to pay their respects to the general. The colonel was not in a good mood when he returned to the camp and was heard fulminating about young fellows born with silver spoons in their mouths. Hamilton dashed in to see the adjutant and heard that Wood had decreed that he didn't see the need to leave a company at full strength (like Hamilton's) behind as a depot; one of the smaller companies coming up could do the job. Once again Hamilton's good connections in the army, based on his sterling military qualities and his personal charm, had given him a great opportunity for further service.

The expedition up the Nile was one of endless days of back-breaking work. Over the next two months Hamilton's company, spread over eleven small boats, was lucky if it came together once in ten days to drag boats and stores past another cataract. It could be dangerous enough; boats were overturned and lost; the men had to be rescued. Heat, sand, flies, monotonous food and brackish water all added to the hardships. For Hamilton the real work was done by the four British battalions and their Egyptian auxiliaries of the River Column, but all the glory went to the Desert Column – the men of the Household Cavalry and the Guards, with a Royal Navy detachment, the KRRC (Buller's regiment) and the Royal Irish Regiment (which Hamilton saw as the usual 'puff' given to the Irish regiments). All the jealousies of the British regimental system came out as Hamilton roundly condemned Wolseley for this fanciful idea of sending a separate column across the desert when all resources should have been concentrated along the river.

At Korti, the base from which the Desert Column was to depart, Hamilton feared that he might be ordered to return to India as his leave would soon be up. Instead Buller, who was reported to speak very highly of Hamilton, said that his services were urgently required until the termination of the expedition. General Earle, the commander of the River Column, then pushed ahead with a personal escort that included Hamilton's D Company, 1st Gordon Highlanders. Hamilton dashed off a letter to his brother telling of this forward movement with a postscript dated at the very hour of Gordon's death at Khartoum (6 a.m., 26 January 1885). On 10 February they reached the village of Kirbekan and found an entrenched Dervish host barring their path.

General Earle, a pleasant old gentleman according to one of

Hamilton's letters home, was of the old school, a martinet on the barracks square but capable of bold and decisive action on the battlefield. For the only time in the Sudanese campaigns the British and Egyptian forces went straight into the attack without receiving the Dervish charge first. The Egyptians, some light guns and Hamilton's company advanced directly along the river bank and opened a steady fire on the enemy to pin them in their positions. Earle led the rest of his force out along a desert valley, got behind the Kirbekan Ridge and stormed the Dervish lines from the rear. The loss to the enemy was tremendous; their commander was killed and part of their broken army fled into the river where many drowned. In the very closing moments of the battle Earle ran up to a small house and looked in the window, to be shot dead by the last Dervish warriors on the field. It was the sad duty of Hamilton's company to bury their general close to where he fell.

After this remarkably successful, if little known, battle, the River Column passed under the command of Henry Brackenbury, one of the finest administrators of the Wolseley Ring. The move upriver was resumed; though Gordon and Khartoum were lost, Brackenbury and Buller between them were still to break the power of the Mahdi. Buller was obliged to fall back with the Desert Column from before Metemma. Though the River Column had almost reached Abu Hamid, where the river became broad and easily passable, when he was offered the free choice of pushing on or falling back, Brackenbury ordered the retreat. He actually took seat in Hamilton's boat, with Ian at the helm, as they began the long, and for some humiliating return journey. Hamilton greatly criticized the distant manner in which Wolseley had directed the campaign, and the division of his forces. He was convinced that Roberts would have been a far more dynamic commander, who would never have permitted the dilettante experiment of the Desert Column.

Ian Hamilton had acquired a good deal of unique campaign experience, another mention in despatches, a medal with two clasps and the Khedive's Star. He received the rank of brevet major and returned to India, to resume his duties as ADC to Sir Frederick Roberts, who was now C-in-C, India. The memoirs of Sir William Birdwood leave us a vivid impression of Hamilton's standing in the army at this time. Sailing to his first posting in India in June 1885 he wrote: 'We had with us also a Captain Ian Hamilton of the Gordon Highlanders . . . In the eyes of us youngsters Ian Hamilton already wore a halo of glory by virtue of his service in the Afghan War, the Boer War of 1881, and the Nile Expedition.'[2] The 1886 social season at Simla was enlivened by the visit of Miss Jean Muir, daughter of a wealthy Glasgow businessman with extensive interests in India. Though she was thought, wrongly, to be engaged to an Austrian prince, Hamilton took his chance at a Viceregal Lodge Ball and jumped through a paper hoop to choose Jean for his dancing partner. They arranged to ride together soon after; Hamilton had made excuses to the Roberts household that he was 'too busy' to attend them on one of their own rides, only to have the entire party meet him on the road while out with Jean. Roberts was not best pleased. He did not want his ADCs going off courting and he made sure Hamilton was kept very busy. But within a fortnight he was engaged to be married. Exile to the plains of Dehra Dun to organize a winter tour of inspection was his reward. The Muir family accepted their daughter's choice with more grace and were ready to take ship immediately for the wedding in India.

A duty call intervened. Roberts was appointed to command operations in Burma, where the military commander, General Macpherson, had died of a fever. Britain had annexed Burma in 1886 after occupying it to avenge several outrages against British citizens and business interests and following the refusal of an offer to establish a protectorate there. Roberts took over from the field commander, Hamilton's old friend from 2nd Gordon Highlanders, Sir George White, now a Brigadier-General. Hamilton was on the staff, ostensibly as Persian interpreter, though he never once met a Persian speaker during his tour of duty. Six brigades of troops were sent out to pacify the turbulent districts of mountain and jungle country. It has to be said that the staff, while enduring some long journeys and arduous conditions, did seem to have their eye on personal enrichment. Hamilton spent some time digging for rubies for his new bride, but had to settle for some topaz and sapphires. Roberts kept his troops out of Mandalay for fear they might loot the deserted palace of King Thebaw. He sent Hamilton, Pole-Carew and Chamberlain in to make a report-cum-inventory of the palace, but the palace was not safe! While Chamberlain behaved correctly, Pole-Carew reportedly filled his pockets with strips of gold peeled off some screens and Hamilton commandeered some soldiers of 5th Gurkhas to escort him some miles through dangerous country to lift a beautiful gold-and-black lacquer seated Buddha from a remote temple. It was shipped home as his personal property, where British Museum experts later confirmed its great antiquity. They wanted to saw open its base, which might have contained jewels, but Hamilton refused his permission. It was ultimately bequeathed to his great friend, Winston Churchill.

Early in February 1887 Hamilton was able to write to Jean that he had been given permission to return to India to get married. Jean cabled a reply by return with comical results. Her handwriting was execrable; even after years of marriage Ian had the greatest difficulty reading it. The cable address 'Hamilton, Mandalay, Burma' was interpreted by the hapless post-office clerks as 'Hamilton, Malabar, Bombay'. The ADC to the Governor of Bombay at Malabar Point was none other than Bruce Hamilton, one of the soldier sons of 'Tiger' Hamilton, Ian's old commander at Athlone. Imagine poor Bruce's shock on reading: 'Will Wednesday 23rd suit you for our wedding in the Cathedral?'[3]

The wedding (in fact on 22 February to avoid Ash Wednesday) was a major occasion in the social calendar of British India. The Viceroy and the Commander-in-Chief attended; the viceregal motor launch took the couple off on the first stage of their honeymoon. It wasn't until they were on the train for Darjeeling that Hamilton discovered that Jean had brought her mother along for the trip! Ian's declared love for originality was being put to the test. Jean brought a considerable private income to the household and, while they were never rich by the standards of late Victorian and Edwardian society, they would always be comfortable. They were married for fifty-five years, until her death. Like most marriages of that length there were years of great joy and excitement, many more of comfortable contentment, some stormy patches, some of frustration bordering on unhappiness, the occasional temptation and the slight hint of dalliances elsewhere. But the union endured and in all Hamilton's correspondence and writings there are constant declarations of Jean's importance to him.

They took a house called 'Stirling Castle' in Simla and enjoyed the giddy summer of 1887 as the Queen's Golden Jubilee was celebrated in a great number of events. Hamilton's reputation as a writer was well established. He had a volume of verse, *The Ballad of Hadji and other Poems*, published in India and England; his brother and some of his fellow artists had added handsome decorative embellishments and it was well reviewed. Perhaps his 'fame' as soldier and writer is nicely illustrated by his becoming the object of addresses from Victorian versifiers. Just the last two lines of one will suffice to give a flavour of this type of literature.

> Ian, to you, from banks of Ken,
> We send you lays of Englishmen.

Ian and Jean were fast friends with the young Rudyard Kipling and his sister, Trix. For a long time Hamilton took lunch every Sunday with Kipling and other literary types at the house of Lord Russell (later the Duke of Bedford). When Kipling wanted to extend his publication record to England, it was Hamilton he approached for advice and help. A manuscript was forwarded to Vereker in London, who showed it to writers of his acquaintance. It was savagely received, with recommendations to 'burn this detestable piece of work'. It was much better liked by Vereker's artist friends and would be published much later in a collection of Kipling stories as 'The Mark of the Beast'. Rather like Ian bouncing back from his first unfavourable reviews, Kipling was not dissuaded from his chosen profession.

In August 1889 Vereker, now a well-respected artist, and his wife arrived on a visit to Simla. Lord Roberts invited him to commemorate the storming of the Peiwar Kotal, even lending him a live Gurkha for a model, and Vereker produced a fine example of Victorian battle painting, the first of several for which he was commissioned. The two brothers and their wives were able to take a long holiday in Kashmir, staying first as guests at the Residency in Srinagar. On arrival at this imposing house, Hamilton was very put out to enter what he thought was his room only to find a lady not known to him getting into her bath. He sought Vereker's help, who authoritatively pointed him towards the 'proper' door, whereupon Hamilton burst in upon the same lady getting out of her bath! They were subsequently the guests of the fabulously wealthy Maharajah of Kapurthala on the occasion of his enthronement.

Jean was slightly asthmatic and occasionally had to leave the heat and dust of India, first in 1888 and again in 1890. Besides conveying genuinely touching expressions of how much they missed each other, the newlyweds' correspondence clearly show that Jean was very well connected in society, with a good ear for the gossip at court and in the drawing rooms, and that she took a very keen interest in the army and the jockeying for available promotions. She was ambitious for her husband and would be a strong pillar of support for him in that respect.

In his military duties Hamilton was still constantly at Roberts's side, especially during the many inspections of the North-West Frontier (four or five times a year for seven years). In July 1887 he received the brevet rank of lieutenant-colonel, just two years after his step up to major. The staff had been joined as ADC by 'Harry' Rawlinson (the future commander of the Fourth Army on the Western Front and C-in-C, India) and as secretary to the Defence Committee in India by Lieutenant-Colonel William Nicholson (a future chief of the Imperial General Staff). These three were good friends and worked well together apparently but, while Rawlinson remained on good terms with Hamilton, Nicholson was to become the deadliest of enemies.

Roberts was as keen as ever on improving the shooting skills of his soldiers. He encouraged rifle clubs throughout India, both military and civilian, running his own shooting team at Simla, which did well in competition and in which Hamilton invariably carried off the top prize. As Commander-in-Chief, India, Roberts could now step up his personal war against the British army's crude 'elementary bull's-eye' course of rifle training. Hamilton was made Assistant Adjutant-General of Musketry for the whole army in India and the principles he had laid down in *The Fighting of the Future* could be more generally applied. As he had predicted in that book, the troops were about to be issued with the first magazine rifles and good and accurate fire control was more important than ever. The Horse Guards were deaf to Roberts's appeals to permit a radical departure in the training. Instead Roberts convinced the Viceroy, Lord Lansdowne, to allow a massive experiment to be carried on throughout the Indian army. In his memoirs, *Forty-One Years in India*, Roberts wrote:

> I therefore gave over the work of improvement in this respect to an enthusiast in the matter of rifle shooting and an officer of exceptional energy and intelligence, Lieutenant-Colonel Ian Hamilton, and directed him, as Assistant Adjutant-General of Musketry, to arrange a course of instruction, in which the conditions would resemble as nearly as possible those of field service, and in which fire discipline should be developed to the utmost extent. He was most successful in carrying out my wishes, and the results from the first year's trials of the new system were infinitely better than even I had anticipated.[4]

Four schools for the officers and NCOs of the native regiments were set up in India, and these men were returned to their regiments to teach the new system to their men. All targets were of khaki figures (no black bull's-eyes on white backgrounds here); every kind of moving and 'snap' target was employed. The Indian press could confidently report that, 'all critics, who know *anything* of the matter, are unanimous that the revised course for the native army is far and away superior to the British course'. Gradually the British authorities were forced to admit that the results proved that the new system was in every way a better one. By mid-1892 an army newspaper could state: 'There is no doubt that the real British School of Musketry is at Simla and not at Hythe.' That year the final proof was offered. A field firing exercise involving British and Indian units was organized at Attock under the most realistic of battle conditions. From deep trenches instructors operated the most complex series of moving, disappearing and reappearing targets, culminating in the release downhill, when the 'attack' had closed to 250 yards, of canvas and bamboo balls that bounded towards the men at great speed. Those units trained in the new system shot these targets to pieces; the others missed them completely. When Roberts returned to England the next year (1893) he was able to present this incontrovertible evidence and finally convince the home authorities of the need for major reform of the British army's training. Hamilton's part in this vital reform cannot be underestimated.

Roberts was certainly doing what he could to advance Ian's career, as well as that of other deserving officers on his staff. In 1890, Lord Wolseley as Adjutant-General had seen through a Royal Warrant to regularize the promotion from full colonel to major-general of those officers who had held certain catalogued posts. Since the first step was to secure promotion to substantive colonel, Roberts duly noted that three of his staff officers were eligible for this advancement – Ian Hamilton as AAG Musketry, William Nicholson, now Roberts's Military Secretary, and Lord William Beresford, Military Secretary to the Viceroy of India. Every qualified officer in England was duly promoted, but not one of these three 'Indians'. This was the most blatant piece of 'African' preferment in the ongoing 'war between the rings'. That Redvers Buller was in high office at the War Office would explain Hamilton's virulent attitude towards him when their paths next crossed.

Roberts kept up a barrage of letters demanding that this injustice be put right. He was making the general point that this was an affront to all British officers serving in India and it would make it harder to get men to serve there willingly. In the course of a long and detailed letter to the Secretary of State for War (28 January 1891), covering the career patterns of many 'Indian' officers, Roberts wrote this warm praise of his devoted servant:

In explanation of my repeated efforts to obtain for Lieutenant-Colonel Hamilton the promotion to which I consider him to be entitled, it is, I trust, almost needless to state that, although this officer is a personal friend of my own, I have selected him for the important post he at present holds exclusively on public grounds. I know of no other officer, either at home or in India, who possesses in an equal degree the special qualifications which pre-eminently fit him for directing the musketry training of the army. Although as a lieutenant he was Musketry Instructor of his regiment for only about 16 months, he succeeded during that period in raising the Gordon Highlanders from seventeenth in order of merit to the top of the list, and equally satisfactory results on a much larger scale here attended his officiating and permanent tenure of the principal appointment on the musketry staff of the army in India ... I should deeply regret to see Lieutenant-Colonel Hamilton, who has devoted himself heart

and soul to this work, and who, in addition, has distinguished
himself in the field, denied promotion which under the provision of the Royal Warrant appears to be his due, equally with
other officers in the Headquarters Staff who hold appointments
certainly of no greater importance and of far less responsibility.[5]

This correspondence went on for months to no avail. An appeal to
the Duke of Cambridge himself was met with the inexplicable reply
that the Royal Warrant would not be applied in this instance.
Not to be outdone, Lord Beresford and Nicholson got to work
through the Viceroy and the Government of India in Council.
Before long the Secretary of State for India had made it a Cabinet
matter and the three men were finally confirmed as full colonels.
Though further wrangling cost Hamilton another year in lost
seniority, he was now the youngest colonel in the British army.

It is hard to exaggerate the devotion Hamilton felt for Lord
Roberts. He would later write:

> Never shall I forget my passionate longing, my prayers, for the
> advancement of Roberts, my hope against hope that he would
> become Commander-in-Chief in India, that he would triumph
> over his enemies and force his way out to South Africa . . . I
> will say this for Sir Fred; he was so charming, so considerate, so
> even in his temper, so wonderful a hero-to-his-valet man . . .
> Lord Bobs was Boss of my Ring and was the man to whom I
> owe militarily everything . . . The things I had in mind . . . were
> his example and the immense pains he took to mould a
> wayward and casual character into his own bright, clear-cut
> image, a task, alas, pathetically impossible.[6]

As Wolseley was nearing retirement in London, and Roberts
expected to succeed him as Adjutant-General, there was some
considerable debate over the successor to 'Bobs'. The Queen,
anxious to keep the royal princes in high command, was set on
having the Duke of Connaught be promoted from C-in-C, Bombay
to C-in-C, India. The Prime Minister, Lord Salisbury, was quite
certain that would not be the case. Roberts, who thought Connaught a perfectly good soldier worthy of the post, was asked to
extend his command in India for two more years to allow more
time for the difficulty to be resolved. Finally in April 1893 Roberts

returned to London after his forty-one years in India. Hamilton, having been twenty years in India and missing his wife who spent more and more time away because of her health, would not have minded being called back to England to continue working with his old chief.

Instead he was appointed military secretary to the new Commander-in-Chief, India, his old Gordons comrade, Sir George White, VC. Hamilton had predicted in a letter to Lady White back in 1887 that Sir George would fill this high office, when for the first and last time White expressed annoyance at Hamilton, deploring his 'insincere nonsense'. White was wrong on both counts and their long friendship was now rekindled. They began a new series of inspection tours which took in Nepal and some spectacular tiger shoots in December 1893. White and his staff were at Calcutta in January 1894 for the ceremonies surrounding the departure of Lord Lansdowne as Viceroy of India and the arrival of his successor, Lord Elgin. A home leave from May to August 1894 made a welcome break for Hamilton from the worst of the hot season in India; he returned in time to see trouble brewing again on the North-West Frontier. Sir William Lockhart of the Punjab Frontier Force had led a successful punitive expedition into Waziristan. Hamilton was disappointed that Sir George White, unwilling to deprive officers on the spot of the chance to serve, had not allowed any of his personal staff to join the expedition. But it did see his chief convert his ideas to a 'forward defence' policy for India. He was won over to the argument that India was best defended against the Russians and their tribal friends beyond Kabul and Kandahar, preferably by tribes friendly to Britain rather than on the plains of the Punjab.

Meanwhile from London, Roberts, who was disappointed in his expressed desires for the Aldershot Command (which went to the Duke of Connaught) and for his appointment as Viceroy of India (which went to Lord Elgin), was writing to Hamilton every week for some four months, pouring out his innermost feelings to his most trusted aide. He detailed the intrigues concerning the failed postings, and the hostility of the royal dukes to Roberts getting on too successfully in any of the home commands, and described how Redvers Buller was seen as the implacable enemy of any officer returning from service in India. Roberts refused the governorship of Malta because he relied entirely on his salary and would be heavily out of pocket if he took the job. This was a continuing difficulty for many senior generals and makes it clear that their long service to their country was certainly not motivated by purely financial considerations. There was also the problem for government of finding 'billets' for these long-serving senior officers, who were frequently too senior for most posts and were all angling for the few available positions equal to their rank and status. It was common for these letters to contain a request for Hamilton to 'look out' for some young officer serving in India and bring him to the Commander's attention and see that he 'got on' in the service; all part of the system of rewarding old comrades in arms by making sure their boys did well. It was 1895 before Roberts was finally offered command in Ireland, by which time he was glad to accept it.

In India active service once again intervened to rescue Hamilton from his desk and keep him up to the mark. As the North-West Frontier's wave of turbulence continued, a British political agent and 400 Indian troops were besieged in the fort at Chitral, far to the north and just fifty miles from the Russian border. A relief force under Sir Robert Low, with Brigadier-General Bindon Blood as his chief of staff, was set in motion on 1 April 1895.

A few weeks later a message reached Hamilton at Simla, just as he was preparing for his summer home leave. General Stedman, QMG India, was commanding the vital lines of communication and he had asked for Hamilton as his Assistant Adjutant-General and Assistant Quartermaster-General. In a very excited letter to Jean, Ian had to apologize for the loss of a home leave but explained how important this opportunity was for him. 'I cannot tell you, darling, what a good thing it will be for me. Just the making of me. Not medals or that sort of thing I don't mean – but teaching me just where I was weakest and afterwards making me just as qualified for service on the home staff as if I had passed the Staff College.'[7] This is the only suggestion we get that he might have regretted his decision in 1882 of throwing up the chance to go to Camberley.

Without doubt Hamilton had made great progress in his chosen profession but he must always have wondered what might have been. From many years of being the personal assistant of a commanding general, carrying out domestic tasks as well as military duties, he was now issuing orders and seeing things, important things, happen at his behest. Stedman had great confidence in him and gave him a 'frightening' degree of independence to organize the tortuous lines of communication between the troops and their bases. Over pathless mountains, bridgeless rivers and snowbound passes, constantly under attack from insurgent tribesmen, he was responsible for the two-way movement of tens of thousands of pack animals and men. At one point, when Low and his deputy were both absent in other parts of the theatre of war, Colonel Hamilton and his clerk were effectively commanding some 15,000 fighting men and all their auxiliaries. When, in May, Stedman was injured in a fall from his horse, Sir Robert Low ordered Hamilton to take full command of the logistical arrangements of the expedition, reporting directly to Low and signing all necessary orders in Stedman's name. Towards the end of the campaign, as it was drawing to a successful conclusion, we once again see Hamilton and his personal aide, 'Jim' Turner, oblivious of their rank and responsibility, taking to the hills to pursue marauding tribesmen reported in the vicinity by British Indian infantry. He was very fit indeed and seemed to thrive on active service. In September he was delighted to receive one of the relatively few 'mentions' in despatches for this campaign. It meant more to him than the CB that came his way, along with the campaign medal; he said he would have preferred the 'lower' order of the CSI, because it had a prettier ribbon.

His plans for the future had undergone a period of upheaval. Just as he was taking up the field posting in the Chitral, Lord Roberts had written asking if Hamilton would return to Dublin to be his Assistant Military Secretary. This was a great embarrassment as the post would normally be filled by a major and Hamilton was a full colonel. To accept it would look like the worst sort of 'jobbery', clinging to the coat-tails of his patron until a better posting came along, especially as it was fairly obvious that Roberts wanted Hamilton's proven literary talents on hand as he wrote his memoirs. He was able to refuse initially because of the active service on hand but Lord and Lady Roberts kept up the pressure on him, through Jean, to accept the call from his old chief. Roberts was hurt that Ian didn't accept willingly; Ian was hurt that his loyalty was being doubted. He then made an error of judgement and wrote explaining why he couldn't accept the post, offering instead to send in his papers and come home on half pay to serve as Roberts's private secretary and help with the book. This drew no reply from Roberts who was, in fact, insulted that Hamilton could believe him capable of such selfishness as to allow such a move. Jean wrote to explain that Roberts had acted out of genuine regard for Hamilton, believing him to be desperate for a home posting. The whole unfortunate episode was ended in August 1895 when Hamilton was offered the important post of Deputy Quartermaster-General, India by Sir George White. This post, once held by Roberts himself, was the best possible for a soldier of Hamilton's rank and experience. He at once telegraphed the news to Roberts, asking if he approved of him accepting the new offer. It was this cable, which Roberts passed to Jean for reply, that brought Jean's letter chiding Ian for misunderstanding Roberts's motives and wondering whether he really wanted to come home at all.

The new and prestigious posting for his dear 'Johnny' did, of course, allow Roberts to withdraw his offer gracefully. Having by then seen a copy of Sir George White's adulatory letter offering the post to Hamilton, he wrote to Jean expressing his delight at the promotion. Hamilton was due to take up the job in October 1895 and would be immediately eligible for two months' privilege leave. Hamilton planned to sail home, spend just three weeks with Jean, most of which would be taken up restoring good relations with Lord and Lady Roberts, and then return to India before the year was out. Instead Sir George White rewarded his recent exertions with a ninety-day leave, which gave him a full seven weeks at home. Much of that would have been spent explaining to his wife why he had accepted another major position in India that would lead to some years more of separation.

From January 1896 Hamilton was serving as Deputy Quarter-master-General at Simla, a very demanding job requiring long hours of paperwork. Later that year the QMG was taken ill and Hamilton took on the full burden of two men's work, needless to say while still only drawing a single pay. In India the QMG's work carried more responsibility than that of a British QMG, also being concerned with intelligence, engineering and medical services over and above the usual duties. However, when the QMG was officially invalided out and Hamilton found himself in sole charge of all those activities in India, he actually found that his workload fell dramatically. Instead of preparing and writing endless complicated memos for the consideration of his superior, he could now make instant decisions of his own, safe in the knowledge that Sir George White trusted him implicitly and would not have wanted to be bothered with masses of administrative detail. Hamilton would never again have sympathy with any 'big man' who complained of being overwhelmed with detail. The solution was to devolve such work to three or four responsible heads of department who could be trusted to get on with the matters in hand, leaving their chief free to address the larger picture.

That year saw the abolition of the separate army commands based at Madras and Bombay and the Commander-in-Chief, India now had direct command of the whole Indian army, organized into four commands each under a lieutenant-general. Hamilton could see that he was next in line for a posting to the most important of these commands, in the Punjab, where Nicholson was coming to the end of his time as Deputy Adjutant-General. This should have brought promotion to brigadier-general and placed him in the service of Sir William Lockhart, himself in line as the next Commander-in-Chief, India. The desire for home service and the prospects of significant advancement in India were once again pulling him in both directions at once. Meanwhile Lord Roberts, still with the former requirement in view, had applied to Lord Wolseley to ask for Hamilton as his Assistant Adjutant-General, Ireland, from 1 January 1897. Hamilton was saved another awkward confrontation with 'Bobs' as Wolseley did not take up the idea. As he travelled home for his 1897 summer leave, Hamilton met for the first time a delightful young lieutenant in the 4th Hussars, Winston Spencer Churchill. Ian already knew his mother socially and they became great friends and were to remain so for the rest of their lives.

He was travelling back to India in September 1897 in the company of Sir William Lockhart (another of those old army friends of his father) and Captain Aylmer Haldane. All were keen

to be involved in a new frontier campaign in the offing, to punish
the Afridi and other tribes in the Tirah region for their continuous
lawlessness. At Aden Sir William received a secret telegram from
Sir George White naming and asking his opinion of two divisional
commanders and six brigadiers for the campaign. Lockhart, who
was to command the Tirah expedition, took Hamilton into his
confidence, bowing to his extensive knowledge of the army in India
and checking on some of the names mentioned. Hamilton was
told that he was to have the First Brigade, a moment of great excitement for him as it would be his first service as a general officer.
By 6 October 1897 he was at Peshawar, organizing his troops for
the advance on Kohat. His provisional brigade comprised the 1st
Gordon Highlanders, the 1st Devons, the 4th Gurkhas, the Nabha
Native Infantry, the machine-gun section of the 16th Lancers, a
British mountain battery and the usual complement of field hospitals and supply troops. This scratch force he successfully led over
the difficult Kohat Pass to join Penn Symons's 1st Division. He was
looking forward to distinguishing himself under the leadership of
Sir William Lockhart, his chief of staff, Nicholson, whom Hamilton
still counted a good friend, and Penn Symons. Success in the Tirah
would mean he could safely leave India for good, return to England
and await the next interesting job that came vacant. His only worry
was that Lockhart's personal dislike of Penn Symons might see his
troops left out of the main events of the campaign. He took
command of First Brigade comprising the 1st Devons, the 2nd/1st
Gurkhas, the 30th Punjab Infantry and two field hospitals; the 2nd
Derbyshires were to join him soon. For the forward movement
Hamilton was asked to command a force much larger than his own
brigade, such was the confidence his divisional commander had in
him. Personal disaster was to end all these optimistic hopes.

On 16 October 1897, riding quietly along, his pony suddenly
shied at some passing veiled women on donkeys and went crashing
to the ground. As he tried to jump free, Hamilton fell heavily,
breaking one leg and spraining the ankle of the other. Sympathetic
telegrams from half the army in India poured in as his brigade
was given to Brigadier-General Hart, VC. Once again he was the
subject of medical experimentation as the 'new' plaster of Paris was
applied to his leg, though the particular batch used was defective

and refused to set, so the whole thing had to be done again. By November, when fever and dysentery also set in, he was very ill indeed, but he was back on his feet by December. When the commander of 4th Brigade, Brigadier-General Westmacott, became unwell, Hamilton was notified by Lockhart that he might be called back to relieve him. This news was as good as a tonic and he passed his medical board inspection satisfactorily, but Westmacott recovered and Hamilton suffered further upset as other expeditionary staff appointments passed him by. In January 1898 he was resigned to something like three more years in India as he tried to boost his career enough to be eligible for a good home posting. A long separation from Jean, who was wavering between expecting Ian home and making and then cancelling plans to join him in India, was adding to his current low spirits.

By February he was back in the field, commanding the equivalent of two brigades (the 3rd Brigade swollen to seven battalions, a battery and two engineer field companies). His camp had to be carefully constructed, with the tents raised over deep excavations. The British had been introduced to the dangers of men armed with modern rifles and the new smokeless cartridges; enemy snipers, deadly accurate at all times, were now extremely difficult to spot. Some important lessons were being learned by the officers serving in this campaign, not just the need to secure their positions with the pick and shovel, but the fatal consequences of moving in close order with such marksmen in the hills around and about. Hamilton was to study this new development carefully; it confirmed everything he had been trying to inculcate through his musketry training for many years. Progressive officers like him would devise new infantry tactics to allow for the increased efficiency of the defender's rifle fire. He would be the first to fight a battle with these new tactics and would not have long to wait for the opportunity.

The campaign was brought to a close, as much by the demands for economy from Simla as by success in the field. The tribes were bribed with large quantities of silver to hand in their modern rifles and desist from banditry. As the British began to evacuate the valleys and march back to their Indian cantonments they were at their most vulnerable. The younger Afghan warriors and some recalcitrant war bands harassed the columns. It was Ian Hamilton's important, if unglamorous, duty to protect the lines of passage for the withdrawal of 20,000 British troops. Based well forward in a fortified camp at Gudda Kalai (Pushtoo for 'Den of Thieves'), he occupied the mountain heights every day with skirmish lines of Gurkha riflemen, covered well by a plentiful artillery, pulling them back each night in what often proved a difficult manoeuvre in the presence of a bold and resourceful enemy.

Winston Churchill, developing a reputation both as a journalist and a notorious 'medal-hunter', had served in 1897 in the Malakand Field Force through the good offices of his family friend, Sir Bindon Blood, but he had been ordered to rejoin his regiment, the 4th Hussars, at Bangalore before he could get involved in the Tirah campaign. In January 1898 he was telling his mother that if troops were sent from India to serve in the Sudan, Ian Hamilton was sure to command them and he had promised to take young Winston out on his staff. (The 'Africans' would, of course, make sure that no Indian troops, however suitable, were used in the recapture of the Sudan). Hamilton had written to him from the seat of the war promising that, if Major Turner got the higher posting he deserved, Hamilton would send at once for Churchill to be his orderly officer. The chief protagonists then present two quite different stories of how Churchill fulfilled his wish to serve in the Tirah. According to Hamilton, Churchill cabled him from Meerut, where his polo team was in competition, begging him to arrange for Churchill an interview with Sir William Lockhart. Because of the family friendship, Lockhart was always kind to Hamilton and agreed to the request. Churchill duly impressed the general and was taken on as an 'extra' ADC at his headquarters. Sir William was promptly ordered back to Simla to take up his new post as Commander-in-Chief, India, leaving Churchill in the theatre of war. Now, according to Churchill's letters to his mother, he travelled from Meerut to Peshawar and simply went to see Lockhart with a request to visit his friend, General Hamilton. (How young cavalry lieutenants gained instant access to commanding generals is not explained.) He says he did not expect employment but, 'to his astonishment', was immediately taken on as an orderly officer on Lockhart's staff. He thought that he owed the advancement to Captain Haldane, Lockhart's remarkably influential ADC. Haldane was a Gordon

Highlander and, of course, knew of the connections between Lockhart, Hamilton and Churchill and may have been just making sure that everybody concerned was pleased with the outcome.

In March 1898 Hamilton was finally presented with the choice he had been skirting around for some years. Sir William Lockhart invited him to become Quartermaster-General, India, at the fabulous salary of £3,000 per annum. On the very same day the Adjutant-General of the British army, Sir Evelyn Wood, cabled him with the offer of the interesting post of Commandant of the School of Musketry at Hythe, Kent, at the more modest annual salary of £800. He chose the latter, once again proving that he was never motivated by the materialism of the age; the acquisition of money and fame for personal glorification was alien to him. As it happened, the decision, in part taken to return him to the side of his dear wife, was to ensure that he would be available for the war that brought him some of his greatest achievements. Lockhart wrote to assure him that he was delighted for him, concluding his letter: 'There is no doubt about the advantage your appointment will be to the service'.[8]

As he prepared to leave India for the last time, Churchill wrote to him asking him to be sure and call on his mother and to 'please say nice things about me to everyone at home'. He closed with the stirring lines: 'Au revoir my dear general – may we meet again when rifles are loaded and swords sharpened – if possible before an audience which will include forty centuries.'[9] (The latter was a reference to the new campaign developing in Egypt for the reconquest of the Sudan, which Churchill was desperate to join.) Hamilton carried back to England the manuscript of Churchill's novel *Savrola* and the text of an article on the forward defence of India for the journal of the Royal United Services Institute. From the ship he wrote a fatherly letter to the younger man warning him that 'you will only be losing time and training if you continue to hang between the two or three avenues which radiate from your feet and lead towards fame each in its own way'.[10] He urged that Winston choose quickly between the army or politics and put all his efforts behind one or the other. While some great military adventures still stood before him, Churchill was firmly set on the path of political advancement.

For the first time since they were married, Ian and Jean were able to set up home together in England. His new duties could not have been more rewarding to him professionally. His ideas on rifle training, which had transformed the Indian army, could now be spread throughout the British army. Realistic battle conditions and individual accuracy summed up the revolution in training instituted by him. He immediately increased the number of full courses at Hythe from four to five a year, and drew the militia and yeomanry into the system for the first time. In the course of a year he visited all eleven military districts of the United Kingdom to inspect their efficiency in musketry, and his annual report covered the shooting prowess of every command, both home and overseas. He wanted all officers to obtain a certificate in musketry to make them all trainers of men in the new principles. New musketry regulations were written and, with the enthusiastic backing of Sir Evelyn Wood, more ammunition was obtained for firing practice. A British soldier fired seven times more ammunition on the ranges at Hythe than any conscript in any other European army. At last Hamilton's great interest, in which he had made a great and original contribution, was being put to the best possible use in the service of his profession and his country. Every commandant of Hythe between the Boer War and the First World War claimed to have created the astonishing efficiency of the British battalions that poured fifteen aimed rounds a minute into the German formations at Mons and Ypres in 1914. All of them built upon the modernizing revolution of Ian Hamilton.

The annual manoeuvres in the autumn of 1898 were the most important for nearly twenty-five years. In these Grand Combined Manoeuvres, 50,000 troops were deployed in the West Country. Hamilton commanded a brigade in the 'Blue' army led by Sir Redvers Buller as it opposed the Duke of Connaught's 'Red' army. The old British square had proved itself useful in the current Sudan campaign and some of the older generals were delighted with the excuse to use it. Buller was comprehensively outmanoeuvred and 'defeated' in the war games, but Hamilton's brigade had been handled very skilfully. From concealed positions he had sent out raiding parties that so repeatedly overran the headquarters and communications systems of the 'Red' brigade opposing him that it was at one stage declared to be operationally out of action. In a move reminiscent of his days as a subaltern at Mooltan, he was reprimanded for using such unorthodox tactics.

Churchill had secured a temporary posting with the 21st Lancers in the Sudan and in September Hamilton wrote for news of the campaign. After a long and vivid reply describing his part in the famous charge of the 21st Lancers at the battle of Omdurman (September 1898), Churchill concluded with a PS: 'I wish you would imitate Sir Bindon Blood and write to me as "Winston". Churchill is very formal.'[11] The friendship was developing apace.

The Commandant of the School of Musketry at Hythe was often replaced after just one year, but Hamilton was doing such a spectacularly good job there that he was given another year's tenure. Thus he was in post when the call to arms rang out again in South Africa.

4

War in South Africa,
1899–1902

It would be hard to imagine a war more cynically contrived than the Second Anglo-Boer War of 1899–1902, as Alfred Milner, the Governor of the Cape Colony, and Joseph Chamberlain at the Colonial Office goaded the Boer republics of the Transvaal and the Orange Free State into a mobilization that many Boers didn't care for, obliging a reluctant British government into despatching reinforcements. The British military commander in Natal, General Sir William Butler, was bitterly opposed to Milner's machinations and was forced to resign in August 1899. No one should ever assume that professional soldiers welcome war at every opportunity. Interestingly, many of the great Boer commanding generals also voted against the war measures being taken in Pretoria.

While an army corps of 48,000 men was drawn together in Britain, to be commanded by the somewhat reluctant Sir Redvers Buller, VC, urgent reinforcements were despatched from India (a brigade each of infantry and cavalry) and the Mediterranean (an infantry brigade), which began to arrive at the Cape in the first week of October. It was news of this that prompted the Boers to deliver an ultimatum to the British Government to have these troops removed by 11 October 1899. Almost regardless of the rights and wrongs of the case, it was impossible within the international politics of the day for an empire of the size and influence of Great Britain to bow to such a demand from such an impudent little adversary. Kruger's government had badly misjudged the situation in expecting Britain to cave in as they had done after their defeats in 1881, and in hoping for more concrete assistance from their anti-British friends in Europe. However, Britain was about to make more than a few misjudgements of her own.

As the political crisis in southern Africa developed, the Secretary of State for War, Lord Lansdowne, appointed the then Quartermaster-General, Sir George White, VC., to be the new GOC, Natal. He was firmly of the 'Roberts Ring', and had been C-in-C, India when Roberts left, and he had 'inherited' Ian Hamilton as his Military Secretary there. They were, of course, old friends from their days of service together in the 2nd Gordon Highlanders. He was therefore very happy to have Colonel Hamilton in Britain available for appointment to his staff as Assistant Adjutant-General. At Hamilton's suggestion he also took with him that other 'Indian', Lieutenant-Colonel Sir Henry Rawlinson. They sailed for South Africa on 16 September 1899, fully aware that their task was essentially defensive, to hold the field until Buller's army corps arrived to deliver the coup de grace. Having been appointed on 12 September, and leaving four days later with no briefing regarding policy, intelligence or strategy, Hamilton was in a curiously similar position to that he would face in 1915.

Arriving at Cape Town on 3 October, they dined at once with Milner. He was very dismissive of the Boers' ability to stand against regular troops. Hamilton swiftly disabused him of this notion, to the apparent annoyance of Milner. Boers in the open might be as vulnerable as any to cavalry and artillery, but on ground of their own choosing they were as formidable an opponent as could be found anywhere in the world, according to this veteran of Majuba.

When the Boer ultimatum expired on 11 October, White and his staff were moving by train to Ladysmith. The Boers had assumed the offensive, presumably to try for a decision before the arrival of the British reinforcements, and struck to the west and the south, hoping to raise up the Cape Afrikaaners in their support. But they were soon tied down to besieging the makeshift British and colonial garrisons at Mafeking and Kimberley. Their other chief offensive was into Natal, with the vital port of Durban as their objective. Military good sense dictated that they would be opposed along the line of the Tugela River. But, as so often in history, the soldiers had to defer to their political masters and the Governor of Natal insisted that the northern part of the colony had to be defended. White would have settled, reluctantly, for Ladysmith as his base, but the temporary local commander, Major-General Penn Symons, had already moved a sizeable force up the railway line to Dundee. It was political expediency that saw a further weakening of White's field force as the Governor insisted that a battalion, two cavalry regiments and a battery were sent back to Maritzburg to give a solicitous display of strength in the provincial capital.

Hamilton was already writing to Jean that he feared they would be bottled up in Ladysmith. He would have preferred it if the whole force had tried to stall the Boer offensive as far forward as possible. Major-General Archibald Hunter had now arrived from India to serve as Buller's chief-of-staff and took over in that capacity to Sir George White until Buller arrived. This freed Hamilton from staff duty and he was delighted to assume command of 7th Infantry Brigade, with the local rank of Major-General. His old battalion, 2nd Gordon Highlanders, was now under his authority, together with two other battalions just over from India, 1st Devons and 1st Manchesters. He immediately began three days' intensive training, free of Aldershot doctrine and able to develop his theories based on his observations of the Tirah campaign and his advanced thinking in the realms of 'musketry', fire control and 'fire and movement'. The brigade was fortunate to have such a forward-thinking commander; it was to prove just what a properly trained infantry could achieve within the next few days. It is entirely to the credit of these infantrymen that they responded so quickly and so well to this new tactical training.

The Boers closed in on the brigade at Dundee and had soon got behind them and cut the railway at Elandslaagte. Penn Symons had been Hamilton's commander in the Tirah campaign and one of his last letters was to him on 17 October, expressing delight in his field appointment. 'If they leave it to you, all will go well . . .'[1] On 20 October Penn Symons was mortally wounded as he led his infantry in the storming of Talana Hill to put the encroaching Boers to flight in a confused and bloody little fight.

The victors were in a poor strategic position and were ordered back to Ladysmith. To cover them, Sir John French's cavalry was ordered to turn the Boers out of Elandslaagte but he found them in much greater force than expected and wired for assistance. White entrained Hamilton's brigade and two batteries of field artillery, which began to arrive in the late morning of 21 October. Many writers state that Hamilton's force arrived in the afternoon but he makes it quite clear in later correspondence that his soldiers were ready to attack at midday. Hamilton would have liked to attack the Boers immediately, but French insisted on a delay to rest and water his horses, which meant the battle could not commence until after 2.30 p.m.

Hamilton swiftly appraised the Boer position and both White and French deferred to his plan of action. The Boers held the eastern arm of a horseshoe-shaped ridge that ended in a kopje. Hamilton set the Devons to assault the ridge frontally while the Manchesters went for the hill, with the Gordon Highlanders on their right seeking to turn the enemy position. They were supported by dismounted troopers of the Imperial Light Horse, while French kept the 5th Lancers and a mounted squadron of the ILH in hand to exploit success.

But if the Boers expected the British to present them with a sitting target they were in for a rude awakening. Hamilton called his soldiers around him and explained to them that they were to put into practice the very wide, very loose formations they had been rehearsing under his direction. He filled the men with enthusiasm, promising them that their fame would be the talk of London the next day. The men dispersed to their duties with many expressions of confidence. 'We'll do it, sir. We'll do it,' is how a war correspondent present at the time reported their eager response. The Devons deployed for a seemingly fatal task in a way never seen in the British, or any other European, infantry until then. There were nearly three yards between each man going forward, and 450 yards between each attacking wave. The depth of the battalion in attack was nearly a mile, and it went forward in rushes, with sections firing and moving alternately in support of one another, while the artillery heavily shelled the ridge with shrapnel. They had to cover nearly two miles thus and, as they drew closer, the Boer Mausers drove them to ground to seek cover and catch their breath.

Meanwhile the Manchesters and Gordons had begun their ascent of the hill at one end of the ridge. Here all the traditional attack methods were given full play. Pipers played 'The Cock o' the North'; officers were well to the fore – the Gordons were to lose thirteen of the nineteen officers employed. Lines of farmer's wire occasionally held up the attackers; a thunderstorm, long since threatening, burst over the battlefield. There was some wavering as the men neared the top of the hill. Hamilton and his immediate aides dashed into the forefront of the fray. He ordered the buglers to sound the charge and the infantry surged forward and gained the crest. On seeing a white flag, the British began to sound the 'cease fire'. There then occurred one of those incidents, common enough in the fog of war, that build into stories of enemy treachery and can generate much hatred and reciprocal revenge-taking. A party of some fifty Boers, led by their venerable chief, Kock, in black frock coat and top hat, refused to surrender (and may well not have understood the Western conventions concerning the flag). Instead they volleyed into the relaxing British and charged, causing a momentary panic that threatened to bounce the attackers off the ridge. Again Hamilton's personal courage and example saved the day as he rallied the soldiers, calling for bugle and pipes to stiffen them. And, at a most fortuitous moment, the Devons completed their frontal assault and came storming up the ridge to put the once-rallied Boers to full flight. As the exhausted and rain-sodden infantry rested, French's cavalry pounced and, in a spirited action that gave great satisfaction to the proponents of cold steel for horsemen, they did great execution with their lances.

The German Great General Staff admired this battle victory with its artillery preparation, skilled assault, defeat of a counter-attack, consolidation of the position and cavalry pursuit. Indeed it was almost the only example they could find in the war to illustrate their idea of a model battle. Together with Talana Hill, it came as a severe shock to the Boers, many of whom were veterans of the war in which they easily shot down red-coated infantry whenever they were attacked. If the khaki-clad British were going to come on like this too often, the war was going to be grim indeed.

French's staff officer, Douglas Haig, carried the news back to Ladysmith and Rawlinson reported how 'Johnny' Hamilton had handled his infantry splendidly, combining great personal courage with great skill. Sir John French personally recommended Hamilton for the Victoria Cross for twice showing the way forward to the attacking infantry. Alas, while he had been too young and junior at

Majuba, Hamilton was now too senior and it was considered undesirable to award the VC to a 'general officer'. (He was, of course, a substantive colonel.) Lord Wolseley, then Commander-in-Chief, did not wish to create a new precedent and declined to submit Hamilton's name to the Queen.

Despite suffering from a bout of influenza brought on by the rainstorm at Elandslaagte, Hamilton saw the troops from Dundee safely back into the lines at Ladysmith, just as the Transvaal commandos under Piet Joubert (some 14,000 men) and those of the Orange Free State under Prinsloo (some 6,000 strong) closed the net around the town.

Hamilton had been keen to attack the Boers' main laager, which his scouts had reported as poorly defended. White originally agreed to an attack by four battalions, which began to assemble at 1 a.m. on the morning of 28 October for a surprise assault. But, with barely two hours to the start, White called off the operation. He had a much larger affair in mind. Later that day he presented a plan to his staff for a large-scale attack on the Boers' main position on Pepworth Hill to the north of Ladysmith. Hamilton objected, arguing that the troops were too played out for such a major attack, which would, in any case, be subjected to deadly enfilade fire from the hills around it. White was not best pleased with this dissent, and chided Hamilton that the victor of Elandslaagte thought he could speak as he pleased to his old chief. But Archie Hunter agreed that the plan was unsound and it was dropped.

Regrettably White next presented, as fait accompli, a much larger and more complex plan of operation, involving several columns moving against the Boers to the north. 'Mournful Monday' was the name given to this sorry battle of Ladysmith on 30 October 1899. Lieutenant-Colonel Carleton had taken two battalions (1st Royal Irish Fusiliers and 1st Gloucesters) and a mountain battery out at night to seize Nicolson's Nek and cut the enemy line of retreat. But in the dark they lost their sense of direction and were ascending Tchrengula Hill when their mules stampeded and crashed back through the infantry, carrying off most of the ammunition and alerting the enemy to their presence. Field-Cornet Christian De Wet's Free Staters soon had Carleton's force pinned down. Meanwhile a scratch brigade of five battalions under Lieutenant-Colonel Grimwood went out to attack Long Hill, newly deserted by the Boers in favour of more formidable flanking positions from which Louis Botha's men were soon pouring a devastating fire into them. Far from being able to attack Pepworth Hill, Hamilton had to use his brigade to cover Grimwood's hard-pressed force. With French's cavalry late getting out to the right, White saw his whole plan crumble. He ordered a retreat around noon.

The Royal Artillery deployed two batteries to cover Grimwood's withdrawal and the King's and the Manchesters formed the inter-mediate line. But Botha's men poured in such a devastating fire that three battalions of British infantry broke and ran for the rear, carrying most of the cavalry with them. Only Hamilton's brigade came away with any semblance of order. To crown the defeat, in the utmost confusion of white flags and calls to surrender, Carle-ton's force capitulated – a thousand of the British passing into captivity in a failure worse than Majuba.

It would seem that Sir George White never recovered from this reverse. He maintained a passive defence and awaited the much heralded advance of Buller's force. Just before the Boers completely invested the town on 2 November, French, Haig and the 2nd Dublin Fusiliers were withdrawn. That left nine battalions, four cavalry regiments and six batteries at Ladysmith, a town not easy to defend as it was dominated by hills to the north and east. Thankfully the Boers settled down to a fairly passive siege.

The perimeter was divided into four sectors and Hamilton was given command of the largest sector, Sector C, some five miles long, including the important southern ridge called the Platrand, a plateau some three miles long with hills at either end, Wagon Hill to the west and Caesar's Camp to the east. With seldom more than 1,000 rifles to defend the position at any one time, Hamilton devised the best defence possible according to the latest precepts. He kept his main forces back in a series of small forts along the inner edge of the plateau, leaving a 500–800-yard field of fire for the defenders whilst sheltering them from the fire of the enemy artillery. The rocky and boulder-strewn ground made entrenchment impossible, but the stone forts, comfortingly similar to the sangars known to these Indian army soldiers, were steadily improved and were quite formidable before long. A line of outposts and sentries watched the outer edge of the perimeter, and a telephone network ran back to White's headquarters in the town.

It is a great pity that an important book like *The Boer War* by Thomas Pakenham should set about the worthy task of restoring some of Buller's reputation by the wholly unworthy method of attacking the reputation of Ian Hamilton at every opportunity. He repeats every known calumny he possibly can without any evaluation of source or motive. His 'critique' of Hamilton's handling of the defence of the Platrand is extraordinary, but it is, of course, written by a general historian and not a military historian. Hamilton is blamed for not digging trenches along the edge of the plateau, which ignores the barren and rocky nature of the terrain, misunderstands the nature of modern defensive fighting with a small garrison to hand, and gives little credit for the prepared fortifications that still existed for the visitor's perusal a hundred years later. Hamilton is both criticized for spending time in a nice house in the town – the old and ill-informed complaint about 'chateau generals' – and blamed for getting too closely involved in hand-to-hand fighting during Boer attacks, which misses the point that this occurred because Hamilton regularly slept up on the plateau amongst his soldiers. (We shall return to this litany of hostile comment later.)

After a skirmish on 7 November, a heavy attack on Caesar's Camp on 9 November, which lasted for most of the day, was decisively repulsed. This both encouraged the defenders after the debacle of 'Mournful Monday' and discouraged the Boers from further attacks for several weeks.

The routine of besieged life set in. The shelling became a backdrop that soon grew familiar. White and Joubert agreed between them that the wounded and civilians could be removed to a camp at Intombi, some four miles away in Boer territory, provided it was kept supplied by the garrison, by way of a daily train permitted to run by the besiegers. Hamilton was a keen advocate of a more active defence, often proposing attacks on the enemy lines, especially after it became clear that some of the besiegers had gone south to face Buller. He was particularly concerned that the cavalry should be allowed to break out and make themselves useful to the field armies gathering to relieve the various besieged garrisons. He carried Hunter and Rawlinson with him, but Sir George White would not agree.

As Buller began his approach march to the Tugela the garrison became more aggressive and carried out some effective raids on Boer gun positions. When it became clear that a battle was in the offing, Hamilton was again proposing and preparing for a breakout battle, though not simply an obvious push to the south, which the Boers would have welcomed. Again White would not sanction such boldness. Expecting an early end to their plight, the news of Buller's heavy defeat at Colenso on 15 December, in the same week as British defeats at Magersfontein and Stormberg, came as a heavy blow to the defenders of Ladysmith. Worse still, but mercifully not known to all, was the extraordinary message that Buller sent into the town by heliograph, telling White that he could not get in to help him and that, if he couldn't hold out, he should fire off his ammunition and seek terms from the enemy. White may have been low in spirits but he had no intention of leading 12,000 British soldiers into captivity and the message was treated with the contempt it deserved.

It should come as no surprise therefore to know that Hamilton was freely expressing his intense dislike of Sir Redvers Buller. He confided to his diary the scathing comment, 'a nation which possesses a Roberts and a Buller and selects the latter for a vital undertaking deserves almost any misfortune which it is possible to imagine.'[2] Buller was the 'evil genius' of the Wolseley Ring. Hamilton was convinced that, as Adjutant-General, Buller had held up the promotion of 'Indian' officers like himself. As theatre commander in South Africa he was also suspected of preventing Hamilton getting his next step in promotion, for he was still a colonel doing a major-general's job. Since the manoeuvres fiasco in 1898, Hamilton had remained convinced that years at a War Office desk had robbed Buller of the will to fight. The ensuing misfortunes of the relief force must have reinforced his fears.

The antipathy was entirely mutual. Buller repeatedly vented his bad opinion of Hamilton to anyone who would listen. Far from congratulating the Natal field force for the victory of Elandslaagte, Buller is reported as saying, 'That fellow Hamilton has forced Sir

George's hand and let him in for this fight.'[3] On 8 November he cabled Lord Lansdowne: 'French is here, conversation confirms doubts I have of White's ability. Besides evident want of military precautions, White seems to have been weak and vacillating and much influenced by Hamilton, a dangerous adviser.'[4] This can have done Buller little good, as Lansdowne was a firm friend of Roberts and favoured his ring accordingly. At Cape Town Buller spoke to Lord Methuen, who reported in a letter to his wife on 12 November that Buller thought 'White was frightened to death, Ian Hamilton mad and French all right'.[5] French himself confirmed these opinions of Buller's in a separate talk with Methuen. Perhaps Buller, who was to show himself to be an excessively cautious field commander, just could not cope with an officer so eager to get stuck into the Boers at every opportunity. Perhaps he still smarted at the humiliation of those 1898 manoeuvres. Certainly we must understand that the officers of the British army were as prone to personal antipathy as any other section of society, exacerbated by the way they all had to compete for a finite number of important appointments as they progressed in their chosen profession.

If Hamilton could take any comfort from 'Black Week' it was in the fact that his adored old chief, Lord Roberts, was placed in supreme command in South Africa, and Buller was left with responsibility for the Natal campaign alone.

The Boers had also taken heart from their string of victories and determined on one major effort to crack the Ladysmith defences. Five thousand men under De Villiers were to assault the Platrand at several points at night in an effort to overwhelm the 1,000 defenders by surprise and main force. Hamilton's quarters in the town, which he shared with Rawlinson, had been so badly damaged in the shelling that he had decided to camp out with his staff in the vicinity of Caesar's Camp. At three o'clock on the morning of 6 January 1900, the Boers attacked both Wagon Hill and Caesar's Camp, with another force moving onto the nek between them. Because Hamilton's defences were so well placed away from the crest the enemy had only the vaguest idea of their composition and there followed a desperate and confused struggle in the darkness. The Manchesters and some men of the Imperial Light Horse absorbed the initial attack. Hamilton was holding three companies of the Gordons as a local reserve behind Caesar's Camp at Fly Kraal, which he used to strengthen the line at about four o'clock. From the town came three squadrons of the ILH to Wagon Hill; the other half of the Gordons came up to the Fly Kraal. The 60th and Rifle Brigade were also sent up and began a series of very costly counter-attacks, which Hamilton put a stop to as quickly as he could, as the Boers were now pinned to the crest line of the ridge and were making no further progress.

Shortly after noon, Hamilton was conferring with local officers at Wagon Hill about an organized counter-attack when a determined rush by the Boers, led by De Villiers himself, broke into the position. Hamilton hurled himself into the thick of the fighting, pistol in hand, and in the ensuing mêlée the Boers were routed and De Villiers was killed. By mid-afternoon a storm had broken over the ridge and the fighting seemed stalemated. The Devons were brought over from the northern defences and White insisted that they be used to attack and clear the Boers off the ridge. In fact Hamilton's conduct of the defence had already pinned the Boers to the outer edge of the ridge and he was convinced that they would be obliged to relinquish their hold before too long. But the orders were firm and Hamilton could only give the Devons another speech of encouragement, as he had done before Elandslaagte, before launching them across a bullet-swept 150 yards in the evening gloom. Despite heavy losses the Devons swept the Boers back and ended any chance they had of holding any part of the ridge. That night they evacuated it completely and made no further effort to storm the town.

Hamilton's force had lost 17 officers and 158 men were killed or mortally wounded. Another 249 men were wounded, mainly in the counter-attacks to clear the ridge. The Boers admitted to 64 men killed and 119 wounded, but are thought to have lost nearer 250 men altogether. These were far greater losses than the Boers suffered in battles like Magersfontein and Colenso. In a letter to his wife, White wrote: 'Johnny Hamilton was in command when the principal attack was made and did invaluable service, and I have reported on him in the highest terms.'[6]

Meanwhile Buller, wracked with self-doubt, was feeling his way forward, suffering defeat at Spion Kop, Vaal Krantz and Hlangwane. Finally his battle-hardened soldiers forced their way through the Boer positions along the Tugela. This coincided with the news of the major Boer surrender at Paardeberg on 27 February. Boer morale in Natal started to crack. Soon they were streaming away from the Tugela and from the lines around Ladysmith.

On 28 February cavalry from Buller's force, under Hubert Gough, ended the 122-day siege. Buller made his formal entry into the town on 3 March. The early euphoria soon gave way to another round of intensely personal bickering. Having been part of the reception committee for the relief force, Hamilton, by now described as 'a regular skeleton', was forced to take to bed as he was ill with a severe bout of 'Peshawar' (enteric) fever. He had a stream of visitors from Buller's force, from whom he learned many details of the half-hearted nature of Buller's campaign. He wrote a particularly vitriolic letter to the leading military writer, Spenser Wilkinson, then military correspondent of the *Morning Post*. He wanted his friends to know of Buller's telegram after Colenso, which he described thus:

> After the battle he wired us that we had better fire off our ammunition and make the best terms we could. We thought at first our cypher and helio must have fallen into the hands of the Boers, it seemed so incredible that General Buller of all men could give such unworthy advice.[7]

(Buller's defenders insist that he meant to advise White that he would not reach Ladysmith in under a month, and that the defenders should seek terms only if they could not hold out that long. It is hardly surprising that the garrison of proud fighting men should have taken such strong exception to the idea.) Hamilton continued to Wilkinson:

> I want you to know sharp, Buller is no use. He is indeed far, far worse than useless, and I write to beg you to use all your influence to get the man recalled before he does more mischief ... generally officers and men have lost all confidence in 'Sir Reverse' as they call him. I should think 100 of his army have been to see me since I have been ill and from General to Subaltern they agree that he is as unsatisfactory as a general

could be . . . except in the case of the Colenso fight, everyone is
confident that the Battalions could in every case have fought
their way through all right had they been given their heads . . .[8]

Lord Roberts urgently called for the services of his trusted
deputy cooped up in Natal and soon Hamilton was on his way
back to Cape Town. En route he wrote to Roberts from Maritzburg
on 10 March 1900, about Buller's entry into Ladysmith. 'Buller was
very rude to Sir George and spoke to him in the vilest way of you
and Kitchener, whom he appears to dislike and to attribute dishon-
est motives to, almost as much as he does you. . . .'[9]

While recuperating at Cape Town, Hamilton was visited by Leo
Amery, war correspondent for *The Times* and future historian of
the war. They were good friends and political allies; no doubt
Hamilton's views on the campaign in Natal did much to inform
Amery's later writing. Roberts offered Hamilton, still only a colonel
but confirmed as a local major-general back-dated to October, a
choice of commands: either an infantry brigade or complete charge
of Roberts's lines of communications. While recognizing the
importance of the staff post offered, Hamilton inevitably chose the
combat command.

With the main army in Bloemfontein and preparing to advance
on Pretoria, the debate developed as to whether the war could be
brought to a speedy conclusion. Hamilton, unlike his colleagues
Rawlinson and Hunter, took a very optimistic view, which was
much appreciated by Roberts. As he travelled to join the army at
Bloemfontein, Hamilton heard that he was to command a newly
created division of mounted infantry and infantry, 10,000 strong,
with the semi-independent task of moving along some ten to twenty
miles east of the main columns, covering Roberts's flank and
uncovering the flank of the enemy facing him. Leo Amery, in the
fourth volume of his history of the war, gives a very perceptive pen
portrait of this rising star.

The choice of so young a general as Ian Hamilton, who was
then only forty-seven and had come out to South Africa as a
colonel, to command that part of the main army which entailed
most responsibility and independence, was a good instance of
Lord Roberts's judgement of character and determination to

give full scope to dash and enterprise. Ian Hamilton was one of those men who had come to the front from his own determination to be there when important work was toward. He had proved himself in India a capable organiser as well as a dashing soldier, had been wounded at Majuba, and had seen campaigns in Afghanistan, Egypt, Burmah, Chitral and Tirah. His record in Natal has been set forth in previous volumes, and Lord Roberts, who had first recognised his ability as a member of his staff in India, had sent for him immediately after the relief of Ladysmith. There were perhaps some more scientific soldiers in the British Army than Ian Hamilton, and some who made fewer mistakes, but he had two great merits which Lord Roberts himself also possessed and could appreciate in others: an eye for country which amounted almost to genius, and a capacity for pushing on and imposing his will on the enemy instead of waiting for them to develop their plans. Also he was willing to take responsibility, run risks, and stake a budding reputation on the venture, a quality too rarely found among officers, or for the matter of that among men of any profession. Though personally ambitious, he was always ready to recognise merit in his colleagues, and like many of the good soldiers whose adventures are recorded by Dumas, fighting and adventure were his favourite interest and his favourite theme.[10]

Hamilton himself would develop the idea that an officer who was overly careful of his own reputation was likely to let many of those fleeting battlefield opportunities pass him by, to the great disservice of his soldiers and his country.

After three weeks of organizing and training his division and several days in action at the end of April recapturing an important waterworks from Boer raiders, Hamilton began the advance to the north on 30 April with a stiff fight to clear the Boer entrenchments at Houtnek and Thaba Mountain. As the general advance of Roberts's army began on 1 May, Hamilton's command was increased until it included a cavalry brigade, a mounted infantry brigade, two infantry brigades (under the superb fighting generals, Smith-Dorrien and Bruce Hamilton), and thirty-eight guns. Colonel Hamilton was doing the work of a lieutenant-general. His fame was to be greatly enhanced by having with him the correspondent of the *Morning*

Post, Winston Churchill, who subsequently expressed his admiration in his book, *Ian Hamilton's March*. It was Churchill who saw in Hamilton that capacity for greater things. 'His mind is built upon a big scale, being broad and strong, capable of thinking in army corps and if necessary in continents, and working always with serene smoothness undisturbed alike by responsibility or danger.'[11] Someone else willing to express admiration was the redoubtable Horace Smith-Dorrien, who later wrote:

> From now on I enjoyed every moment of the campaign. He was a delightful leader to follow, always definite and clear in his instructions, always ready to listen and willing to adopt suggestions, and, what is more important, always ready to go for the enemy, extremely quick at seizing a tactical advantage, and always in a good temper.[12]

What a splendid pen portrait of a warrior in his element.

Having turned the enemy out of strong lines along the Zand River, Hamilton's column moved closer to the main army as it drew near to Kroonstadt. Roberts halted there for ten days' to rest and resupply. After just three days rest, Hamilton was sent off to the right again to take the important town of Lindley. It was here that the Boer leader Piet De Wet first intimated that he would surrender his commando if they could all return to their farms. Hamilton strongly favoured the lenient approach to the Boers, but Roberts would not agree. He took the line of insisting on unconditional surrender, especially for prominent Boer leaders. Hamilton's strong opinions on using leniency to shorten the war and secure a lasting peace date from this incident.

His pursuit of the forces of Steyn and Christian De Wet, forcing them out of their strong positions around Heilbron, completely uncovered the flank of the Boers facing Roberts and ushered in the final stages of the advance to Pretoria. That task accomplished, Hamilton's force was now switched to the left. Churchill has left us a dramatic description of Hamilton's dusty veterans passing across the railway line from right to left in full view of Lord Roberts's main army. Hamilton's soldiers had that grudging respect for the tough commander; their nickname for him was 'Old Full Complements and Half Rations'!

Passing the Vaal River on 27 May, Hamilton came up to the Boers strongly posted at Doornkop, key to the Witwatersrand position, and most significantly, the scene of the defeat and capture of Jameson's raiders in 1895. Hamilton's men were low on supplies, having marched unrelentingly ahead of their wagons, but there was a Boer depot at Florida, beyond Doornkop. French and Hamilton renewed their battle co-operation and soon agreed that the cavalry would turn the position by a wide movement to the left while the infantry pinned the enemy frontally. But an hour after the cavalry had moved off, Hamilton suddenly unleashed his two infantry brigades in a frontal assault. Again it was an attack taking fully into account the demands of the new warfare, for each brigade was deployed on a frontage of two miles, with anything up to fifteen yards between each man. In this widely dispersed formation the approach to the enemy was accomplished with relatively light casualties. The heaviest losses were suffered by the Gordon High-landers as they closed with the strongest part of the enemy position, confused as they were by the Boers abandoning a false crest and continuing to resist from 200 yards further back. In a magnificent effort the Gordons, the regiment of both Ian Hamilton and his father before him, fought the Boers out of the position and completed a victory that uncovered the entire enemy defences of Johannesburg.

Johannesburg fell on 30 May; by 3 June the advance on Pretoria was renewed, with Hamilton's force in the centre. Having shelled the Boers off the last ridge before their capital, the British took Pretoria on 5 June. It is possible that some of the leading Boers were ready to surrender at this stage of the war, but the stunning successes of Christian de Wet against the over-stretched British lines of communication stimulated further resistance.

Botha's 7,000 men was one such force that abandoned plans to surrender and instead made a stand east of Pretoria, occupying a line of hills covering the railway line to Delagoa Bay. With Pole-Carew's division holding the enemy's attention in the centre and French's weakened cavalry moving on his left, Roberts once more depended on Ian Hamilton to force the decision on the day of battle, 11 June 1900, by turning the enemy position from the right. Hamilton's cavalry brigades, in much better shape than French's troopers, were drawn into a series of hard-fought encounters with aggressive Boer commandos thrown forward from their main position. As Bruce Hamilton's infantry brigade came into action in support of the hard-pressed cavalry, Ian Hamilton quickly realized he could best relieve the pressure by hurling his infantry at the Boers holding the tactically important Kleinfontein kopje, which covered the main position at Diamond Hill. The Boers fell back in some confusion and Hamilton would have pursued them closely with unforeseen results had Roberts not ordered him to fall back until reinforced. Too late, Roberts realized that he had misread the situation and gave Hamilton the all-clear to renew the attack. Sadly the moment of opportunity had passed and the Boers were too strongly posted to risk a charge. On the other flank, French's cavalry had been thrown entirely onto the defensive by the Boers and were holding their ground with difficulty.

During the night Hamilton's force was able to improve its position, seeing some of the foremost Boers slipping away and moving the infantry up into the shelter provided by Kleinfontein. Roberts ordered Pole-Carew to support Hamilton in a renewed attack on Diamond Hill, but a delay in transmitting the orders meant that the attack could not begin until midday. Again what looked like a suicidal assault was carried off because of the extreme dispersal of the attacking infantry. The stubborn enemy were driven off the first crest by excellent artillery support but resisted very strongly from the true crest, where they were brought under punishing fire by British field guns manhandled into the front line by Hamilton's infantrymen. At this stage in the battle De Wet, having discomforted French on the other flank, was prepared to deliver a violent attack on Roberts's depleted centre, which could have been extremely embarrassing. Just then success crowned Hamilton's efforts as De Lisle's mounted infantry, attacking with intervals of thirty yards between men, stormed another important kopje and the Boers began falling back.

During the night Botha's force retreated and was able to get clean away on 13 June, as Roberts was unaware of the success that had been achieved. It might seem a poorly won victory but it did end forever any hopes the Boers may have had for the recapture of their capital and the prolongation of their main resistance. Roberts began the slow and deliberate pursuit along the railway line towards the eastern frontier of the Transvaal. Once again personal injury kept Hamilton out of the field when, on 23 June, he broke his collarbone in a fall from his horse. While he was recovering, his troops were used by Major-General Hunter in the great sweep through the north-east of the Orange Free State, which resulted in large-scale surrenders of Boers in the Brandwater Basin.

Hamilton was back in the saddle, literally, by 14 July and was given command of a division of infantry and mounted infantry in the push along the railway line to the east. He had, at last, been made a local lieutenant-general and was able to write to Jean that any money worries were now over as his pay jumped to £7 a day. In his letters to his wife he was again fulminating against the folly of demanding unconditional surrender of all the Boer leaders. Many would have thrown in their hand at this stage of the war and the years of guerrilla warfare might have been avoided if a more enlightened policy had been pursued. Instead the main army was tied down to pushing the Boers ahead of them along the railway, until Middleburg was taken on 27 July.

Because De Wet was on the loose in the British rear, having escaped the British columns in the Brandwater Basin, Hamilton was recalled and given a force to secure the mountain passes in the Magaliesberg range to the west of Pretoria. His usual vigorous style of attack cleared the Boers out of Zilikat's Nek on 2 August. He then gathered in the force under Baden-Powell, which had been operating around Rustenburg and, on the orders of Lord Roberts, began to fall back towards Pretoria. Then came word that De Wet was heading for the Magaliesburg, pursued by columns under Kitchener and Methuen. Hamilton was ordered to head him off and was directed towards Olifant's Nek. His troops were exhausted by their extensive marches but it might have been expected that he was the man to finally put De Wet 'into the bag'. His critics have made much of the fact that the Boers were able to escape him. Rawlinson confided to his diary: 'We ordered Johnny to go to Olifants Nek but he did not go there and in consequence De Wet has eluded us. This will prolong the war considerably, I fear, and we are all down on our luck . . .'[13] Roberts's silence on the matter is held up as an example of the favouritism he showed towards

Hamilton. However, a careful reading of the files covering this operation reveals that the daily intelligence passed to Hamilton from headquarters at Pretoria did not make it clear that it was always a day late in reaching him in the field.[14] More crucially, just as Hamilton was in a position to seal Olifant's Nek he was informed that the enemy was heading for the Magato Pass, the next one to the north. As Hamilton tried to redirect his troops accordingly, De Wet's commando escaped through Olifant's Nek on 14 August. While Hamilton should have been sufficiently alert to cover both such important passes, he was a victim of the poor standard of British scouting and field intelligence work at this stage of the war. He pursued and shelled De Wet's rearguard but the Boers were able to disperse into many small and trouble-some bands that would plague the British Army for months to come.

With no rest at all, Hamilton was soon back at Roberts's side in the final advance along the railway line to Komati Poort, on the border with Mozambique. He wrote to Jean: 'I am in rags and very dirty with no soles to speak of to my boots. These smart Head Quarters' Staff make me feel what a state I am in . . .'[15] Buller's force now came into the fighting alongside Roberts, and Hamilton was able to render him signal service by forcing the Boers to retreat from his path as they jointly closed in upon Lydenburg on 6 September. They fought side by side over the next few days and so it is somewhat gratifying, in view of their earlier exchanges, to read in a letter to Jean:

> Buller was most generous in his expression of thanks and had me to dine and all sorts of things. Really, if I had not known he was my deadly enemy I should have thought he was my very good friend. However, he certainly was generous in his acknowledgements and I am glad to say that I can no longer feel that strong dislike of him amounting to hatred which I have hitherto.[16]

It was 24 September when Hamilton and Pole-Carew finally arrived at Komati Poort, to find that the Boers had fired their supply depot and fled, Kruger for Laurenco Marques and Europe, Steyn and

Botha for the rugged interior from whence they would keep the flame of resistance burning for many a long month.

It was about this time that Roberts wrote the following report:

> Ian Hamilton is quite the most brilliant commander I have serving under me. He shares with Pole-Carew the love and admiration of all his force. He takes infinite trouble in matters of detail and knows his work thoroughly. He is most careful to assure himself exactly what he is required to do. He is very intelligent, untiring in the performance of his duty and he has that military instinct which would enable him to appreciate when a risk should be run in order to achieve some given object. I would select him before all others to carry out any difficult operation.[17]

Roberts heard from London that he was to succeed Lord Wolseley as Commander-in-Chief, and he asked Hamilton to be his Military Secretary. Hamilton agreed if the posting was limited to two years; he was reaching that stage in his career where he expected more important and independent roles than this endless 'devilling' for Lord Bobs. He was offered a KCB to go with his official advancement to major-general (at last!). He told Jean that he could do without the knighthood and would prefer further steps in rank, but Roberts was not be gainsaid in this, as in most other things.

Firmly convinced that the war in South Africa was all but over, Roberts left Cape Town for London on 11 December, taking Ian Hamilton with him. Lord Kitchener was left in command of the army; a long and thankless task lay ahead of him.

Hamilton was back in London on 2 January 1901, sharing the tumultuous welcome accorded to Lord Roberts. He was lionized by high society as one of the most successful of generals in a war where many reputations had foundered. His work as Military Secretary included a great deal of influence over promotions and appointments. He was a man who was very useful to know! Many friendships would be cemented at this time, but those disappointed could become enemies. Hamilton was very supportive of the reforming efforts of St John Brodrick, the Secretary of State for War.

But it was not long before he was required for active service again. The guerrilla phase of the Boer war was proving exhausting, costly and politically disastrous as the policy of 'concentrating' Boer civilians into camps led to deaths on a large-scale among the non-combatants. In a letter to Kitchener, Roberts made the tentative suggestion that he might like a senior officer for a chief of staff, and he mentioned Hamilton's name. The offer was accepted with unexpected alacrity. Kitchener cabled back, on 5 November: 'I am extremely grateful; there is nothing I would like better. He is just the man I want. Hamilton will be a great help to me.'[18] By 9 November Hamilton was on his way back to South Africa.

Kitchener was certainly feeling the strain of conducting the war in his usual way, making all the decisions himself and leaving very little for his staff officers to do. Hamilton's years as Roberts's right-hand man in India, where he undertook extensive staff duties on behalf of his chief, made him perfect for Kitchener's chief of staff. Kitchener had been showing signs of distress at some of the disasters befalling British contingents out in the bush. From his ship Hamilton had written back to Roberts listing his priorities as he saw them: first, to reassure Kitchener that he had the full support of the War Office; second, to let Hamilton take the burden of staff work and free Kitchener for operational duties; third, to try for a one-month armistice in the Transvaal and Orange River Colony, to break up and demoralize the commandos; and lastly, to improve the deplorable level of British musketry.

As soon as he arrived at Cape Town, Kitchener welcomed him with open arms and before long he was running the day-to-day details of the war, the organizing of patrols between blockhouses and the sweeps of columns, which he reduced from large-scale efforts to more concentrated work against particular local commandos. As he was still Roberts's Military Secretary he was also passing back to London regular reports on the officers serving in South Africa. He noted the improvement in the performance of Rawlinson, who had gone through of a period of sluggish activity; admired Sir John French but regretted that he surrounded himself with personal friends rather than competent staff officers; and could find little to say about Douglas Haig because he did so little with his troops, who might as well have been in winter encampments, so reluctant was their commander to use them in action!

He did, however, admire him as 'one of the most thoughtful, educated and large-minded of our staff officers'.[19]

As some of the Boer leaders began to enquire about the possibility of meeting for peace discussions, Hamilton conveyed to Roberts the feelings of the British commanders in the field concerning their dislike of the policy of unconditional surrender, which was playing into the hands of the extremist Boer leaders and prolonging the war merely to serve the interests of Milner's friends, the Johannesburg capitalists. Roberts firmly suppressed a letter of this character (dated 17 January 1902) that Hamilton had drafted for presentation to Brodrick at the War Office. An even more outspoken version of the letter had been sent to Winston Churchill, to see if he could influence the policy-makers in London. But he did ask Churchill to be careful in how he used the letter. 'I do not in the least mind your showing it to any of your Hooligan friends, who are also friends of mine, as I am sure that they will understand that I am writing, not from any personal motive, but merely *pro bono publico*.'[20]

Hamilton's great aim was to incorporate the Boers into the British Empire with the least possible delay. He, in common with large numbers of British officers, admired them as a race of people, intelligent and industrious, and greatly preferred them to what he regrettably persisted in calling the 'Jewburgers', who had started the war in the first place. Kitchener was firmly of the same opinion and together they did everything they could to encourage the Boer moderates to begin the peace process.

Meanwhile he continued to correspond with Roberts on the practicalities of the war and how it should affect British army training. He began to formulate his ideas for a much improved staff college, with less historical theory and much more practical work, using officers who had done well in South Africa as guest lecturers. He proposed for the first time an idea that he developed in the future: that staff officers should be seconded to industry for some months to learn how mass organizations should be run.

In February 1902 a series of huge drives directed against the best of the Boer leaders, Christian De Wet, saw him escaping with barely fifty men at his side. But in March things flared up in the Western Transvaal as De La Rey inflicted a series of defeats on the British

forces, even wounding and capturing Lord Methuen. This came as
Kitchener was meeting Lucas Meyer, Schalk Burger, Reitz and other
Boer leaders who were willing to discuss peace. It strengthened
their hand in demanding a peace with honourable terms before
they could call on the commandos to lay down their arms. What
they really wanted was the promise of the restoration of representative government in their provinces within, say, three years. This
was vigorously opposed by Milner, whom the soldiers increasingly
viewed as the chief stumbling block in the path of peace.

As the focus of the war centred more and more on the hunt for
De Wet and De La Rey in the Western Transvaal, the British
column commanders took the unusual step of writing a 'round
robin' letter to Lord Kitchener asking if he could send Ian Hamilton out into the field to act as a local commander-in-chief to
co-ordinate the work of their several columns. What higher praise
could have been bestowed on a soldier by his comrades? Kitchener,
until then determined in his usual way to control everything from
his office in Pretoria, saw the wisdom of the suggestion. Hamilton
later recalled before the Elgin Commission that one day before
breakfast Kitchener simply said to him, 'I think you had better go
out to the Western Transvaal.' Apparently there was no further
discussion on the topic. Was this to investigate, to advise or to
command? Hamilton just packed his valise and left, with just one
ADC, for the theatre of war.

Thus it came to pass early in April 1902 that Hamilton was
directing the movements of thirteen columns as they manoeuvred
De La Rey's commandos into a tighter and tighter corner, even as
the negotiators were gathering at Vereeniging. Finally Hamilton
directed four 'super columns', composed of his best veteran troops
under the most tried and trusted commanders, in a drive towards
the Boers' last refuge, the Great Hart's River valley. Several commandos were in the field against him. In a superb reading of the
situation that would have earned the praise of the great Sun Tzu,
Hamilton saw through a feint in one direction by one group under
Kemp and warned his column commanders to be ready for an
attack at any moment. On 11 April he was with Kekewitch's column
at Rooiwal (also known as Roodewal) when he saw the astonishing
sight of many hundreds of Boer horsemen charging across the veld,

knee to knee and rank upon rank. He and his fellow generals realized that this was a less than flattering display of Boer contempt for British marksmanship! But the enemy had badly miscalculated the situation; the British were not taken by surprise. The charge was shattered; the leader, Potgieter, was killed; the commandos flew asunder and were pursued, losing what remained of their artillery.

When this news reached the envoys at Vereeniging it was the decisive turn of events for many of the Boer leaders, who could now tell their fighters that there was no point in further resistance. Kitchener seized the moment and made proposals of a generous nature, offering to make good the losses to Boer farms and the like, which drove the wedge deeper between the moderates and the die-hards in the enemy delegation. Hamilton, 'acting the locust' in his own words in the fertile lands of the Western Transvaal, had the satisfaction of noting that he had been deeply involved in not only the first great victory of the war (Elandslaagte) but also the last (Rooiwal).

During May, as the British kept up the military pressure, Kitchener having refused the request for an armistice, Boer dele-gates went out to all the commandos in the field, gathering their opinions on the peace negotiations. At the various dinners with the Boer leaders Hamilton was delighted to get details of the various operations he had been involved in. From them he learned that he had killed and wounded more Boers on Wagon Hill than they had lost in the great battle at Magersfontein, and that his seizure of Diamond Hill had turned a powerful counter-attack into a retreat.

On 31 May 1902, the Boer leaders, having been promised representative government at the earliest possible time, won for them by Kitchener's insistence over a reluctant Milner, signed a peace treaty to end the war. In his letters to Roberts and Churchill, Hamilton expressed his admiration for the 'rifles and religion' stance of the Boers and his contempt for the blather and self-interest of Milner's cronies. He would have immediately accepted Boer leaders into the British army as colonels and generals: Louis Botha would have made a great impression at Aldershot in com-mand of a brigade; he would have had Smuts as Attorney-General in South Africa and De La Rey as Governor in the Transvaal. He genuinely felt no malice towards these former enemies and sought only to ensure that Britain would never have to fight them again. How little it would have cost to invite the defeated leaders to Britain, to be dined and fêted, instead of letting them take up invitations to visit Germany, where they would be the focus of much anti-British agitation.

Hamilton's return to London saw him at the very height of his fame; he seemed to be going from success to success. His victories in the field were complemented by his brilliant staff work; he was in liaison with powerful figures in the Liberal Party; his ideas on policy show him to be a far-sighted thinker on military and imperial affairs. He was surely destined for high office.

5

Quartermaster-General and Service
in Manchuria, 1902–5

Hamilton badly needed a rest. It was his fondest wish to take a long
sea voyage via Japan to the United States and unwind by visiting
the Civil War battlefields. But Kitchener, like Roberts before him,
had discovered in Hamilton the perfect staff officer for the drafting
of documents and speeches, adding literary lustre to whatever went
out in the name of the 'Chief'. Kitchener insisted that his 'bloody
poet' (a pet name that Hamilton delighted in) must not leave his
side for the return to Great Britain; there was an important final
despatch to write. For the second time Hamilton experienced the
adulation of the British public as he returned in triumph from
South Africa in the company of Lord Kitchener and General Sir
John French. Besides writing speeches for Kitchener, Hamilton was
soon in demand as a speaker in his own right. Milner is on record
as saying how greatly audiences appreciated Sir Ian's sparkling
impromptu delivery.

After attending the Coronation of King Edward VII (9 August
1902), Hamilton left on 4 September in the company of Lord
Roberts, Sir John French, General Kelly-Kenny and the Secretary
of State for War, Brodrick, to attend the annual German
manoeuvres as the guests of the Kaiser. In his later report Hamilton commented that Britain could use Germany's education,
prevision and planning but that their order and system lacked all
pretence at initiative. To correct this he admired the way the
officers conducting the exercises would throw unexpected problems at the participants to see how they would react. He was
confident that the British volunteer was a better raw material to
work with; if Britain had Germany's method that superiority
would be unbeatable. He was not impressed with what he later

described as the 'offensive-at-any-price' tactics, which he saw spread through European armies over the next few years.

Before he left he was given the Order of the Crown of Prussia and, on his return to Scotland, the King ordered him to attend him at Balmoral and particularly asked to see the new Order. A slight panic ensued as Hamilton had to cable his London household to forward it immediately. One of his able parlour maids checked with Lord Roberts on how his Order of the Black Eagle looked and sewed Sir Ian's ribbon in similar fashion before despatching it north with all speed. Before an important dinner, with many dignitaries in attendance, including Lord Rosebery, Arthur Balfour, Sir George White and Winston Churchill, the King took Hamilton to one side for a long, seemingly intimate conversation. Hamilton enjoyed the thought of his social barometer rising as the courtiers gazed upon the sight. If they only knew that the King, who took the greatest care in all matters relating to social etiquette, as Hamilton would find out one day to his cost, was patiently pointing out the errors in the way his ribbon was being worn and was recommending a royal tailor who would put Sir Ian right!

In August 1902 Botha, De Wet and De La Rey were in England looking for further concessions to help the Boers rebuild their country. Hamilton lobbied Chamberlain on their behalf, an act entirely in keeping with his views while the war was being fought, and once again showing how freely officers could make political points at this stage in the British army's history. When Kitchener departed for high command in India in October, Hamilton reverted to full-time duties as Military Secretary at the War Office. He resumed his literary ambitions but was not sufficiently pleased with his work to see it published.

In April 1903 he was appointed Quartermaster-General of the British army in what turned out to be a very busy year as the civil and military establishments turned their attentions to the need for reform of the many failings the army had displayed in South Africa. The Royal Commission on the War in South Africa, chaired by Lord Elgin, sat from October 1902 to July 1903, putting some 22,200 questions to 114 participants in the recent war. Hamilton was still Military Secretary when he was interviewed by the commission twice, first in December 1902 and again, after he had prepared an extensive document proposing major reforms, in February 1903.

During the first session he was questioned on the performance of British officers in general. In a published appendix to the commission findings, he first gave a very useful summary of the duties of the Military Secretary as 'everything related to officers' appointments, promotions, education, retirement, rewards and honours'.[1] He pointed out that during his tenure of the post under Lord Roberts the workload had increased enormously because of the extra regiments raised for the war and for the garrison in Egypt and the new regiments being raised in Africa, such as the West African Frontier Force and the King's African Rifles. He began his campaign for the encouragement of public school and university graduates to enter the army by accelerated routes, perhaps being commissioned directly as lieutenants to allow for their age and learning on entry to the service. The army needed men capable of independent thought and they were not getting that type through Sandhurst. The academy would be of great service if it functioned as a university, but it did not and probably could not. The army needed to increase the pool of reserve officers by encouraging regulars to transfer on half-pay into the militia while retaining their place in their regiments. They would thus improve the militia while new young officers were replacing them in the regular army. The best schools should all be encouraged to raise cadet units, and he would allow for paid training in the army during vacations. The military education of officers should take the road of encouraging independence of thought and action, and of decision in cases of emergency, of which there had been plenty in the recent war.

He faced a series of questions that implied that the mounted infantry in South Africa might have performed better if they had been armed with swords as well as carbines, because the enemy became excessively bold in their presence knowing that they had no 'personal weapon of offence'. Hamilton countered smartly on two fronts. If the Boers grew overly bold in the later stages of the war it was because they knew they were in little enough danger from the very bad shooting of the British yeomanry. He remembered how the Boers had charged en masse at Rooiwal for over a mile and hardly lost a man because of the lamentably inaccurate fire they faced until they drew too close and were cut down in swathes. He also insisted that the mounted infantry were seen to use their bayonets very effectively in several battles but only when fighting on foot, which was their primary function. He was prepared to let the regular cavalry keep their swords but only because it was their whole raison d'être after hundreds of years of history and tradition. He said that 'morally, it gives them an idea that they can do things which they really cannot, but still they think they can, and therefore it enables them to act really with greater boldness than they otherwise would'.[2] Faint praise, indeed!

Hamilton had obviously spent some time thinking over the experience of the war for he laid before the commission a sixteen-page document packed with comment and suggestions for reform.[3] The late-eighteenth century had seen the end of the era of ultra-disciplined warfare typified by the army of Frederick the Great. The French Revolution had ushered in the age of the mass army, of the whole state becoming involved in war. Throughout the nineteenth century most European powers had opted for mass conscription and the creation of large reserves of trained men ready to be mobilized in time of war. The training of the masses took pre-cedence over the skills of the individual. The war in South Africa had changed all that. Now the skilled individual, armed with the wonderful modern rifle and able to use his initiative and thus turn the terrain to his best advantage, was a formidable soldier. A battalion in the attack fetched up before its objective in great disorder. Then was the time for individuals and small cohesive groups to go forward using cover, to penetrate the enemy position and establish enfilade fire. Self-confident soldiers with a strong sense of personal discipline and esprit de corps would carry the infantry through all danger to victory. New magazine rifles and smokeless cartridges might make the defence formidable but only against the old attack in massed formation. The new dispersed attack gave opportunity for manoeuvre, for turning flanks, for fighting patrols to continually stretch the defence ever thinner until it broke. A determined attack invariably overcame a passive defence. Attacks could be commenced in the late afternoon so that the moment of decision would occur as dusk fell, or night marches could be made for attacks in the early dawn. Advantage should be taken of fog, rain or dust clouds. One has to remember the dread of most generals at that time of night fighting, with its concomitant loss of control, to realize just how radical and far-thinking these views were. Hamilton urged the army to pay higher wages to fewer but better and more realistically trained soldiers, skilled in the use of deception. The sporting young men turned out by British public schools and universities should be the perfect officers for this free-ranging style of war. 'Quality above quantity should be our motto.'

Hamilton was unforgiving in his critique of the cavalry in South Africa. Their one advantage, that of mobility, was lost because of their poor standard of horse-mastership. Given that their enemy rarely faced them on open ground, their recourse to fire tactics was of little use given the low standard of shooting among the regular cavalry. They were inferior as scouts to the colonial units raised for the war. In short their cohesion, steadiness and drill, all that made them regular cavalry, was a source of weakness, as it simply provided the enemy with a solid target. 'Compared to a modern rifle, the sword or lance can only be regarded as a medieval toy.' Mounted infantry were superior to them in the field.

These comments were anathema to many of the leading generals of the day. Hamilton wrote a note in the margins of his own copy of the commission's report: 'This infuriated Haig and French beyond measure.' Nicholson reportedly annotated a copy with the statement: 'This man has a tile loose!' This clearly signifies that Nicholson had entered into that frame of mind that made him one of Hamilton's deadliest enemies, with significant ramifications for Hamilton in the future. It is hard to pinpoint the exact reason for the split but Hamilton thought it might be simply that Nicholson felt himself unduly neglected by this erstwhile friend and colleague who was now cutting such a figure in society and the army.

Hamilton would have had every battalion of the army send one company for training as good mounted infantry, at permanent schools running three-month courses for each army corps. The field artillery as then organized was too mobile for the infantry and not mobile enough for the mounted arm. He tentatively suggested a 'position artillery' to assist the infantry, heavier guns that would rarely have to move much faster than a walk but big enough to give more meaningful support to the infantry as they developed their attack on any enemy position encountered. Once again, if we think forward to the desperate lack of heavy artillery in France and Flanders in the early stages of the Great War, we can see Hamilton's prescience at work. The fact that British divisions in 1914 each had a battery of 60-pounder guns shows that this line of thinking was developed to some extent.

Hamilton was very impressed with the way the British infantry adapted their tactics to the new conditions as the war progressed. The early days of volley firing and of always waiting for orders to come up from the rear were replaced by the infantry developing attacks by company and double company 'rushes' – the evolution of a fire-and-movement style of tactics familiar to all modern soldiers. He advocated the keeping of plenty of entrenching tools with the battalion transport and had the ingenious idea of perhaps shaping the butt of the rifle so that it might be useful for scooping earth into some personal protection for the rifleman. This led on to the well-known recommendation for which Hamilton is some-times regarded as an early proponent of the armoured fighting vehicle (tank); at the least it shows that his questing mind was proposing solutions for future problems that would beset the army in its next and greatest ever conflict. 'Another point to which I would draw attention is the desirability of having two or three steel shields on wheels with each infantry battalion; under cover of this half a dozen men at a time might be worked across the open into some angle of the enemy's position, where they would make their presence very unpleasantly felt.'

Hamilton took his 1903 leave in September and October and went to America with Jean's brother, Kay Muir. On the ship he wrote up reports of his part in Roberts's march on Pretoria for Leo Amery's *Times History of the War in South Africa*. He visited West Point and the eastern battlefields of the American Civil War.

The final report of the Elgin Commission, published in August 1903, was a severe indictment of Britain's military system and the need for reform of the old War Office was obvious. Lord Esher was asked to chair a commission to advise on the creation of an army board nearer in style to the Admiralty. It met for the first time on 1 January 1904 and spent a month drawing up its proposals without calling for any witnesses at all. In the meantime Hamilton, who knew that his job as Quartermaster-General would end on 1 February 1904 and could see nothing immediately available that took his interest, staked his future on his estimation of how things were developing in the Far East. He confidently predicted a war between Japan, a new ally of Great Britain since 1902, and Tsarist Russia. He decided to take some leave and sail for Japan (on 6 February 1904) in the hope that he would secure the prestigious posting as British observer with the Japanese army on campaign.

As a serving soldier Hamilton had to seek permission to make the voyage. Lord Roberts promised to speak to the King on Ian's behalf and royal approval was secured. Sir William Nicholson also encouraged Ian to set off at his own expense and promised to do all he could to see that he got the cherished appointment, which would be cabled out to him en route. Arnold-Forster had offered to write to Lord Lansdowne on Hamilton's behalf, but Nicholson, whom Hamilton still held in high regard, thought this might leave it open for a flat refusal as the government could hardly appoint a military observer to a war that hadn't even started yet.

From Marseilles he wrote to Jean of how anxious he was that Lord 'Bobs' clear things with the King. With the expected upheavals in the high command of the army as a result of the Esher Committee findings, he wrote with feeling: 'This is a most critical period in our fortunes; perhaps the most critical.'[4] He recounted how he had tried to secure friends in the right places – Ewart, a candidate for Military Secretary, Davidson, the King's Equerry, and Lord Esher himself, though he did not consider him 'reliable'. But to show how important a socially successful wife was to an Edwardian general, he also asked Jean to 'see something' of the Arnold-Forsters (the current Secretary of State for War) and the Dilkes (a possible candidate for that office). 'Every little helps,' as he wrote. The next day he added a request that Jean should go to see Sir George and Lady Clarke, as he could be the secretary of a powerful new defence committee of the whole empire. He could also recount how he was making the journey on as little money as possible as his salary would only continue at £175 per month until

1 June, after which he would go on to half-pay unless he won the
Japanese attachment, in which case he should be solvent again.
Being a British general was certainly not riding a gravy train.

He closed this letter with a reflection that whatever the conclusions of the Esher Committee, he thought that the changes
would reflect a 'court and political intrigue'[5] to have a clean sweep
of the current office-holders at the War Office. He had received a
long letter from Lord Roberts talking of the indecent haste with
which Esher was trying to remove him, Nicholson, Kelly-Kenny
and others from office. Hamilton agreed that they had all been
badly treated, but he favoured the reforms themselves, which
called for three major changes in the higher organization of the
army: the creation of a Defence Committee under the Prime
Minister; the formation of an Army Council of three civilian and
four military members under the Secretary of State for War; and
the abolition of the post of Commander-in-Chief, with the possible
creation of an Inspector-General to co-ordinate the work of the
field commands.

On 9 February his daily letter to Jean gave her his opinions on
the new changes so that she might be well informed for her busy
schedule of 'networking' lunches, teas and dinners. Ian had earlier
asked her to 'try and see something of the proper men as you may
get news out of them to give me'.[6] He was referring to influential
Liberal journalists such as Leo Amery and Alfred Spender. He was
genuinely disappointed that Nicholson had lost his place to his
intellectual inferior, Lyttelton, who was straight and kind but had
'neither force of character, industry or brains'. Douglas would be a
better Adjutant-General than Kelly-Kenny, and he was sure that
Plumer was a good man who would do well. He was very anxious
that the new Inspector-General should be Lord Roberts, and not
that 'authority on buttons', the Duke of Connaught. What is most
fascinating is the rider that 'you might give these as my views to
any member of the Opposition – Dilke, Asquith, Winston Churchill
– if it comes naturally. If you see Mrs Leo [Amery's wife] you
might tell her. To members of the Government you will be more
careful. To Royal circle people still more so.'[7]

On 11 February, from Port Said, he could write to Jean that she
should have joined him on the smooth voyage thus far and that he

felt a mere nineteen years old. A few days later a bombshell struck. He saw a Reuters report that Lieutenant-General Sir William Nicholson – jobless after the 'clean sweep' at the War Office – and J. A. L. Haldane had been appointed as the official British observers with the Japanese army. Small wonder that he asked Jean if she was surrounded by 'snakes and lions'.[8] He remembered that 'Nick' had especially advised him not to use Arnold-Forster's influence to land the post. 'Hardly is my back turned when Nick steps forward and secures the very position he had taken pains to assure me I should get!' He was quite sure that 'our luxurious friend' would not brave the hardships of campaigning in a Manchurian winter; no 'rice and rotten fish' diet for him. He had a letter from Lord Knollys stating that the King 'entirely approved' of his going to the front and he hoped that he would still get a billet, even as a junior observer or, at worst, with the Russian army – 'an unpleasant billet for an Englishman'. His anguish was increased when he heard a few days later that the Duke of Connaught was lobbying for Kelly-Kenny to get the 2nd Army Corps (Southern Command) which was exactly the posting that Hamilton expected to get on his return to the United Kingdom.

Subsequent letters show him resigned to his ill fortune. He was greatly improving his French through reading and conversation with French passengers, so there was some gain 'even if my great schemes are destined to fall through owing to the cleverness of mon ami Nick'.[9] This bitterness continued to rankle as he wrote from Singapore that he knew the Japanese military attaché in London so well that he could easily have received a letter of introduction to the Japanese high command: 'How much better I could have arranged matters had I at all suspected Nick.'[10]

On 5 March he received a cable while steaming between Saigon and Hong Kong that totally transformed the situation yet again. To Jean he wrote: 'Whom have I to thank for it after my better half?'[11] In London Jean had been lobbying furiously on Ian's behalf and she had got Lord Roberts to see the Secretary of State for India, St John Brodrick, who had consequently appointed Hamilton as the representative of the Indian army to the Japanese. Hamilton received the official cable on 7 March, telling him he was on the fabulous salary of over £3,000 per annum and that a staff officer and ADC would be sent out to join him from India. He was almost beside himself with excitement at this change in his fortunes and was determined to make a success of his mission.

He was in Japan a long way ahead of Nicholson and spent his time, while staying with the British ambassador at Tokyo, in getting to know the Japanese commanders and their troops. His fluent command of both French and German gave him much greater access to information than many other foreign observers. He passed back a stream of intelligence to official circles, but sent summaries of his correspondence to Jean who was empowered to release them to friends in London such as Leo Amery. Hamilton was predicting that the present British government would not last long and he was determined to use his connections with the current opposition to his best advantage. A letter to Winston Churchill in April summarized his admiration for the Japanese:

> The Jap is the fighting man *par excellence* of the future. He has the quick practical grasp of the situation; the initiative and the instinct of ground and cover which are everything to the private soldier under the dispersed conditions rendered necessary by modern rifle fire. He is extraordinarily amenable to discipline. He is intensely patriotic. He is hardy – quick on his feet – sound in his stomach and absolutely fearless of death. What more do you want? I admire the Generals immensely and they have the precious advantage of recent war experience.[12]

He found the Japanese were brim-full of confidence, sure that they would thrash the Russians or any other nation in the world bar Britain and, possibly, America.

By the end of March Nicholson had arrived with his staff; Haldane had persuaded him that he would need to be seen at the front. Before too long Hamilton could write to Jean that he might have misjudged 'Nick', whom he had always regarded 'with friendly wishes and feelings' and with whom 'we never came into any sort of competition, not even the vaguest'. Apparently Arnold-Forster had spontaneously offered the post to Nicholson, who was without any prospective employment, and so he had felt obliged to accept. He did reveal, however, that 'the faithless Rawley (Henry Rawlinson) went to him immediately after seeing me off and advised him to get himself appointed'.[13] Hamilton believed Nicholson's assertion that he did no such thing, and he urges Jean to 'chaff Rawley about this the next time you see him!' Once again Hamilton urged Jean to lobby on his behalf in London, this time instructing her to get a promise from Arnold-Forster that, should his government fall and he be turned out of office, that he would tell the incoming Secretary of State that Hamilton had been promised a corps command on his return from the Russo-Japanese War. She was to 'tell them (the Arnold-Forsters) I have played the game fair and square and that to all my sympathising friends, many of them very powerful, I have always said that I had been well and properly treated by the War Office and had no complaint'.[14]

One other small cloud passing over the horizon illustrates how this busy manoeuvring for friends and influence could occasionally backfire. Apparently St John Brodrick had read something into an official letter of Ian's as a criticism concerning his work as Secretary of State for War, and he had remarked on this to Jean at a dinner. Jean duly reported this to Ian, who thought that he had been accused of disloyalty and sent an angry letter to Brodrick. In his lengthy and very patient reply Brodrick pointed out that Hamilton too often appeared as all things to all men, to the sometime detriment of his reputation. He said he was deeply hurt that Hamilton could think that he (Brodrick) had imputed Hamilton's disloyalty to Lord Roberts and himself, 'but your manner of dealing with people with whom you often did not agree, and the tact and courtesy which you always showed, had I thought caused you at times to agree with their opinions, or to seem to do so, when that agreement was in opposition to what you had expressed to others'.[15] He noted that Hamilton had agreed with Arnold-Forster and Lord Knollys over the personnel changes at the War Office and had then used 'intemperate language' about it to others. 'Honestly I think you would have stood better with all parties if you had said what was the fact: that although perfectly willing to acquiesce in the decision, you felt it somewhat hard that your appointment should be so terminated.' He complained that Hamilton had expressed criticisms of War Office work to Arnold-Forster within three months of Brodrick leaving office there, on matters where they had worked in full agreement for some years. He went on to warn him of being too friendly with Leo Amery; he would openly use Hamilton's opinion to attack and embarrass the government. He stressed that he often defended Hamilton against his detractors; against 'those who do not know you as well as I or have such confidence in you ... When a man reaches one of the highest positions in the Army, he cannot afford to let a hastily written letter ... or a few pleasant words in society, handicap him to the extent which, as a friend of yours, I could not conceal from myself some of your recent utterances or the utterances imputed to you appear to have done.' He closed with the earnest wish that Hamilton would write to him personally to clear up any misunderstanding, but there is no doubt that this was a thorough-going slap on the wrist for Hamilton's inveterate politicking. The unpleasantness blew over; Hamilton accepted that there was no personal bitterness in the exchange of letters and, while he still harboured some resentment, he was prepared to read Brodrick's letter as a withdrawal of any imputation against his character.

Hamilton used the period before fighting broke out to familiarize himself with the Japanese army and its generals. Invited to visit the Marquis Oyama, he was surprised to be ushered into the general's bath-house, where he was making his ablutions. Hamilton later recounted that, in the steamy interior, he at first had difficulty in distinguishing between a sponge floating in the water and the pock-marked face of the Japanese general. This innocent witticism was to land him in very hot water with the King of England when it found its way into print.

Hamilton's earliest despatches all predicted victory for the Japanese, and many of his critics delighted in the prospect of him being proved wrong as the Russian masses crushed their smaller adversary. His first despatch was received just as the announcement came of the Japanese victory at the battle of the Ya-lu River (1 May 1904), which allowed the Japanese to pour out of Korea and into Manchuria itself. It was 3 May before Hamilton was able to leave Japan, the most senior officer in a large group of British and foreign attachés, to join the headquarters of Kuroki's 1st Army. The Japanese paused for a month as they built up their strength, which enabled Hamilton to make a number of visits to the Ya-lu battlefield with officers who fought there to enable a detailed study of the action and to begin to draw lessons from it. It was his weekly task to write letters home to the King, Lord Kitchener, to the two Secretaries of State for War and for India, and to the QMG, India, as well as almost daily to Jean and frequently to his old chief, Lord Roberts. He had also learned, from some of the wildly inaccurate reports that later circulated about events in South Africa, to keep a very careful daily diary, which would provide the basis of the two-volume study of the war, *A Staff Officer's Scrap Book*.

While he was impressed with the way the Japanese massed 40,000 men at the Ya-lu to overwhelm the thinly stretched 6,000 Russians defending the river line, he deplored the way their excessive caution and need for certainty let slip the chance to win an annihilating victory. But the moral advantage of winning this first battle was incalculable in the effect it had on the minds of both the Japanese and the Russians.

Hamilton lived very modestly at the headquarters, eating the boiled rice served to the Japanese soldiery and trying to experience the war as they saw and felt it. He greatly admired their infantry in particular, for their dogged quality and natural patriotism. If he found the ordinary Japanese officer overly secretive, he saw that as more of a virtue than a fault. By contrast he thought that the British 'not only wash all their dirty linen in public, but implore all passers-by to take a hand in the process'.[16] He saw in Japanese society just that sense of honour and duty that he professed himself and that he tried to instil in his fellow citizens through thought, word and deed. His crusade to get schoolchildren imbued with this spirit of service before self drew much inspiration from the way Japanese mothers raised their children within a strict honour code.

While Kuroki's 1st Army, Oku's 2nd Army and Nodzu's 4th Army began the Japanese offensive in the general direction of the Russian's main base at Liao Yang, Nogi's 3rd Army completed the investiture of Port Arthur. Relentlessly the Japanese pressed back their enemy. They were baffled by the ease with which the Russians were turned out of strong defensive positions. Because they had a high regard for General Kuropatkin, they came to believe he must be planning some devilish counter-stroke and themselves became more careful in their advance. Hamilton's early experiences were frustrating as the Japanese tried to control very closely the movements and reporting of the foreign observers. He wrote a fiercely critical letter home, safe in the knowledge that the press censors would pass it immediately to the high command. Without a word of reference to this letter, he was soon visited by Fuji, the chief of staff, who could not have been more friendly. He had two Japanese officers assigned to him to explain everything he desired to know about the army and its movements (this was just as well as Nicholson had refused the two Indian army officers assigned to Hamilton permission to accompany him); his subordinates were free to visit any part of the army; Hamilton himself had Kuroki's permission to attach himself to any formation at any time.

After Kuroki had seized the important Mo-tien-ling Pass on the road towards Liao Yang (30 June 1904), the Russians made two strong efforts to recapture it. Hamilton was shocked to see the crude, mass tactics of the Russian infantry: brave men brought on shoulder-to-shoulder to be destroyed by Japanese artillery and rifle fire. What use was the 'misguided, spurious gallantry which impelled Russian officers to stand up, not only exposing themselves unnecessarily, but also disclosing the exact position of their sections, and thus drawing fire upon their men'?[17] During the second Russian attack Hamilton heard that some Japanese had given way before a particularly strong attack and he immediately rushed towards the scene of fighting, anxious as ever to be in the thick of things. He rode his horse to the point of exhaustion and raced forward on foot. As he drew near to the front he fell in with a Japanese infantry battalion pressing into the firing line. He was greatly impressed by the joy with which the soldiers advanced; these men seemed not to shun battle but to glory in it. 'Here all is natural.' It is in keeping with Hamilton's dislike of what modern capitalism could do to the working people that he could remark that the 'ragged unemployed in Mayfair' were more to be pitied than the soldier wounded in battle. The Russians were in full retreat before Hamilton got too caught up in the battle.

It is also of interest to note how honest and self-critical Hamilton could be about his own character. When he saw white men being rounded up as prisoners of Asiatic men, he confessed inwardly to an innate racism that made him hate the sight of it. Instead he vowed to strive harder to understand the Japanese and their outward coldness towards him and all Westerners. He began by accepting that the Japanese were scrupulously clean and fastidious, and that most Westerners smelt like carnivorous savages to them! He greatly appreciated the artistic nature of the Japanese: the simple pleasure some soldiers took in a nightingale singing; the lovely gardens created out of nothing during any pause in the operations. As a soldier-poet, he contrasted Japan's admiration for them with the mild form of amused contempt that greeted them in Britain.

On 31 July 1904 Hamilton witnessed the battle of Yoshirei, in which the stubborn Russian defence brought some of Japan's best troops to a standstill, before relentless pressure all along the line forced the usual collapse of resistance. He was to draw some important theoretical lessons for the conduct of modern battle from what he saw, to be published in *A Staff Officer's Scrap Book*. During the subsequent battle of Liao Yang, which was fought on a massive scale between 26 August and 6 September, Hamilton noted a marked improvement in the Russian performance. They had done away with useless volley firing and were giving greater scope to individual shooting, some of it quite good. But it was too late to prevent the inevitable defeat and it took all the Russians' legendary stubbornness to secure their safe retreat towards Mukden.

A stray Russian shell had destroyed most of Ian's personal kit and many of the reports he had prepared, but he had acquired a pet on campaign. After Yoshirei he came upon a little fox terrier being attacked by some wild dogs. The animal, which had a chewed string halter around its neck, followed him back to his camp; Ian was convinced that the inconsolably unhappy dog was looking for European company. It later transpired that it was the pet of the Russian Count Keller, who was killed in battle on 31 July. The Japanese had planned to give the dog an honourable death and bury it with its master, but the little bitch had other ideas and made its escape. Ian adopted the sad creature and christened it 'Rooski', and it was often photographed at his side for the rest of his stay in Manchuria. It lived for many years with the Hamiltons in England.

After the battle of Liao Yang, Hamilton met Marshal Oyama, the Japanese commander-in-chief in the field, who offered him champagne. Hamilton replied, 'I can not restrain my smiles on

seeing the face of an old friend.' On this being translated into
Japanese it made a perfect example of the thirty-one syllables of an
ancient form of poetry, to the huge delight of the assembled staff.
It would be hard to imagine a British staff recognizing poetic
language in quite the same way.

It was at Liao Yang that Hamilton finally met Nicholson,
Haldane and the other attachés who had been moving with the
2nd Army. On hearing Haldane apologize for the quality of what
Hamilton thought was perfectly good bread, he realized that they
had had all the advantages of service with an army operating along
a railway line, always better supplied than the 1st Army as it
manoeuvred in the Manchurian mountains. The officers with the
2nd Army had enjoyed none of the freedom accorded to Hamilton
and his aides. Nicholson had been taken ill and left for Japan,
leaving Hamilton as the senior British officer in theatre.

The armies went into winter quarters and operations were
sporadic. On 7 December 1904 he had the enormous pleasure of
being made the Honorary Colonel of the Gordon Highlanders, the
family regiment. In a shooting competition between teams armed
with captured Russian rifles, it was two members of Lord Roberts's
famous Indian team that carried off the prizes – Colonel Hume
came first and Ian Hamilton second, his prize a barrel of pickled
cabbage! When Port Arthur surrendered on 1 January 1905, Hamilton was able to visit the 3rd Army and study the siege and the
battles that led up to its investment. He returned to the 1st Army
by the end of January, and on 2 February he received orders to
return to Britain to take up the Southern Command, the army
corps he had longed for.

Even here the path to Hamilton's advancement had been far
from smooth. Since October 1904 he had been hearing 'on the
grapevine', via Brodrick at the India Office and Kitchener in India,
that he was to be offered one of the army corps commands at
home, only then to receive a mysterious cable saying that the
proposal to relieve him had been cancelled. He had no idea what
this meant. Had his continued attacks on the cavalry alienated
senior army figures like Sir John French? He confessed to Jean that
he had been scathingly sarcastic about the role of horsed cavalry in
Manchuria and this may have done him harm but he had no

regrets; he was not going to accept any promotion under 'false colours'. Were the military authorities trying to get another general into his 'billet'? We know from the private journal of Lord Esher that there was in fact, an attempt to reward the good and faithful general, Kelly-Kenny, who was near the end of his career, with a year at Southern Command to see him into his retirement. Kelly-Kenny made it quite clear that he could never afford to accept the post. Hamilton once estimated that it would cost him £3,000 a year of his own money to entertain at Southern Command, when the allowance for it was £1,000 a year. At one stage he was writing to Jean that he might have to go on half-pay the following summer, though the money he had saved in his present job would see them through any difficulty. He then told her that both Henry Wilson and Henry Rawlinson were writing to him very freely and amiably and that 'as they are each in their line as selfish and cunning as foxes I take this as a good omen that my star has not yet set!'[18] Instead it seems that the sheer excellence of his regular letters and reports were so pleasing to the King that this is what kept him in Manchuria. It was in January 1905 that he was informed via the ambassador at Tokyo that the King's private secretary, Lord Knollys, was asking if Ian would prefer to come home by 1 April or to see the Manchurian campaign through to the finish. After careful thought Hamilton replied that he felt he should be of greater service putting his experience to practical use in Southern Command. His wish was granted immediately.

Before he left Manchuria he received the most felicitous visits from the Japanese generals he had come to know and respect; they clearly appreciated his good manners and good grace. On his arrival in Japan he was fêted by the Emperor, who gave him the Grand Cordon of the Sacred Treasure, and by the War Minister, who made him choose as a gift between two magnificent examples of the swordsmith's art. Hamilton again charmed all present by appealing for help in the choice to a venerable general who shared with him the order of the Sacred Treasure referred to above. He finally left Japan on 4 March, stopping off at Calcutta to visit Lord Kitchener, then Commander-in-Chief, India, who had requested an opportunity to discuss the war with him. It is thought that Kitchener raised the question of Hamilton succeeding him as

C-in-C, but Ian knew that the home authorities tended to rotate the command between Britain and India and that it was the turn of a local man to command there. He dined with Kitchener and the Viceroy, Lord Curzon, at the height of their famous feud over the relative powers of the two office-holders over the army in India. Only Hamilton's skills at the dinner table rescued the event from being a complete disaster.

He arrived back in Britain on 23 April 1905. What he had seen in Manchuria had reinforced many of the lessons he had deduced from the South African war. A well-trained infantry, skilled in the use of the rifle and in widely dispersed formations could dominate the battlefield. Artillery was of increasing importance. Cavalry was in terminal decline; its great contribution in Manchuria had been to carry the great iron kettles in which the infantry cooked its rice. He was keen to distil these lessons, publish his findings and put them to test on the training grounds of Salisbury Plain.

6

Southern Command,
1905–9

Some two years after he had been promised an important home command, Ian Hamilton finally took over as GOC, Southern Command in April 1905. While in this post he would be promoted, in October 1907, to the rank of full general. Besides being a major part of the home army, this command also included Portsmouth, the principal route for visiting dignitaries, and the recently acquired Salisbury Plain, of increasing importance to the training of the army. Hamilton was, of course, very keen to apply his newly won experience of modern war to the training of his troops. As well as paying his usual and beneficial attentions to the standard of musketry of his soldiers, he set a thoroughly modern programme of training for his gunners, with special emphasis on indirect fire and on the timing of fire to support infantry assaults. Based on his experiences in both South Africa and Manchuria, and on his evidence to the Elgin Commission, he was an early practitioner of the deployment of heavy guns in a support role in the field. He was the first to make use of Salisbury Plain to improve the all-arms co-operation of the troops under his command. He also made a special point, when exercising his troops, of inviting naval officers from Portsmouth to watch the manoeuvres and join the discussion afterwards. He was part of the (regrettably) small group of army and marine officers and military and naval thinkers who were keenly aware of the special need for Britain, if not to integrate its armed forces, at least to improve their mutual understanding. He also entertained several German observers, including a Captain Schroder of the Saxon Army, who was desperately worried about the possibility of a great war breaking out in Europe and who actively sought the maximum number of contacts between Britain and Germany in order to prevent it.

Hamilton's principal staff officers at Salisbury were Brigadier, later Major-General, E. C. Bethune, who shared Hamilton's enthusiasm for volunteer troops and would be Director-General of the Territorial Force in the Great War, and Brigadier Richard Haking, a gifted trainer of men and future corps commander on the Western Front.

His duties were many and various besides the principal one of commanding his troops and preparing them for war. There was a high degree of ceremonial duties concerned with important visitors passing through Portsmouth (the King of Spain in 1906, the Kaiser in 1907); his official residence, Tidworth House, Andover, a huge mansion that he once told Churchill rivalled Blenheim Palace and was about as ruinous to his pocket to furnish, was often used to accommodate and entertain these dignitaries and those waiting upon them, including domestic and foreign royalty. He was regularly used, because of his experience and his linguistic skills, to watch and report upon foreign military manoeuvres, and he was consulted for evidence by various commissions. He was in great demand as a public speaker by both military and civilian bodies, and was bombarded with letters asking his opinion on matters military, past, present and future. He was, of course, also writing important books of his own during this time. Finally, he led the busy social life of an Edwardian gentleman such that once, on his way down to dinner, he had to ask his wife to remind him who exactly they were staying with that weekend!

Hamilton had always intended to write a book about his experiences in Manchuria. *A Staff Officer's Scrap Book* is one of his finest works, a marvellous combination of witty observation and profound analysis of Japanese society and modern warfare. It both greatly increased his fame and added to his social and professional enemies. Like all serving officers who venture into print, he had to be very careful about getting official approval for the publication. In August 1905 he was aware that Nicholson, now an implacable foe, had lobbied the Secretary of State for War, Arnold-Forster, against the writing of such a book. The manuscript was sent to Viscount Hayashi, the Japanese ambassador, who read it to ensure, in the words of Arnold-Forster, that it was accurate, fair and harmless. The first volume, covering his early impressions of the Japanese army and the fighting to the end of July 1904, was published in November 1905.

Drawing on his deep knowledge of military history and his decades of experience in India and Africa, he used the war in Manchuria to discourse on the fitness of nations for war and on the harsh reality of war for the men engaged in the fighting. This interest in the intensely personal and psychological demands on the individual soldier figures very greatly in Edwardian military writing and some of the finest of its type is penned by Hamilton. But he prefaced his book with some wonderfully erudite remarks of use to all historians, especially military historians. Military history must be always to some extent misleading. The facts 'known' instantly are often neither well balanced nor exhaustive and soon the story is being shaped by 'the susceptibilities of national and regimental vainglory'. The historian may reconstruct events with skill 'but to the hopes and fears which dictated those orders, and to the spirit and method in which those movements were executed, he has forever lost the clue. On the actual day of battle naked truths may be picked up for the asking; by the following morning they have already begun to get into their uniforms'.[1]

His first appeal was to the British nation, to learn from the ancient virtues of the Japanese people, and in particular how the women did such a great service by raising their children with such a profound love of country that no sacrifice was too great in its name. He was voicing a concern felt by an entire generation of military leaders when he wrote:

> It was because of my conviction that up-to-date civilisation is becoming less and less capable of conforming to the antique standards of military virtue, and that the hour is at hand when the modern world must begin to modify its ideals, or prepare to go down before some natural, less complex and less nervous type. City-bred dollar-hunters are becoming less and less capable of coping with Deer-slayer and his clan.[2]

This argument, though not always presented with such literary flourish, was common in the years before 1914. The extraordinary staying power of the mass citizen armies of 1914–18 suggests that the worry was somewhat premature.

When he made psychological observations on the role of the individual in battle he was again exercising a concern common to many writers of the period and which showed that professional soldiers were far from being the mindless 'butchers and bunglers' that some would have us believe. We can give two examples, both involving that most formidable of infantry, the Japanese Imperial Guard, to illustrate the point. In describing a lull in the fighting at the battle of the Ya-lu River he asked if the infantry were too tired to go on.

> If this is to be taken literally, as meaning that these troops were so exhausted that they could not march a mile or two further to keep at close grip with the enemy, then the statement is nothing less than a libel on the sturdy Japanese infantry; but if it means that the minds and energies of the Generals and the Staff were fairly used up, then, I believe, we have here the secret not only of this, but of many another, strangely inconclusive ending to a very decisive initial success.[3]

Once again Hamilton supplied a gem of wisdom for the military thinker and opened up fruitful lines of future enquiry. It is hard not to read forward in history and consider some of the subordinate command failures that dogged his efforts in April and August 1915 when reading this passage. He concluded with this wise and humane observation:

> It is perhaps necessary to have been a responsible commander during an attack to realise the immense reaction of relief when success is attained, a reaction coincident with an intense longing to tempt fate no further. 'You have won your battle', a voice seems to whisper in your ear; 'the enemy are going; for God's sake let them go; what right have you to order still more men to lose their lives this day?'[4]

How rare it is to find the commander who can look beyond the immediate battle to the developing campaign and demand a higher level of instant sacrifice to avoid future losses in a prolonged struggle.

Discussing the battle of Yoshirei and the failed attack of the Imperial Guard, Hamilton again wrote with compassion:

> There is no more trying demand which can be made upon the soldier than to ask him to resume the advance when, after once being checked, his blood had cooled down and he has had time to realise that the first man to stand up must, in all human probability, be bowled over like a rabbit. The Japanese did not make the attempt, not seriously that is to say, and confessed by the languor of their fire that the ardour of the attack had now burnt itself cold.[5]

The Japanese commander put in reserves and did call for another effort:

> Their bolt was shot, however, and they could not, or would not, respond. It is human nature: that poor human nature against which officers in wartime and priests in peace time have constantly to struggle. Struggle as they may, it is never quite defeated, and is sure to break out just at the most crucial moments. When men have been glued to the ground for three mortal hours, during which time continuous streams of bullets have been passing just over their heads, it is very difficult to get them to rise simultaneously and dash forward with the bayonet. A few specially brave individuals get to their feet and are instantly shot, which encourages the secret idea in each man's breast that he will make his start just one moment after his neighbour. As the neighbour cherishes precisely the same private intention, the result is that nothing can be done unless fresh troops are brought up and led right forward without any pause or hesitation at all. It was, perhaps, natural then that this order to advance had not the slightest effect.[6]

The book contained the usual scathing criticism of horsed cavalry in modern war, guaranteed to irritate those already inclined to criticize him. Its publication was generally well received but Nicholson roundly condemned it as an abuse of Japanese hospitality. He may well have drawn the attention of King Edward VII to that unfortunate little joke about the Marquis Oyama and his bath sponge which went down very badly indeed as an offensive remark on all the world's aristocracy. The King and some of his advisers so feared upsetting their Asian ally that in January 1906 he was prepared to forbid the publication of the second volume, and took the opportunity of meeting Hamilton in February at the launching of HMS *Dreadnought* at Portsmouth to give him a good telling-off and a warning to be very careful. Small wonder that Hamilton was writing a few weeks later that he was relieved to be 'winding up this blessed book which is practically finished'. The final manuscript was vetted by the Foreign Office and there were further excisions of comments on Japanese society and manners. Hamilton's friends in Japan hinted to him that certain foreigners in their country, mainly German but 'even some Britishers', had spread malicious misunderstandings and falsehoods about the book amongst some important people in the country and this is what caused the furore as much as anything Hamilton actually wrote. The fact is that the Japanese liked the book enormously once the son of General Kuroki had translated the first volume into their language in 1906.

The second volume finally received official approval in January 1907 and he warned his secretary 'to keep this permission absolutely private until things have gone so far on that they cannot be stopped'.[7] It was published, at last, late in February 1907, by which time translation rights in the first volume had been widely sold. The first 5,000 copies sold out immediately. He again appealed for service to the public good:

If life is to be lifted out of the dull, ordinary rut, there must be some ideal in the background which, in moments of illumina- tion, may reveal the possibility of existence on a higher plane. What is 'right' compared to 'duty'?[8]

He did get a little carried away by the sheer élan of the attacking Japanese infantry and at one stage suggested the British should revert to carrying their regimental flags into battle, so inspiring were they as an emblem. He was writing straight from the heart to a clique-ridden army when he commented on how well the Japan- ese staffs served their generals:

If I ever get back safe to England and people ask me, 'What are the lessons of the Manchurian war?' I ought, if I have the pluck

of a mouse, most certainly to reply, 'To change our char-
acters, my dear friend, so that you and I may become less
jealous and egotistical, and more loyal and disinterested towards
our own brother officers.' This is the greatest lesson of the
war.[9]

One final passage shows how Hamilton revealed so much of himself
in his writing. He described how an expected Russian offensive had
fizzled out. 'When it fell dusk I returned to Taiyo rather disappointed at having seen no serious fighting. I fear it is my sin to love
the noise of war. I do not quite know, though I often consider,
what I shall say when I am called to answer for it at the long
account.'[10]

It should be said here that Hamilton had a tower of strength in
his literary secretary, Miss Nellie Sellar, the daughter of an old
friend, who worked for him for many years. He bombarded her
with letters, addressed to 'Beloved Nellie!' or 'My dear old girl',
asking for advice on the drafting and redrafting of manuscripts, to
chase down references, even to think up whole themes for speeches
to such groups as the Women's Institute; he often gave her full
credit for the success of his speeches. Jean always thought they got
on very badly but it seemed to work. She certainly could be forceful
in her replies to Hamilton and he once chided her for a 'very nasty
epistle', asking her if it had been written 'the morning after the
night before'!

The point they had been arguing over was whether he should
talk of a possible 'divorce' between Britain and Japan if their
mutual understanding was to be overwhelmed by 'flatteries, cajol-
eries, exaggerations and insincerities'. While he greatly admired the
Japanese for their devotion to duty and their spirit of self-sacrifice,
he always saw them as a deadly menace to Britain's long-term
interests in the Pacific. When he was serving as Adjutant-General
in 1909 a series of newspaper leaders that were particularly friendly
to Japan drove him to distraction. In July he wrote to his friend,
Leo Amery, contrasting the happy, contented and prosperous
people who lived in Manchuria under the Chinese administration
with the bloody tyranny and cruel bullying and oppression that
went on across the other side of the Ya-lu (where the Japanese had

seized Korea). 'It is truly appalling that kow-towing to Japan should be carried to such lengths.'[11] In August another broadside was fired. 'Obviously the writer cannot be aware of the anti-British policy steadily pursued throughout China by Japanese agents.... My own belief is that we have no more deadly enemies in the world than our Japanese allies ... I would rather see Russia, or even Germany, influencing the counsels of China than our brave but thoroughly perfidious allies, the Japanese.'[12] In the argumentative letter with Nellie Sellar referred to above, written in February 1907, Hamilton makes this prescient observation. 'We have our rupture with Japan. If it comes it will be definite and instant, i.e. in what is apparently time of peace, a Japanese Fleet will sail for, say, Hong Kong or Singapore, to strike the first blow.'[13] This is surely as chilling a prediction of Japan's role in 1941 as one could wish for.

A Staff Officer's Scrap Book was a huge success worldwide, drawing great praise in reviews and letters to the publishers and the author. His Russian translators insisted that his conclusions were 'not considered too hard by anyone'. His publisher, Methuen, wanted him to write a study of late-nineteenth century campaigns (Moltke, Skobeleff, and so on). Hamilton made a thoroughly practical reply, checking on the financial and publishing terms and offering a two-volume study of the Russian army through its leaders, Skobeleff and Kuropatkin. Methuen readily agreed to the proposal.

The exchange of letters on this project in January and February 1908 reveal the difficulties under which intellectual soldiers laboured in Edwardian England. On 16 January Hamilton wrote to warn Methuen that the War Office would have to vet the work before publication. '... my investigations may lead me on to rather thin ice, and I have never been noted for mincing matters, so that there is always just the possibility to be considered that some of the most interesting parts of my work might not bear the official scrutiny'. He reminds them that 'many of the most telling passages were excised' from A Staff Officer's Scrap Book.[14]

The internal politics of the army were again alluded to in his otherwise enthusiastic letter of 26 January 1908:

Please bear in mind that seeing there are unfortunately in places of power a fair sprinkling of individuals who would gladly put a spoke in my wheel, whatever my undertaking might be, it will be most desirable to treat this matter as entirely confidential in the meantime . . . At the best, I know well some of my friends would say I was neglecting my official work in order that [sic] (for they would put it at its lowest) to make some money.[15]

The army once again mirrors society in this frank admission of the existence of intense personal rivalries and cliques in its higher echelons.

By 15 February he was writing to put a stop to the venture entirely, depriving us, no doubt, of a valuable work of military history:

I have taken the advice of one or two of my best friends, and they tell me that it might so happen that any rumour that I was going to touch the Russo-Japanese War in any form or shape, might have the most prejudicial results to my career. Even, they tell me, to ask permission to write the life of Kuropatkin would very likely have the effect of putting me out of the running for the command in chief in India, for instance. I do not seek such a post, and I would not manoeuvre to get it. But, on the other hand, I do not think it would be right were I consciously to handicap myself in the consideration of those who will ulti-mately fill the appointment.[16]

At this time Methuen also sought his advice on the translation and publication of a book thought to be by Kuropatkin himself on the Russo-Japanese War. It was effectively a work smuggled out of Tsarist Russia and its provenance was slightly suspect. Hamil-ton certainly encouraged the publication of any observations by Kuropatkin on the late war. After some strong moral objections to publishing a smuggled work, and a side swipe at the 'polite Russians' who blithely pirated A Staff Officer's Scrap Book, Hamilton made a more serious point. If the book was banned in Russia, Kuropatkin, however much he would like it published in England, would have to say no. In a typically witty flourish, Hamilton concluded, 'otherwise the poor devil might find himself shut up in a fortress, which is the Russian equivalent for the King here not asking one to a Garden Party'.[17] These little joking asides reveal what a minefield was the etiquette and lifestyle of the Edwardian power élite.

The earlier reference to the post of Commander-in-Chief, India, is important. There can be no doubt that Hamilton was a leading candidate for the post, perhaps the most obvious choice. Lord Esher confided to his journal on 13 January 1908:

> Tonight dined with John Morley at the Ritz ... We discussed the future Commander-in-Chief, and he recognises Ian Hamilton's Gaelic charm: what an asset it is with natives and how atmospherically attractive it makes him compared with Duff or Barrow – the ordinary 'linesmen'.[18]

Esher, the archetypal 'eminence grise' with very strong links to the Court party, was an admirer of the soldier-poet, Ian Hamilton, and would have done what he could to advance his career. But it seems clear that Hamilton declined any advances on the question at the time, apparently because his wife, Jean, who was not in good health at the time, was definitely set against a return to India.

In January 1906 the Liberals won a huge victory in the general election, a real landslide. Hamilton took care to write an immediate letter of congratulation to Winston Churchill.

> How I exult with you in your victory. As to your deportment under these triumphant conditions, better read old Bacon's essay on envy. You will see there are two methods;- one to ride rough shod, the other to take your hat off and be unusually humble and polite. I prefer the latter myself although I am aware it does not really blunt the eager fang of jealousy.[19]

It was in keeping with Hamilton's literary tendencies that he thought the resoundingly good reviews for Winston's newly published biography of his father, Lord Randolph Churchill, was even better than the political victory and 'more worth doing'.

The Hamiltons' friendship with Richard, later Lord, Haldane began during Hamilton's tenure of Southern Command. In March 1906 Haldane, the surprising choice as the new Secretary of State for War, made an official visit and gathered much material from Hamilton for speeches concerning the upcoming army reforms. He was back in July for a two-day visit in which Hamilton found him 'full of confidence and go'. Another member of the powerful new Liberal government, the Labour leader John Burns, visited Southern Command for the autumn manoeuvres and was a great delight with everyone. Hamilton got on particularly well with people like Haldane because of their shared strong belief in the superiority of the volunteer over the conscript army.

Many of Hamilton's speeches were directed towards volunteer groups and the fostering of the volunteer spirit. They frequently drew upon his love of the common people and could sound dangerously radical. In December 1906 an address to the officers of the Midlands Volunteer Association called for the volunteer movement to modernize itself and recognize that the age of mass democracy demanded not merely 'noblesse oblige' but also the willingness to defend one's freedom in arms if needs must.

> At present I fear we are a good way behind that conception. I saw the other day that a certain labour association had pledged itself to oppose any scheme by which the boys of England, Scotland and Ireland should learn to handle a rifle. Now I can understand a canny old millionaire chuckling as he observes the decline of the military spirit in those whom he would often have liked to dragoon into his workshops on his own terms, but when the rank and file of our people adopt such a view it is a sure sign that Great Britain is suffering from not having been invaded during recent times.[20]

He predicted that Britain would have to face armed despotisms and barbarisms and would need 'a million modern rifles in the hands of a million free men who know how to use them'.

In March 1907 he developed this theme in addressing the Boys' Brigade and asking them to emulate the youth of Japan in their devotion to the service of their country. After quoting a passage from Tennyson on 'airy navies grappling in the central blue' he made another of his accurate predictions about the shape of things to come in modern war. 'Once flying machines are perfected you may see armed men dropping like locusts on to the smiling meadows of England.'[21] In May 1908 he was, with Haldane, addressing students at Oxford to encourage them to volunteer for the Officer Training Corps. Hamilton welcomed the fact that graduates were not so easily assimilated as RMA cadets or militia officers but that they brought a deeper education and wider outlook of life to the services. Army officers were not just leaders of men but teachers of men 'who are drawn from the very poorest class in the land'. He had heard some laughter when Mr Haldane mentioned the modest income of officers. This brought another outburst of anti-capitalist scorn. 'What is the motive that drives a man from bad to worse until he becomes a millionaire? God knows!'[22] and the professional soldier was basically unselfish. He appealed to finer feelings when he asked the Oxford students to join the OTC and be ready to join up in the hour of need.

A constant theme in the training he imparted to the troops serving under him was the need for intelligent initiative as well as obedience. He was fortunate in having General Haking under command when he produced the standard textbook on 'Company Training'. In his introductions to Haking's lectures Hamilton would stress that manuals were not absolute prescriptions for behaviour in training and war but were guides to thought and appreciation of the situation. He feared that regulations tended to kill thought rather than quicken it. The enclosed nature of the English country-side should make them strive even harder to foster local initiative down to the level of the company, battery and squadron. He realized that fear of failure was a paralysing influence.

> But in war, as I have said over and over again, give me the Failure if he has failed in an honest attempt to do something, rather than the man of reputation who has only succeeded in keeping it unblemished by avoiding whenever he could put his fortunes to the test.[23]

All ranks must be taught self-confidence and an understanding of ground and its possible uses in attack, defence and outpost work, especially the intelligent use of dead ground. All training had to be realistic, always 'in the presence of the enemy', by which he meant soldiers armed with blank ammunition always there to dispute any movement being practised. He firmly believed that the attack carried enormous moral superiority that counter-balanced many other drawbacks. Defensive fighting was often nervous in character; with the attack came the adrenaline rush that often prevailed.

This line of thought was fairly prevalent in the Edwardian army; part of a large debate on how to get men to press home the attack in the face of the increasingly deadly firepower available to most armies in the world. One particularly striking passage is quoted by Tim Travers to put Hamilton firmly in the camp of the 'attack or die' school of generals. 'War is essentially the triumph, not of a chassepot over a needle-gun, not of a line of men entrenched behind wire entanglements and fireswept zones over men exposing themselves in the open, but of one will over another weaker will.'[24] Read out of context, this passage does not relate to the stress laid on the high motivation of the volunteer soldier and the fostering of his individual intelligence by the most realistic of training before bringing him to the ultimate test on the modern battlefield. Rather let this passage from his reminiscences equally stand for his real views on war:

> Because Japanese as well as Russians occasionally like to revert to cold steel, do not let it be forgotten that Suvaroff's saying must now be reversed and that it is the bullet which invariably makes a fool of the bayonet provided only the trigger is pulled by a practised marksman ... It seems to me sometimes as if this childish nonsense about the bullet being a fool has been as much responsible for the misfortunes of Russia as all her bad diplomacy and unsound strategy put together.[25]

Hamilton sat on the Advisory Council for the new Territorial Force and the very first camp for them was set up in the autumn of 1908 on Salisbury Plain under his overall command. After only a week he had them performing well in manoeuvres with his regular divisions. At a review held on Whit Monday 1909, the East Lancashire Territorial Division moved with such precision that a French observer of the exercises mistook their artillery for regular soldiers. Hamilton was to devote many lectures to encouraging the development of the Territorials, and was destined to oversee their mobilization and expansion in 1914.

In one exchange of letters with a journalist Hamilton showed how he, with all his colleagues, was having to cope with the increasing pace of inventions and how they might impact upon his profession. Asked his opinion of dirigibles and the new flying machines, he began with very sceptical observations. He first of all deplored the usually faulty intelligence gathered by observation balloons, based on his own experiences at Ladysmith (where herds of cattle were regularly mistaken for mounted troops and vice versa) and Manchuria (where the raising of balloons by the Russians merely told the Japanese where to expect the next Russian activity). If they gave good information during home exercises, it was because the participants were wholly familiar with the terrain already. Powered dirigibles had not yet been used in warfare and he could only see the many technical difficulties preventing their use for dropping explosives or attacking enemy fixed balloons. As for the new aeroplanes, they were not capable of carrying anything like the weight that a balloon could and they required a great deal more ground support in the way of service crews, transport and so on. He ended by admitting that he was a good deal more pessimistic about these developments than many of his colleagues, with whom he frequently discussed the matter. As men became more expert in these things and better machines might emerge, they might 'attain a perfection at present undreamt of'. Within three or four years Hamilton would become one of the foremost advocates of the development of air power.

In this period of considerable intellectual activity concerning the defence requirements of the British Empire, one growing school of thought was calling for the closer integration of the army and the Royal Navy. The naval historian, Julian Corbett, had published in 1907 his two-volume study, *England in the Seven Years' War*. A masterly analysis of the higher direction of a worldwide war, laying great stress on the close and successful co-operation between the armed services for the achievement of great ends, it was a clarion call to the contemporary services to emulate their forebears. There had also been an effort at the Staff College, Camberley, to deepen the understanding between the two services. When Henry Rawlinson became Commandant in December 1903 he quickly recruited the Royal Marines officer, George Aston, to lecture on Imperial and

Naval Strategy with the express intention of fostering better co-operation.

In addition to his lectures, in 1904 Aston conducted the first of a series of annual 'Staff Rides' along the south coast to study theoretical landings at anything up to corps level. At first the Royal Navy just provided officers to give background lectures. They invariably assumed an unopposed landing; it was already thought that modern firepower would make an opposed landing next to impossible. The British army manoeuvres of September 1904 included a major sea movement of troops from Southampton to Colchester, which revealed just how badly these things were understood and how much more needed to be done. In 1905 a joint War Office and Admiralty committee studied these exercises and their report provided the basis for the *Manual of Combined Naval and Military Operations* that was published in 1911 and which was the guiding manual for the detailed planning of the Gallipoli landings. The Camberley studies went on each year until 1908, sometimes involving naval ships but usually not. It is interesting to note that two men on the teaching staff at Camberley, Walter Braithwaite and Frederick Stopford, would play important roles in the Gallipoli campaign. Indeed, Braithwaite's experience in these matters may have been the reason why Kitchener insisted that he go out as Hamilton's chief of staff in 1915. When Henry Wilson became Commandant in 1907 he was more interested in preparing the British army for direct intervention on the European continent and interest in combined operations fell away. Aston kept up his studies and published *Letters on Amphibious Wars* in 1911. Based on studies of four modern wars from 1891 to 1905, one of his main deductions was the futility of warships attempting to silence modern fortresses. What a pity he was not on the directing staff of the Admiralty in 1914–15 when such large claims were being made for a naval attack on the Dardanelles. Hamilton would have been aware of these efforts to increase army/Navy understanding and did what he could within Southern Command to foster these ideas.

Hamilton was always in demand as an observer of foreign manoeuvres; his reports were particularly well written and of the most penetrating and progressive type. In 1906 he was in Austria (from where he claims to have introduced the green trilby hat into London society!) and in German Silesia, where he again criticized the propensity to move in dense masses and to ignore the 'effects' of machine-gun and shrapnel fire in the exercises. In 1908 he visited Austria again, still deploring their use of shock cavalry on the battlefield, then on to Hungary to witness their practice mobilization, together with trips to Bosnia, Serbia and Turkey. He also managed a two-week visit to Russia, where he was able to dine with Generals Kuropatkin and Stakelberg and discuss the Manchurian campaign.

7

Adjutant-General and GOC, Mediterranean, 1909–14

On 1 June 1909 Hamilton was appointed by Haldane to be the new Adjutant-General of the army and Second Military Member of the Army Council. He was working again from the War Office and moved to a house overlooking Park Lane. The Hamiltons were a great success in society, especially as the Liberals commanded such power in the land. His friend, Winston Churchill, was Home Secretary. The Secretary of State for War, Richard Haldane, greatly admired him and drew heavily upon his support for the recent army reforms.

As Hamilton's responsibilities included all matters relating to personnel and recruitment, one of the first things Haldane asked him to do was write a defence of the volunteer principle to combat the strident advances made by the pro-conscription lobby led by none other than Lord Roberts. With no sense of divided loyalty, for Hamilton felt himself to be his own man, he wrote a spirited defence of his long-held and cherished beliefs under the confusing title *Compulsory Service*. At least one bibliographer has assumed this to be a defence of conscription, rather than a sustained attack on it.

To Hamilton's text of some one hundred pages, Haldane prefaced an introduction of thirty-two pages stressing that the Royal Navy was the principle defence of the United Kingdom and that a mass home army would simply be a drain on the budget. The British army's duty was first to garrison the Empire, and second to create a highly trained expeditionary force for joint operations with the Navy, made up of men who had served much longer with the colours than the mass conscript armies of the continent. The Territorial Force was of sufficient size either to handle any enemy landing itself or else to force the hostile power to send such a large force that they would become a sitting target for the Navy. He could see no point in fielding a million partially trained men when the money they would cost would be better spent on the Royal Navy, the Territorial Force and an expeditionary force of regulars capable of carrying the war to the enemy as in the days of Pitt and Nelson.

Hamilton began his argument by saying that conscription was a great leveller, but it worked in a downwards direction. A nation committed to the defence of a great overseas empire needed long-service volunteers for the purpose. Conscripts had a poor record in such campaigns, and he could draw on the recent experience of the Spanish-American War in Cuba and the Italian defeat in Abyssinia for examples. He used the quotation from Bacon so beloved by Basil Liddell Hart as spelling out a peculiarly British way in warfare: 'He that commands the sea is at great liberty, and may take as much and as little war as he will.'[1] The British people did not want to pay for a mass army. Showing how he always thought of the larger picture, Hamilton noted that while the army might draw off some 60,000 men a year to the great benefit of the labour market, recruitment significantly above that figure would disrupt it. Germany, with its enormous army, could barely find 3,000 men to serve overseas. She had to find double rates of pay to get men to serve outside the home country. France was in the same dilemma. How would Britain find the 117,000 men she maintained in imperial garrisons using the same system?

He insisted that the British detested compulsory service as being against their history and their nature. All that would be accomplished by a massive army would be the destruction of the magnificent six divisions of the regular army at home as it was broken up into a training organization for the annual intake of recruits. Better by far to strengthen the Territorial Force and its support troops. He believed deeply in the moral superiority of the volunteer; he had both faced them in battle and commanded them in battle and thought he could speak with some authority as to their worth. Numerical mass was no guarantee of success in war; highly trained and enthusiastic forces could defeat mere numbers.

This was, of course, a line of argument that was bound to appeal to British tax-payers and to their political representatives in the Liberal government. What it also did was grievously disappoint Lord Roberts, who felt betrayed by his great protégé. Some said it was a blow to him second only to the death of his son in the South African War. It would take a good deal of toing and froing at the domestic and social levels before this sad division was healed. It helped that in so many other ways they agreed completely: in encouraging the membership of the Territorial Force, of university Officer Training Corps, of boys' organizations and rifle clubs. But Hamilton absolutely insisted on the voluntary principle. Conscripted masses would simply wreck all the careful re-organization of the Haldane reforms.

As the debate about the value of the new Territorial Force continued, a journalist on *The Spectator* wrote deploring the failure to set up a Territorial Force organization in Ireland and suggested that at the very least that a Veterans' Register be drawn up there. Hamilton's reply must have been something of a shock and not quite what his correspondent intended. Hamilton stated he was all in favour of setting up the Territorial Force in Ireland: 'If they want to rebel, my theory is it is better that they should do so with arms in their hands than by tortuous and embittering political methods. We would then give them a jolly good licking, and bloodshed – as you know from the case of the Boers – is the best possible cement of friendship.'[2] It is hard to know if we are meant to take this seriously as Hamilton concluded the letter by saying that he found little sympathy for these views and didn't expect any!

With *Compulsory Service* written but not yet published, Hamilton embarked on a long overseas tour of foreign manoeuvres. A few weeks before his departure for Russia he had been asked to take over from Lord Roberts as President of the Army Temperance Association. He gave an exuberant inaugural address at the end of which he promised that, if fifty men would join him that night, he would forswear alcohol for a twelve-month. As he inspired over one hundred men to come forward, he was forced to sign the pledge himself, just as he was leaving to visit the hardest-drinking army on the planet, where he had to endure a vodka-soaked extravaganza drinking only ginger pop and mineral water!

He was very warmly received at St Petersburg, meeting the Tsar and the Grand Duke Nicholas on 18 August 1909. Of all the military attachés visiting for the annual manoeuvres he was the only one invited to the special field day (19 August) where the Grand Duke Sergius was being examined for his promotion. He was astounded at the way the Russians freely referred to the 'enemy' side as the Germans, which would never have been allowed during British exercises. He was impressed at the way the veterans of the late war in Manchuria were striving to teach the lessons of that conflict, while recognizing that they had an uphill struggle against a military machine greatly set in its ways.

The full army exercises lasted from 21 to 28 August. At the regimental level he detected an improvement in the conduct of the infantry, with more dispersed tactical deployment (although their fine young officers still swaggered about too much during fire fights) and in the artillery, with the excellent use of concealed positions and indirect firing. The cavalry remained a 'suicide club', still charging recklessly, such that an entire brigade was ruled to have been wiped out as it attacked a fully deployed brigade of artillery protected by skirmishers. In a barbed aside Hamilton remarked that in British manoeuvres it would have been the umpires who were 'wiped out' for making such a ruling! His more serious criticism was reserved for the Russian commanders.

A false principle seemed to underlie the tactics of both Commanders, the principle namely that any and every problem can be solved by the adoption of a rash and desperate offensive. The idea is so diametrically opposed to that which actuated Russian commanders during the Manchurian campaign that I, as a foreigner, was at first astonished. On reflection I understood that I was witnessing a peace reaction against the main fault of the war, only it was being carried too far . . . Several of the commanders were led into disaster during the big manoeuvres entirely because of their blind adherence to the principle of attack at all hazards, for so afraid were they of being thrown on the defensive by even a little hesitation or delay, they did not ever seem to pause to make a thorough reconnaissance or to give their cavalry time to bring them in reports. A few of the enemy's scouts on the horizon or along the outskirts of the forest were enough to make them rush like mad bulls with the whole of their force deployed for the attack in that direction.[3]

Hamilton spent much of the time with the new Minister for War, General Sukhomlinoff, whom he relentlessly lectured on the true lessons of the manoeuvres. Apparently the Minister was put under such pressure by Hamilton's inquisition that he had to get the visitor's Russian aide, a Captain Golejewski, to brief him on how to cope with the 'impossible questions' of the 'infernal Englishman' (sic)! Hamilton was particularly delighted with Golejewski because he had been so disgusted with the performance of the cavalry in Manchuria that he had resigned from the hussars and joined the Pavlovski Guard Infantry Regiment.

Hamilton was impressed by the way that many officers who had served in the recent war with some degree of success had been promoted rapidly in the Russian army. Thus a Muslim leader of Cossack cavalry had been elevated to command the Guards cavalry regiment that was the equivalent of the Britain's Horse Guards (the Blues); a commander of the best of the East Siberian rifle regiments was given the Pavlovski Guards Infantry. Hamilton noted that in a democratic Britain such promotions would be utterly unthinkable. With his tongue firmly in his cheek he reported that he was assured that all the noble officers of the Russian Guards passed over by these two 'had all taken their supersession by Cossacks and Siberians in perfectly good part'![4] He was a good deal less impressed with the enthusiasm with which Russian officers would proclaim their admiration for his *A Staff Officer's Scrap Book*. Thirty thousand copies had been printed and sold in Russia, by both government and private presses, all of them pirated and for which Hamilton received not one penny in royalties!

On his last day in Russia he spent a great deal of time with the Tsar and the Grand Duke Nicholas and firm friendships were sealed. The Tsar spoke warmly of his admiration for the English. Hamilton had never met anyone who loved England so much as the Tsar, a man he felt was so good in himself as to be almost saintly. He was kept apart from his people by court functionaries, which was a tragedy. The Tsar was partially aware of the problem as he remarked to Sir Ian, 'Diplomatists are the only class of human

beings who are equally out of touch with the rank and file of their
own people and with the rank and file of the nation they are
accredited to.'⁵ They reminisced fondly about their time as regimental officers, which both agreed were the happiest days of their
lives. The visit left Hamilton longing for the chance to serve as a
'British adviser' to the Tsar and his court. He was sure he could
revive the dream of Peter the Great, that England and Russia could
draw ever closer together for the mutual benefit of both nations,
and most others besides.

From St Petersburg he travelled by rail to Berlin, where he was
immediately interviewed by von Moltke, anxious to hear his opinions of the Russian army. It was Hamilton's intention to see the
Saxon army manoeuvres but, since Saxony was not as 'independent'
from Prussia as Bavaria, it did not normally issue invitations to
foreign observers. He wrote a private letter to his old acquaintance,
Captain Schroder, and very quickly received an official invitation to
attend, with the full sanction of the War Ministry in Berlin. The
Saxons took the latter literally at their word and over the next two
weeks attached Hamilton to the staff of an infantry brigade, then a
division and, finally, an army corps. He was treated as a native
officer and saw every document and took part in every discussion
(greatly assisted by his fluent German, of course).

The manoeuvres were in and around Chemnitz, 'in the most
socialist part of socialistic Germany'. He found that the officers
loved having these Social Democrats in the ranks; they were highly
intelligent, amenable to discipline, and Germans first, Socialists
second. Their party approved of military service in defence of the
Fatherland and encouraged the men to do their duty gladly. It
made the army hugely popular in the country.

The Kaiser attended the last two days of the exercises. On seeing
Sir Ian so well integrated into the proceedings, he exclaimed, 'Here
you are again, Hamilton, searching out what you can about our
armies'. He made some gallant reply about being on a pilgrimage
to a military Mecca. The Kaiser asked him what he thought of the
new Prussian heavy howitzers serving with 19th (Saxon) Corps, to
which Hamilton replied tartly that he had not been allowed within
a hundred paces of them. The Kaiser laughed and said, 'Quite right

too; a man must keep a few secrets even from his best friends.' Hamilton then reminded him that, as GOC, Southern Command, he had encouraged German officers to inspect Britain's first use of heavy artillery in the field. On the principle that one good deed deserved another, the Kaiser then gave him free reign to see the new howitzers. 'Stick your head down the muzzles if you like!'[6] Hamilton subsequently sent in a separate, and highly secret, report to the War Office about these powerful new weapons being added to every corps in the German army, but he never heard any more about it.

During the discussions after the manoeuvres von Moltke deplored the tendency of attacking infantry to bunch up as they closed on their target, but the Kaiser objected to them being over-extended! He thought some of his officers were being led astray by the British experience in South Africa to favour wide dispersion, but he was sure personally that such experience was altogether exceptional. Hamilton took a full part in the debate and thought the attacks were delivered with more weight and depth than he had witnessed in 1906, but he still criticized them as being too conventional and formal, ignoring the ground and failing to make use of cover. He predicted terrible casualties for such attacks in war. At one stage he was handed a document that roundly condemned cavalry for charging artillery batteries in the field, containing the hauntingly familiar slogan, 'Don't fight them; fight shy of them.' He was astounded to realize that it was his own report of the October 1908 Salisbury Plain exercises, a secret document circulated to 3rd British and East Lancashire (TF) Divisions that had been acquired, translated and distributed by the German Great General Staff!

Edward VII died in May 1910 and, in accordance with tradition, Lord Roberts was despatched in August as a King's Messenger to several of the crowned heads of Europe to announce the accession of King George V. He chose Hamilton as his General-in-Waiting (this was before the publication of *Compulsory Service*) and together they visited Russia, Austria, Romania, Serbia and Germany. They were journeying home laden with expensive gifts and Hamilton declared to Jean that he could hardly remember being so happy.

He returned to Britain and stepped into something of a political furore when he negotiated an excellent new posting as his time as Adjutant-General came to a close.

Haldane had created the new post of General Officer Commanding, Mediterranean back in 1907 and the first appointee to the Malta-based command was the Duke of Connaught, who had just handed over as Inspector-General of Forces to Sir John French. It was widely felt in the army that the post had no real function as there was already a Governor of Malta and the bases at Gibraltar and in Egypt were not in real contact with each other. Connaught felt that the 'backwater' posting had been created just to sideline him from the army's affairs and he let his dislike of it be known to all and sundry. (It is worth noting here that the Duke's long-serving chief of staff, Major-General John Maxwell, shared his chief's resentment at this treatment and probably harboured a long grudge after the matter was resolved to the government's satisfaction.) When he resigned in 1909 it created something of a problem for the government, which they thought they could resolve by appointing Lord Kitchener to the vacancy. Kitchener, a thoroughgoing Tory and opponent of the Liberals and all their military reforms, had set his heart on becoming the next Viceroy of India and had no intention of going to Malta. The Liberals offered many inducements for him to accept and the King himself (still Edward VII at this time) appealed to him to take it, as it would not prejudice his chances of higher office in the future. Kitchener went on a long leave and tour of inspection in the Far East and in the meantime the Secretary of State for India, Lord John Morley, made it clear that he thought Kitchener would interfere with Liberal reform measures in India and was completely unsuitable for the viceroyship. Kitchener returned to England in April 1910 and matters came to a head.

It was just at that time that Lord Haldane engaged Hamilton in a cryptic conversation at the War Office. Haldane began by 'fishing' for a name of someone to take the post if Kitchener refused it; Hamilton was sure he meant himself as a contender. Haldane stressed that it was easy work, requiring only four months a year at Malta, something of a 'lagoon' but that it could be made more interesting with some overseas inspection duties. Hamilton insisted that if they wanted 'an energetic keen man to take it you will have to put thick butter on the dry bread'. It would require lots of interesting travel and inspection work. Kitchener's plans were undone by the sudden death of the King. Morley moved quickly and forced the Cabinet to agree to the appointment of Sir Charles Hardinge as the next Viceroy of India. Kitchener refused the Malta post in high dudgeon and, in fact, remained out of employment for over a year before he returned in triumph to Egypt. The Conservatives were delighted with the government's difficulties and looked to make political capital out of the whole sorry business. To their great chagrin it was announced that Sir Ian Hamilton would take over as GOC, Mediterranean in October, but that he would also be appointed Inspector-General of Overseas Forces. The order creating this important role, covering all the forces of the Empire outside the United Kingdom and India, made it clear that it was a position of such seniority that its holder could expect high command in the event of war. Hamilton was virtually second-in-command behind the putative head of the British Expeditionary Force, Sir John French. This made it a vastly more interesting and prestigious job, one that Kitchener would probably have accepted gladly had he realized its potential. All this irritated the Tories to distraction and we know from Jean's diaries that the Hamiltons paid a heavy price in snubs and cuts in the heady atmosphere of high society.

Politically, these were turbulent times and Hamilton was to get caught up in yet another tussle between the reforming Liberal government and their irascible Tory opponents, now buoyant after their success in the January 1910 general election, when they made up much of the ground lost in the Liberal landslide of 1906. During the constitutional crisis engendered by the opposition of the House of Lords to the 'People's Budget' of 1910 and the subsequent Parliament Bill, which was designed to curb the Lords' power to interfere with the work of the Commons, the Liberals threatened to create 249 new life peers to flood the upper house with government supporters and break forever the Tory stranglehold on that chamber. In his superb biography of Asquith, Roy Jenkins reproduces the powerful and representative list of possible new peers that Asquith drew up in 1911. It included thirteen military figures and the most senior serving officer among them was General Sir

Ian S. M. Hamilton, GCB, DSO. Hamilton had always declared that he did not want a peerage; a step up in rank was always to be preferred. As the political crisis was resolved with the passing of the Parliament Bill in August 1911, he was not put to the test but clearly the Liberals had thought they could rely on him.

The Hamiltons took up residence in the Palace of San Antonio in October 1910 and it was the start of a very effective period in his career. His chief of staff was Gerald Ellison, who had been Haldane's military secretary and was a leading light in the army reforms of the period. They embarked on a punishing schedule of inspections that would, by mid-1914, cover every overseas garrison in the British Empire and all the forces of the Dominions. There would also be serious research going on into the nature of armies, war and generalship that would add greatly to our theoretical understanding of the reforming side of the Edwardian army.

He first got to know the garrison at Malta and renewed his acquaintance with an old friend, Sir Lesley Rundle, the Governor of the island. The Devons were on duty there and together they celebrated the anniversary of Wagon Hill at a great dinner on 6 January 1911. One of the orders Hamilton posted at Malta shows how deeply he thought about the needs of the Empire and about the nature of the society he lived in. He was shocked to hear that officers of the Maltese volunteer forces were barred from the Union Club and that the force was looked down upon in general.

Fortunately these prejudices exist in their acute form almost entirely amongst the more thoughtless youngsters of the Services who have not yet learnt that if we are to maintain our position in the world it has now become a matter almost of life and death that the local resources of the component parts of our Empire should be stimulated and developed. The very first step furthering such a conception is that young Britons should learn to put some curb on their exuberant manifestations of racial superiority. To draw attention to the evil is easy. To suggest a remedy for a chronic constitutional failing would be beyond the scope of this brief statement of the case. I will only at present then express my belief that a strong example set by senior officers may do much to strengthen the bond between the British garrison and the local forces and that I will consider the matter further and do what I possibly can towards such a desirable result.[7]

His first overseas inspection was a two-month tour of Egypt, Cyprus and the Sudan. In Cairo he visited the new Combined Operations Command, and watched combined operations exercises, with the usual post-exercise conference. The War Office had just issued the first *Manual of Combined Naval and Military Operations*, with which Hamilton would become much more acquainted before too long. After only six days in London in March he was then off to the first ever inspection by a British general of the West Indies garrisons. He was at the Coronation of King George V in June and then left for a four-month tour of South Africa, taking in West Africa on the way back. His visit coincided with Jan Smuts beginning to take over responsibility for South Africa's defence from the imperial government. Hamilton was delighted to see the progress made in Anglo-Boer co-operation and he greatly encouraged the new military forces there. In 1911 alone he wrote eleven official reports on the results of his inspections.

The annual inspection of Egypt began the 1912 season. In April he carried out test mobilizations at both Malta and Gibraltar, watching the garrisons and the Royal Navy as they responded to mock invasions. He was again increasing his experience of the problems of amphibious warfare, seeing it on this occasion from the point of view of the defenders. He made great play in his report on the important role of submarines in defeating attacking fleets. In May 1912 a major visit by the Board of Admiralty to Malta brought not only Winston Churchill and his admirals, but the Prime Minister and Lord Kitchener too. Besides the big reviews there was further recognition of the importance of combined operations as further joint exercises were carried out. Jean Hamilton confided to her diary that Kitchener was perfectly livid (with himself) when he saw what a great success her Ian was making of the new Inspection. Hamilton returned to England to attend meetings of the Committee of Imperial Defence and various field training days. At the end of September he travelled via Berlin and Moscow to take the Trans-Siberian railway to begin his inspection of Far Eastern garrisons. After seeing the British and Indian troops in northern China, he visited the Japanese General Sato at Tientsin. Sato was a gunner who had served at Port Arthur and their conversation turned upon the superiority of land forts over ships trying to attack them, which must have given Hamilton something to reflect upon in March 1915. After Peking and Shanghai he sailed for Hong Kong, enjoying the company en route of American General Jack Pershing, who was going to Manila. At Hong Kong Hamilton was critical of the land defences, which were far too extensive for the small garrison to defend. Moving on to Singapore, he pointed out the complete absence of landward defences and warned that if it was to be a great Far Eastern base, it would always be vulnerable if the land defences were neglected. His secret reports on these visits regularly referred to the danger posed by a potentially hostile Japan and he was anxious that Britain made full use of the resources of the Malay peninsula to secure the safety of the Singapore base. He also suggested that Ceylon be built up as an alternative Far Eastern base should Singapore be lost. Less than thirty years would see these warnings justified.

Hamilton was impressed with the keenness of the local volunteers. In the Malay States he noted that 36 per cent of all males between the ages of twenty-five and forty-five volunteered for service. He reminded the readers of his reports that that would give the United Kingdom a Territorial Force of some 3 million men. Again he watched an amphibious exercise that involved British, Indian and Malay troops landing from open boats in a mock assault landing. The men had to go ashore in waist-deep water and he saw one British soldier lose his nerve (and his rifle) and Indian troops mill about chattering and shouting, needing to be shepherded by their British officers. The Malay Volunteer Company behaved splendidly, dashing ashore with great élan, where they formed up and pressed inland in good order.

By the end of 1912 Hamilton had inspected Ceylon and Aden and was back in Egypt for its annual visit. After some weeks in Egypt and the Sudan he strongly suggested that the defence of the latter should be placed under the care of the Indian Army, and he predicted that their presence in the region would be of immediate and considerable benefit to Great Britain in a future large-scale conflict (which is roughly how things turned out in 1914 once

Turkey had entered the war). He then returned to Malta. March and April 1913 saw a series of combined exercises with the Royal Navy and troops of the Malta garrison. He watched three infantry battalions and two batteries embark on five capital ships and sail to the bay to be 'attacked in secret' – it was for the garrison to detect them and respond accordingly. Two cruisers put ashore a covering force ahead of the main landing; they landed unopposed but were soon resisted as they moved inland. All this was a practice of the new *Manual of Combined Operations*; Hamilton had as much theoretical experience of this type of warfare as any general alive. He again reported on the efficacy of submarines as a defensive weapon; they got in amongst the attackers and 'sank' their battle-ships.

After an official visit to Gibraltar and a few days' leave in southern Spain, Hamilton and Ellison were back in London for a series of meetings before a major tour of Canada during the whole of June and July 1913. His visit was hugely popular; the Canadian press hailed the arrival of this 'great soldier', their 'blue-eyed general'. With Canada's Minister of Militia and Defence, Sam Hughes, he inspected 112 military units, covering 14,000 miles in the process. At the time Canada had a permanent force of only 250 officers and 2,500 in other ranks and had a further 44,000 men fully trained through their active militia system. But they had plans to raise nearer 150,000 men organized in six infantry divisions, seven mounted brigades, three mixed brigades and other supporting units. Hamilton recommended that the divisions be organized around their own divisional instruction schools and that every man in the militia be thoroughly familiar with his depot and the routine of mobilization. He greatly favoured national cadet training for all boys rather than compulsory training for all men. Giving the greatest encouragement to this volunteer effort, Hamilton stimu-lated all concerned to renew their efforts and, while there was not time enough for all these plans to come to fruition by the following year, there was a full division of Canadian infantry mobilized in England by January 1915, to be joined by three more for service on the Western Front.

The final report was to have been written in Canada but the hectic schedule meant Hamilton had to complete it during the return sailing to Britain. It was addressed to Minister Sam Hughes and set Canada's home defence efforts in an imperial context.

> Immense forces, some of them mortal enemies to all our most cherished conceptions of life, are now stirring in Europe, Asia, and in the New World itself . . . A thousand years scarce serve to form a State ; an hour may lay it in the dust . . . for the ways of war are changing just as fast, or faster, than the ways of peace. Operations which formerly took months are now carried out in weeks, and will be carried out in days – perhaps hours![8]

He assured Canada that she could expect help if she was attacked, but he was clearly making sure that Canada was in a position to come to the aid of the mother country in what many were seeing as an inevitable conflict between the great powers of Europe in the not too distant future.

On his return the Army Council tried to make him submit his report for their approval before sending it to Canada. He argued vigorously, and successfully, that the report was commissioned by Prime Minister Borden and his Defence Minister and it was to them that he would submit it, unaltered. But the Army Council did forbid him to make his general observations on military policy and modern war. His subsequent reports were restricted to technical details only and are much the poorer for that.

After a further round of War Office, Committee of Imperial Defence and Army Selection Board meetings, Hamilton spent his next full leave with Ellison as an observer of the Swiss army manoeuvres. He made it quite clear that he did this expressly so that he would be the better prepared for his next visit to a great citizen volunteer force – Australia in 1914. In the autumn of 1913 Hamilton was again considered for the post of Commander-in-Chief, India, but he had made it clear that his main interest lay in the developments in Europe and that he wanted to complete his programme of overseas inspections. At least one of his friends thought the government should have sent him to India regardless. Sir Lesley Rundle wrote that 'his picturesque personality and distinguished career as a soldier' was perfect for the Indian Army.[9] After the British army's autumn manoeuvres in September 1913 there was a long spell of office work during which he wrote an important report on *The Establishment and Distribution of Troops in Overseas Garrisons*. Once again his opening thoughts showed just how clearly the professionals were working towards what seemed an inevitable outbreak of war, and with whom:

> Several new factors have begun to make themselves felt in our Councils. A great naval power has arisen beyond the North Sea threatening the heart of our Empire. The danger clouds which have darkened the Himalayas and the Suleiman range for a generation have, for the time being, entirely dispersed.[10]

He used this as a basis to argue for the more positive use of local defence volunteers around the Empire and the freeing up of British battalions to provide more of a striking force for use in war. He was again foreshadowing the emergency creation of five new divisions of regular troops from the overseas garrisons during the manpower crisis of late 1914.

In December 1913 he left, via Gibraltar, for his extensive tour of Australia and New Zealand. He spent nearly three months in Australia alone (2 February to 24 April 1914), making the most exhaustive inspection of all their military forces and facilities. He reckoned he lost a stone in weight during the punishing schedule of travelling and inspections, which must have left his wiry frame almost skeletal. Australia had just passed a Defence Act designed to create six field divisions and one brigade of infantry, eight brigades of light horse and other supporting units by the year 1919–20. Of this projected 153,000 men, barely one-third were being trained at the time of Hamilton's visit. He was impressed by the quality of the men he found under arms:

> I freely confess that my recollections of South Africa, coupled with the assurances of numerous Australian friends, had caused me to feel sceptical regarding the quality of the discipline I should find regulating the ranks of the Army. But if I came here prepared to ban, I can only say now – I was mistaken ... the Australian soldier is very amenable to discipline.[11]

Expressing a keen admiration for the infantry he saw, and ever mindful of the impending conflict, he wrote, 'I wish very much I could transplant 10,000 of these young soldiers to Salisbury Plain.

They would do the croakers good, and make them less frightened of other nations, who have no overseas children getting ready to lend them a hand.'[12] Of the Australian Light Horse, whose forerunners had served with him in South Africa, he said they were 'the sort of men that any commander would like to have at his back in war'.[13] The new officer cadet training college at Duntroon drew his praise; almost the entire product of its first two years would soon be serving with him at Gallipoli. He wrote to Lord Haldane saying how he would like to make Sandhurst a free institution, open to all social classes based on talent alone, as part of a programme of democratizing the army.

The officers and men of Australia's citizen forces had been looking forward to this visit for months. One brigade commander in particular had been carefully rehearsing his men in a battle drill designed to impress their most distinguished inspecting general. John Monash was a civil engineer, of German Jewish extraction, who took his part-time soldiering seriously. At Lilydale, just outside Melbourne, Monash put his brigade through a rigorous exercise before Hamilton, the Governor-General and a number of senior officers. Hamilton called one of his typical lunchtime conferences to discuss progress and admitted that he was expecting an excess of politeness to outweigh much intelligent criticism. Instead he was treated to a forceful exposition by Monash on how things had gone and how they ought to progress; 'he stated his opinions in the most direct, blunt, telling way.'[14] When Monash was criticized in the press for driving his volunteers too hard, Hamilton (known by Tommy Atkins in the South African War as 'Old Full Complements and Half Rations') supported him to the hilt. These men would need all the toughening they could get and they would not have to wait long to put their training to the test. Hamilton remembered for years afterwards how, in the shade of a gum tree at Lilydale, he marked Monash down as a man to watch; his 'outstanding force of character' would make him a fine commander. He praised him both to the Australian authorities and in a secret report to the War Office. Monash always credited Hamilton's reports with securing for him the command of 4th Australian Brigade when war broke out later that year. Hamilton had every right to be proud of his advice, for Monash would turn out to be one of the truly outstanding exponents of the new industrialized warfare of 1914–18 and in the later stages of the fighting on the Western Front would have few equals in conducting the all-arms offensive that defeated Imperial Germany there.

Hamilton went on to New Zealand, where his visit was received with some trepidation because, alone of all the dominions, New Zealand had opted for conscription and the Inspector-General was a known enemy of such military systems! In fact, Gerald Ellison had privately told General Godley that, with Japan and China to be watched in the Pacific, Sir Ian was not about to be too critical. He visited every single military and cadet unit on the two islands and was deeply impressed by the quality of the men he saw there. He did recommend that the officers spend more time getting to really know their men, advice that would never be needed in the British regimental system and reflecting his very real worry about the nature of a conscripted army compared with a volunteer force. He urged the military authorities to press on with realistic training so that the only difference for the citizen soldier between peace and war would be 'putting ball cartridge into their rifles instead of the customary blank'. He left New Zealand on 4 June 1914, after nearly six months on tour.

During his absence a great crisis had gripped both the government and the army at home. After the passage of an Irish Home Rule bill through Parliament, which would have come into force in 1914, Sir Edward Carson had led the increasingly strident movement on behalf of the mainly Northern Irish, mainly Protestant opponents to Home Rule. An armed militia, the Ulster Volunteer Force, made open preparations to fight to stay out of any such constitutional arrangements; a nationalist militia, the Irish Citizen's Army, was raised in response. Ireland had all the makings of a bloody civil war. When some troop movements were ordered to increase the garrison in the North of Ireland, this was seen as an attempt to coerce the Unionist population into accepting the Home Rule bill. Some officers of the 3rd Cavalry Brigade, stationed at the Curragh barracks, in Kildare, and, like so many officers in the army, with strong family connections and loyalties to Ulster, preferred to 'send in their papers', to resign en masse, rather than march against their kith and kin. If this wasn't actually a mutiny it came close to looking like one, and the disaffection spread quickly through wider sections of the army and the Royal Navy. In the frantic negotiations to defuse the situation, promises were made to Brigadier Hubert Gough and the other ringleaders that were repudiated by the Asquith government, leading to the resignations of the Secretary of State for War (J. E. B. Seely), the Chief of the Imperial General Staff (Sir John French) and the Adjutant-General (Sir John Ewart).

On 29 March 1914 Hamilton wrote to his friend, Seely, commiserating with him over the 'terrible strain and anxiety' he was going through.

> In some ways I wish very much I was at home just now so as to be able to hold out a helping hand to you, for whatever it might be worth. On the other – and this from the personal or selfish point of view – I take it for God's mercy that I am as remote from the scene of internecine strife as it is possible for any man still alive on this earth to be.[15]

In a postscript he says he has heard the 'painful and distressing news of your resignation'. He had always found Seely easy and straightforward to work with. The crisis, which rumbled on for some weeks, was somewhat resolved when Prime Minister Asquith himself took over the duties of the Secretary of State for War and two fairly unremarkable men, Sir Charles Douglas and Sir Henry Sclater, were installed as CIGS and AG respectively.

Though Hamilton had expressed relief at being away from the storm centre, there can be no doubt that this was his great chance to fill the one great office that had eluded him so far – Chief of the Imperial General Staff. If he had been available in London he would have been a strong candidate; there was no other officer more suitable by dint of experience or seniority. This is, of course, pure speculation, but he had turned down other promotions, notably C-in-C India, and it does seem as if he had set his sights higher. Many officers in this clique-ridden army would have viewed his advancement with alarm, but he also had friends and admirers. Winston Churchill is on record as thinking he would have made a fine CIGS; he said Hamilton thought in terms of army corps and continents, exactly what was required of such a strategic, directing post. Sir Lesley Rundle, writing from Malta to Hamilton's personal secretary in London, said, 'I had great hopes that Sir Ian would have been Chief of the General Staff, a much more fitting appointment . . . than the present one.'[16] He had hoped that he could then renew a good working relationship by becoming Hamilton's Adjutant-General. What a blessing this would have been for the army in August 1914 if these two men, both used to working with Kitchener and taking over important tracts of work from him, had been in place to take up the burden and perhaps reduce the sense of chaos created in the War Office at the outbreak of the war.

An interesting exchange of letters with Jean gives us an idea of the disruptive influence of the 'Curragh incident' and a clear indication of how Hamilton saw his career developing. On 2 April 1914, Jean had written to Ian in New Zealand telling him of the gossip going about that he had written to London asking for the jobs of either French or Paget. Ian replied on 11 May during a train journey to the town of Hamilton, where the New Zealanders were going to name a mountain after him! He assured her that the story was a malicious lie and thanked heaven that neither job had been offered to him, though he knew Jean 'hankered after me getting French's job'.

> You could have replied, 'In over forty years service my husband has never asked for an appointment and he is not likely to begin now.' Never that is, in peace time. I've often asked to go on active service. But you seem to have quite forgotten this grand appointment promised me for 1st August – it is to my thinking ever so much above either Chief of the General Staff or C-in-C Ireland.
>
> But most likely the best of all would be to be left in peace to enjoy a quiet life and write.[17]

From 1910 to 1914 Hamilton kept up his theoretical studies on military history, military organization and the nature of modern war. He wrote one book that was ready for publication in the summer of 1914 and had gathered material for at least three others. The most complete of these, *The Soul and Body of an Army*, would be revised in the light of his war experience and published in 1921, but the manuscript prepared before 1914 reveals the progressive nature of his military thinking.[18]

The book was aimed to address the abysmal ignorance of military affairs amongst the Anglo-Saxon people and his desire was to explain 'what a wonderful, moving, living, inspired creation is an Army'. He deplored 'mere brute force' and the 'stupid brutality of numbers'; his central argument was that 'nowhere in the world does quality stand so far above quantity as on the battlefield'. Using mechanical similes, very much in the spirit of his age, he described the army as a gleaming locomotive constructed from the scrap iron of the individuals included in it. Organization, training and discipline were the harmonious assembly and machining of its parts, but all would be inert without the inner fire, the moving spirit variously called morale or patriotism. Britain had very belatedly learned the value of organization; the six divisions of Mr Haldane's British Expeditionary Force were its living embodiment. Discipline, much detested by free-born Britons, was not the old corporal discipline of the horse-and-musket age but that new sense of self-motivation that kept a man true to his task on the 'lonely battlefield' dominated by the magazine rifle with its smokeless powder. It was entirely typical of Hamilton that he drew examples of altruistic discipline and loyal concern for one's fellows from the work discipline of the coal miner and the deep-sea fisherman, whose very lives depend on solidarity with their neighbours. Iron discipline and years of training were not enough: 'the latchkey to success in modern war is a high patriotic spirit abiding in the hearts of the people.' He went on to attack Britain's national school system for failing to inculcate this love of duty, honour and sacrifice, and saw it left to the army, with its officers drawn from the public schools where those virtues were upheld, to become the school of the nation. The army taught the people the civic virtues of active citizenship.

He would have liked to have seen all adult males registered for 'National Manhood Service'; not the loathsome conscription, but a way of organizing future mobilization in time of peril. He expected the Royal Navy, the regular army and the Territorial Force to hold the line for some six months before this mass could be deployed effectively – which is something like what happened in 1914–15. But he did greatly favour a compulsory cadet scheme – more Boy Scout than military in character – to teach the whole youth of the nation to serve their country. Some of this reads and sounds positively militaristic, and when he talks of 'race and place consciousness', it is almost fascistic; when his mainspring motto for this newly inspired Army is revealed as *Dulce et decorum est pro patria mori* modern readers might be forgiven for writing him off as a dreadful old reactionary. But we must remember this was written in the years before 1914 and in some deeply moving passages he talked of the blighted existence of the 'poor little slum kids' of Britain. He was trying to instil some nobility into their lives; to rescue them from the cruel fate of servitude to the money-grubbing capitalists that Hamilton felt were a living disgrace to a great nation.

The final additions to this manuscript were written in the summer of 1914 and they possess an increased sense of urgency, though, of course, the outbreak of war would prevent its publication. When discussing the importance of genius in command and the need to actively embrace modern innovation, Hamilton's own imagination took flight. He envisaged a highly mobile army of mounted riflemen, cyclists, armed motors and armoured trains, backed by 'flying machines by the thousand', and fleets of 'diving dreadnoughts'. 'We could give wings to a division, wheels to an army corps, fins to a fleet'; in one sweep he was predicting air-mobile troops, the mechanization of the army and the powerful influence of the submarine. This came from a general who, in 1908, thought the aeroplane was not much better than an observation balloon. He welcomed and embraced every modern development; he approved of the prospect of 'night fighting on a grand scale', something regarded by most of his contemporaries in 1914 with absolute horror. If only these ideas had been given fuller reign in the years before 1914, the British armed forces would have been in better shape to adapt more quickly to the shock of modern industrial war. That they adapted as quickly as they did is to their credit; but the process could have been less painful and bloody.

Hamilton had also gathered material for a book to be entitled *On War*, which suggests that he wanted to leave for posterity a work to rival that of Clausewitz, but little came of it. He also began some more philosophical reflections around the title *The Millennium*. He was well on the way to preparing a study of command in war that he greatly expanded in the 1920s but did not complete. It was ably edited after Hamilton's death by Major (later General Sir) Anthony Farrar-Hockley and published in 1957 as *The Commander*. In February 1912 he had sent to Nellie Sellar a first draft of the main theme of his study.

> There are three clear types all muddled up by the public under the word 'General'.
> 1) There is the personally magnetic leader.
> 2) There is the chess brain mover.
> 3) There is the administrator.
> No one has ever worked out this idea. One and Two very rarely combine. Both One and Two may have a smattering of Three. Three when in high degree is a quality apart; rarely co-existing with Two; practically never with One. One, Two and Three only combine once in 200 years, forming a Napoleon, Caesar etc.[19]

All this theorizing and writing of necessity came to a stop soon after he returned to England in that glorious summer of 1914.

8

The World War Spreads,
1914–15

Hamilton arrived back in England on 15 July 1914, to a country seemingly more concerned with the ongoing troubles in the North of Ireland than with the European crisis developing since the murder of the Archduke Franz Ferdinand and his consort at Sarajevo on 28 June. His current appointment as Inspector-General of Overseas Forces was due to end on 1 August. He had made a great success of the job over the previous four years and the War Office had decided to combine it with the role of Inspector-General of Home Forces to create a single authority responsible for the standardized training and equipment of all the forces of the British Empire. 'Jack' Seely had as good as promised the position to Sir Ian before he quit as Secretary of State for War. No other general could bring more practical experience, theoretical understanding and intelligent thought to this important new task. He approached the new appointment with the greatest excitement; the ideas he had been developing in his projected book, *The Soul and Body of an Army*, would soon be spread throughout the regular and volunteer forces of the Empire.

Within a fortnight of his return his hopes seemed to be dashed. There had been unofficial talk at the War Office that he might be asked to take the post of GOC, Ireland, for which he had no desire whatsoever. It seemed another senior officer was in the running. On 28 July Sir John French called on Sir Ian to explain that he was not to get the new post of Inspector-General after all. Once again in his career he was being asked to stand down to assist the War Office in finding a posting for another officer who required employment. This time it was Sir John French himself, no longer Chief of the Imperial General Staff since his resignation over the 'Curragh incident', who had been appointed in his place two days earlier. Hamilton was deeply disappointed but in his typically loyal fashion he wished French well. Knowing that Sir John French was still the commander-designate of the British Expeditionary Force, Hamilton wrote the very next day offering to serve under him in any capacity he saw fit.

From 27 July, without any firm decision to enter the almost inevitable general European conflict, Britain began to respond to the gathering crisis. In particular the First Lord of the Admiralty, Winston Churchill, began to make the Royal Navy ready for war – guards were placed, minesweepers collected, the Home Fleet moved to Scapa Flow. A seemingly routine order to absorb into the Royal Navy two fine battleships nearing completion for the Turkish navy was to have profound ramifications. On 29 July all regular soldiers were recalled from leave; next day Sir John French was confirmed in his post as C-in-C, BEF, and Ian Hamilton was told that he was to command the Home Army. Full mobilization of the fleet was ordered on 2 August and the army began its preliminary moves for the same eventuality. Field Marshal Lord Kitchener, to his great chagrin, was refused permission to return to Egypt on 3 August. On 4 August, as a British ultimatum requiring Germany to respect Belgian neutrality expired, war was declared and the Expeditionary and Territorial Forces were mobilized.

That evening the Hamiltons and their friend, Henry Rawlinson, dined together and the two soldiers planned to speak separately to Haldane and Kitchener respectively, to try and get the two great men to work closely together for the national good. Early on 5 August Hamilton received a note from his friend, Lord Haldane, to the effect that he expected to relieve the Prime Minister of the duties of Secretary of State for War, the implication being that he would do the actual work even if Asquith retained the nominal title. It also implied that this would be a more satisfactory arrangement than bowing to the mounting popular campaign, driven by the press, to appoint the 'national hero', Kitchener of Khartoum, to the post. It would certainly have been greatly to Hamilton's advantage to have such a firm friend in this vital war post. That very day the pro-Kitchener campaign became a specifically anti-Haldane movement, with allusions to the latter's 'German sympathies'. It should go without saying that these 'yellow press' accusations were completely without foundation. It must remain a matter of interesting speculation as to how well the mobilization of the nation might have gone under this most meticulous of planners, rather than under the overwhelming personality of Kitchener.

The cabinet met with its military advisers and commanders in the afternoon of 5 August to begin the monumental task of organizing the nation for war. That day Asquith had finally persuaded Kitchener to serve as Secretary of State for War. Admiralty and War Office officials joined the field commanders of the BEF at the meeting. Hamilton attended in his capacity as C-in-C, Home Forces. In the discussion about deploying the British army to France, Hamilton joined Sir John French in favouring the more cautious assembly point of Amiens, rather than Maubeuge, which was required by the pre-war plans laid with the French army. It was at the meeting the next day that Kitchener astounded the assembled politicians and many of the service chiefs, by predicting a long war that could last three years and require an army of up to 3 million men. It is fair to say that prevailing military orthodoxy expected a relatively short but violent war, of great encounter battles in north-western Europe in a campaign that really could be 'all over by Christmas'. Kitchener's reputation was so great that the Cabinet left most of the major decisions concerning the prosecution of the war to him.

Hamilton's immediate duties were to prepare the defence of the home country against the possibility of German raids or invasion and to oversee the mobilization of the Territorial Force. Out of fear of the former it was decided to hold back two of the six infantry divisions of the BEF until regular units returning from overseas service could be reorganized and the existing divisions released for service in France and Belgium. By a happy chance the Territorial Force had just at that time been assembling at its summer camps and it was able to mobilize very quickly. Fourteen infantry divisions and fourteen brigades of yeomanry cavalry, organized on the basis of strong regional connections, were instantly available. With something like 120,000 men under his command, Hamilton organized a Central Striking Force to be on hand to move wherever it would be required in the event of a German descent on the coast. He brought them so quickly to a high state of readiness that he was reportedly keen for the Germans to try a landing anywhere they liked. Apparently some confusion arose subsequently as to whether he was in command of the whole Home Army or just this Central Striking Force. Kitchener merely 'thought' that Sir Ian was the commander of the Home Army and Hamilton records his dismay at the depth of Kitchener's ignorance of the very whereabouts of places and locations they had to discuss. The official Orders of Battle show that he was commander of both, and his friend and colleague of many years, Major-General Gerald Ellison, was his chief staff officer.

Kitchener began immediate steps to increase the size of the army by 500,000 men, and an appeal for the first 100,000 volunteers to fill out the ranks of the regular army appeared on 7 August. It is widely accepted that, having little experience of the developments in the Home Army for many years, he had little or no faith in those 'new inventions', the General Staff at the War Office or the Territorial Force. It had been the intention of Haldane and the coterie of officers supporting him, including Hamilton, Haig and Cowans, that the Territorial County Associations would oversee any future expansion of the army by replicating – 'stamping out' was the phrase used – the existing divisions and brigades of the Territorial Force. This might have alleviated a great deal of the disorganization and distress that attended that unique phenomenon in British history, the rush of volunteers of 1914, when a regular army happy to deal with 30,000 recruits in a year found itself absorbing such numbers by the week and in two remarkable instances that number in a single day! To be fair to Kitchener it has to be said that when the Territorial units were invited to volunteer for overseas service the response was very patchy and not at all as automatic as many would have wished. Their primary function was home defence and it would seem that many of the men wanted it to stay that way.

On 12 August Lord Esher wrote in his journal of his anguish at Kitchener's proceedings, and added some interesting observations on Ian Hamilton himself.

Our military arrangements are thrown into confusion owing to our Secretary of State's inexperience of our organisation at home. If he persists in raising this new army, I am afraid he will destroy the morale of the Territorial Force. His new army should be raised behind, not in front of, the Territorials ... Ian Hamilton, it is thought, will be appointed Commander-in-Chief of the Home Forces, a post he is sure to fill admirably.

He is so brave and gallant that his non-employment against our enemies seems an error of judgement. His Celtic nature, that of the soldier poet, does not appeal to the sober English character. Ian Hamilton is brilliant, and a leader of men, rather than a planner of battles. His genius would have been well suited to the wars of the seventeenth century. Wherever he has served, or wherever he may command, men have followed him or will obey him with ardent affection. Confidence is a plant of slower growth, and I am uncertain of its ever blooming in the sunny atmosphere of his impetuous personality.[1]

Hamilton would, of course, have been delighted by the rush to join up – the vindication of his beloved volunteer principle – but he regretted that the Territorial organization was thrown over by Kitchener's 'bull in a china shop' approach. As the volunteers were organized into 'service' battalions of the regiments of the regular army and then into divisions of the New Army, the existing Territorial regiments also found themselves overwhelmed with new men arriving at their establishments. By the end of August it was decreed that wherever 60 per cent of a Territorial division had volunteered for overseas, it would be filled out with volunteers and a second-line formation would be created for home service. The force under Hamilton's command was in the process of doubling itself.

Initially Kitchener used Hamilton rather as he had done when he was his chief of staff in South Africa, sending him hither and thither to 'get things moving', which Hamilton suggests meant rather more of interfering with the proper movement of the BEF in favour of assembling Kitchener's 'first hundred thousand'. It is generally forgotten that it is to Hamilton's credit that, under his command of the Home Forces, the Territorial Force was so quickly mobilized and trained up so that it was able to despatch many formations – battalions, brigades and whole divisions – to replace regulars in overseas garrisons and fill up the shattered ranks of the BEF after the grim fighting of the late summer and autumn of 1914.

While Hamilton could always be relied upon to do his duty in whatever capacity he found himself, he was first and foremost a warrior and he wanted a fighting command. On 17 August Lieutenant-General 'Jimmy' Grierson had died suddenly en route to take up the command of II Corps in France. Hamilton immediately offered himself as a replacement, putting aside the fact that, as a full general, he was technically stepping down a rank. Sir John French opted for General Sir Horace Smith-Dorrien, an equally splendid fighting soldier, to take the corps. This is one of those ironic twists of fate, given that French and Smith-Dorrien were to become the most ferocious of enemies over their conduct of operations in 1914 and 1915.

There was to be yet another occasion when Sir Ian might even yet have served on the Western Front, in an even more exalted role. Kitchener was not completely satisfied with French's command of the BEF, having more than once admonished him over his conduct of operations. It was not good timing, during the critical battles around Ypres, that Kitchener should have met the French Commander-in-Chief, Marshal Joffre, at Dunkirk and proposed to replace Sir John French with Sir Ian Hamilton as C-in-C, BEF. Joffre, greatly influenced by Sir Henry Wilson, insisted that he required no change in the leadership and the matter went no further. No doubt the idea of 'Kitchener's man' in command of the BEF did not appeal to Joffre and his chief British supporter, Wilson. Again we can only speculate on how this would have changed the course of history. We have already seen that Hamilton was as committed to the cult of the offensive as most of his colleagues, and the imperatives of being a junior partner in a great coalition war would have been the same for him as for French and Haig. But in March 1915, while Hamilton was bringing some of the first-line Territorial divisions to the peak of perfection in their training for war – he described the 1st London Division (TF) as a 'beautiful' division of exceptional value – he was writing to Churchill about his ongoing correspondence with Canadian and Scottish officers serving on the Western Front. From various perspectives all were agreed that the defence had a superiority over the attack in the order of five to one. From this Hamilton deduced that the solution was to 'fight elsewhere in the meantime so as to gain as much

1. Lieutenant Ian Hamilton, Gordon Highlanders, (left) barely distinguishable from his Indian guides and bearers on a record-breaking hunt in Kashmir, 1876.

2. Colonel Hamilton (mounted left) commanding a brigade in the Tirah, 1897.

3. Major-General Sir Ian Hamilton as Commandant
of the School of Musketry, Hythe, 1898.

4. Lieutenant-General Sir Ian Hamilton (centre) with foreign military
observers to the Japanese army, and their Japanese liaison officers, 1904.

5. General Sir Ian Hamilton in conversation with the Tsar of Russia at the Russian manoeuvres, 1909.

6. A sketch by the renowned military artist, Richard Knotel, of General Sir Ian Hamilton in conversation with Prince Ernst Heinrich of Saxony at the Saxon manoeuvres, 1909.

7. An Indian mule company bound for Gallipoli preparing for embarkation at Alexandria, April 1915. (IWM:Q13216)

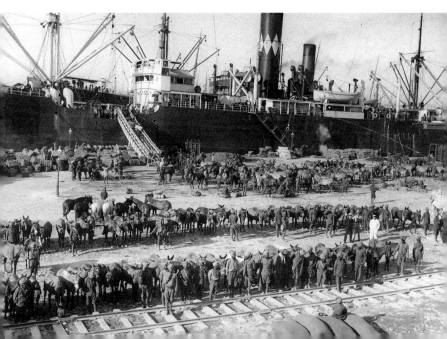

Above: 8. General Sir Ian Hamilton and his chief of staff, Major-General Walter Braithwaite, being rowed ashore at Gallipoli, 1915. (IWM:Q13343)

Right: 9. A typical scene of the 'safe' rear area at Anzac Cove, where the Australians were landed in error in April 1915. (IWM:Q13603)

Below: 10. General Sir Ian Hamilton bestowing medals on his French liaison officers at GHQ, Imbros 1915. His Military Secretary, Captain Pollen, attends him as Braithwaite looks on. The Guard of Honour shown were from the Sussex Yeomanry and the Royal Naval Division. (IWM:Q13509)

11. General Sir Ian Hamilton leading cheers at the medal ceremony. The men of the RND were clearly enjoying the occasion. (IWM:Q13516)

12. Major-General Walter Braithwaite and his son and a.d.c., Lieutenant V. Braithwaite, MC, Somerset Light Infantry at GHQ, Imbros, 1915. 'Val' Braithwaite was killed on 1 July, 1916, the first day of the battle of the Somme. (IWM:Q13521)

13. Lieutenant-General E.A. Altham, Inspector-General of Communications, MEF (centre) visiting Suvla, 1915. This master organizer ended any supply chaos at Gallipoli once and for all. (IWM:Q13553)

14. Major 'Jack' Churchill, Winston's brother, serving as Camp Commandant, GHQ Imbros, 1915. (IWM:Q13619)

15. Putting a brave face on it. General Sir Ian Hamilton taking leave of his staff at GHQ Imbros, October 1915. With his back to the camera was Hamilton's good friend, Brigadier-General Gerald Ellison. (IWM:Q13548)

16. A battery of 60 pounder guns in action at Cape Helles. Only eight of these precious heavy guns were available in July 1915. By the beginning of August all but one had broken down for lack of spare parts. (IWM:Q13340)

17. Commodore Roger Keyes, Vice-Admiral J. De Robeck, General Sir Ian Hamilton and Major-General Walter Braithwaite on HMS *Triad*, October 1915. (IWM:Q13560)

18. General Sir Ian Hamilton (aged 90) toasting pipers of the Gordon Highlanders at his London home, 1 Hyde Park Gardens, 1943.

19. General Sir Ian Hamilton at the grave of Lady Jean Hamilton, Doune, Scotland, 1944. The ceremony was to open a memorial plaque to her adopted son, Captain Harry Knight, Scots Guards, who had been killed in action in North Africa in 1941.

20. General Sir Ian Hamilton (aged 93) taking the salute at the Whitehall march past of veterans of the Boer War, London, 1946.

territory and glory as possible, whilst the Germans are hardening their hearts to make a terrific onslaught upon defences which need no reinforcements to be able to hold them'.[2] Later we shall see that the experience of battle in 1915 would convince him that a more measured approach to seizing terrain and inviting the enemy to make costly counter-attacks was a more profitable way in warfare than general offensives looking for that elusive decisive break-through.

By the end of October 1914 the main armies on the Western Front were entrenched from Switzerland to the North Sea. A largely unexpected, baffling and deeply frustrating deadlock had set in. The Germans were content to remain on the strategic defensive in France and Belgium while they assisted Austria-Hungary to settle the account with the Russians on the Eastern Front. The French, of course, wanted the Germans out of their country and expected their British allies to assist them in a series of offensives during 1915 to achieve that goal. It must be stressed that the great majority of the British military establishment entirely agreed with this analysis.

There were some, however, who were already looking for some other way of breaking the deadlock. Winston Churchill, with the world's greatest navy at his disposal, was hoping to find some other use for it than chasing commerce raiders and blockading the enemy coast. Lloyd George was already looking for a great Balkan alliance to assail the Austrian empire from the south. Maurice Hankey, Secretary to the War Cabinet, was also proposing a solution to the problem by attacking the enemy coalition other than frontally at its strongest point.

These alternative ideas all gained credence with the entry of Turkey into the war. When Britain had commissioned the two 'Turkish' battleships into the Royal Navy she took no cognizance of the fact that they had been paid for in a bout of nationalist fervour with the savings of the common people of Turkey. The disappointment at their loss was thus a huge blow to Britain's otherwise good standing in the country. The Germans, who had been wooing Turkey away from its pro-British sentiments for some years, were able to step up the propaganda war against 'perfidious Albion'. When two German warships, the *Goeben* and the *Breslau*, gave the Royal Navy the slip in the eastern Mediterranean in August 1914, the Turks allowed them to escape through the Dardanelles and dock at Constantinople. The Germans then 'sold' them to the Turkish government (the price was nominal) and German-Turkish friendship was sealed. A German admiral replaced the British Admiral Limpus in command of the Turkish navy; hundreds of German specialists and advisers headed for Turkey. With a British fleet at the mouth of the Dardanelles watching for the German raiders, and the Turks manning their forts and closing the straits to all shipping but their own, the crisis mounted. The Turkish army mobilized in September; in October the Turkish fleet attacked the Russians in the Black Sea and from 1 November she was at war with all the Entente powers. While this greatly added to the military burden of the war for Britain, with the threat to Egypt and the Suez canal a particular problem, others saw it as an opportunity to carry the war to the enemy coalition where it was more vulnerable than on the heavily fortified Western Front.

Early in November, just to show the Turks that they had erred in choosing Germany as their friend, the British fleet, soon to be joined by a French squadron, bombarded the forts at Sedd-el-Bahr at the tip of the Gallipoli peninsula, blowing up one of the chief magazines. This merely announced Britain's interest in the area and reminded the Turks that they, under German direction, should get on with improving their defences in the area.

On 2 January 1915 a request was received in London from the Grand Duke Nicholas, Commander-in-Chief of the Russian forces, for a British demonstration of force against Turkey to relieve pressure on the Russian armies currently being heavily assailed in the Caucasus Mountains. The first of many tragedies associated with this campaign is that, by the time the appeal was placed before the War Council, the Turks had suffered a crushing defeat in the snowy wastes and were in full retreat. There need never have been a Gallipoli campaign at all. But this, of course, was not known at the time and there was a strong moral obligation on Britain to assist an ally that had selflessly sacrificed hundreds of thousands of soldiers by attacking in 1914 before they were truly ready in order to help the greater Allied war effort.

Kitchener made it quite clear that there were no troops available for an attack on Turkey, so Churchill undertook to seek professional advice on the feasibility of an all-naval attack to clear a path through the Dardanelles and threaten Constantinople itself. He cabled Vice-Admiral Carden, commanding the Eastern Mediterranean squadron, for his opinion 'if forcing the Dardanelles by ships alone was a practicable proposition'. Carden, who had been the Superintendent of the Naval Dockyards at Malta, had not been the first choice for this command; it had been offered to the victor of the battle of the Falklands, Vice-Admiral Sturdee, who had turned it down. After consulting his captains Carden replied that the operation could not be rushed but that the Dardanelles might be 'forced by extended operations with a large number of ships'. He envisioned four phases: the reduction of the outer forts; overcoming the intermediate defences up to Point Kephez; conquering the forts at the Narrows; and, finally, sweeping the minefields and allowing the fleet through to reduce the forts above the Narrows and enter the Sea of Marmora. He asked for twelve battleships, three battle-cruisers, three light cruisers, sixteen destroyers, six submarines, twelve (only twelve) minesweepers and sundry auxiliary ships.

At this stage the First Sea Lord, Admiral Fisher, was greatly in favour of a bold stroke against Turkey and encouraged Churchill's scheme, but he demanded at least 75,000 BEF veterans, to be replaced in France by Territorial divisions, to support the attack as a proper combined operation. The Admiralty offered the new *Queen Elizabeth*, who had to register her tremendous 15-inch guns and might as well do that on Turkish forts as on a floating target at sea. The rest of the ships were old, surplus to the requirements of the Home Fleet, and could be 'spared'. It makes poignant reading to see the journals of the naval officers as they sailed towards the Dardanelles knowing that they were officially classed as expendable. Twenty-one trawlers were commissioned into the Royal Navy and sent out as minesweepers. Churchill was clearly confident that the heavy guns of his ships could overwhelm the Turkish forts. He could quote the destruction of the great Belgian forts at Liège by heavy howitzers to prove his case. But there was little enough expert opinion to back his claims. Traditionally the Navy had been extremely reluctant to pit ships against forts. Naval guns fired tremendous distances but at a flat trajectory and could easily whizz over forts rather than hit them. Churchill had missed the point that it was heavy howitzers that proved their worth against forts, not guns. Sir George Aston had made a detailed study of the failures of ships against forts but his advice was never called for.

When Churchill attended the War Council of 13 January he waited until the meeting was nearly over before presenting his scheme for a naval assault on the Dardanelles. The force of his personality and the extravagance of his claims allowed Churchill to carry the plan through. Kitchener agreed to everything as long as it cost him no troops. Churchill actively sought more French participation. They readily provided more ships and, after reflecting that the British were getting overly involved in a part of the Mediterranean that the French considered lay within their sphere of influence, they were soon anxious to get more involved themselves. The War Council gave its agreement for a naval attack to commence in February, with Constantinople as the target. As the fleet continued to mass in and around the islands at the mouth of the Dardanelles a certain degree of panic developed in the Turkish capital. Our witness is the neutral American ambassador, Morgenthau, who described Turkish and German officials as preparing for a hasty exit. They expected the Anglo-French fleet to batter their way through the straits in ten hours. Only one German general in the Turkish service, Liman von Sanders, thought that such a fleet would be cut off, isolated and doomed.

The Admiralty realized that a strong force of marine infantry would be a useful adjunct to the naval attack and had to hand the Royal Naval Division, a mixed force of marines and naval reservists who, being surplus to requirements as far as the fleet went, had received a rudimentary training as infantry and a baptism of fire at Antwerp in 1914. From 6 February 1915 the division began to be despatched to the island base of Lemnos. Based on a thorough report by Admiral Jackson the naval authorities, led by a now reluctant Fisher, had begun to demand military assistance, initially just to occupy the forts as they were reduced to prevent them being reused by the Turks. The drift into a much larger campaign had begun.

9

Attack at Gallipoli,

1915

The naval attack opened on 19 February with the bombardment of the four outer forts, two on the Gallipoli peninsula and two on the Asiatic shore. The results were disappointing, with the Turks fighting back vigorously. Bad weather set in and prevented further operations.

Although the War Council of 16 February had agreed to send the 29th Division, formed from British regular infantry battalions returned from overseas garrison duties, to Mudros, Kitchener revoked the order a few days later. He was under enormous pressure from the army and the French to send them as reinforcements to the Western Front and it was not until later in March that he determined to send them to the Dardanelles. Instead he proposed releasing a still larger, if less experienced, force.

On 20 February Kitchener cabled Sir John Maxwell, GOC Egypt, to tell him that 2,000 marines were at Lemnos, with another 8,000 due there by 13 March, to assist the Navy and 'occupy any captured ports'.[1] Maxwell was ordered to prepare 30,000 men of the Australian and New Zealand Army Corps (Anzacs), currently training in Egypt under their commander, Lieutenant-General Birdwood, to be ready for this service. Full transportation for such a force would not reach Alexandria until 9 March at the earliest, so Maxwell was expected to find local transport for an infantry brigade, with 'special, competent officers', plus mountain guns and 'sappers competent in demolition' to go as soon as possible to assist Carden's efforts. Meanwhile the War Office staff began the process of building up Egypt as a base of new military operations, sending out ordnance companies, food, forage, hospital stores and

disinfectants for two months, as well as two months of flour and
frozen meats and one month's wood for fuel.

A breezy cable from Kitchener to Maxwell on 22 February asked
if everything was working all right and 'have you got all you want?'[2]
The staff got on with building a forward base around the harbour
at Mudros, on Lemnos, with all its necessary depots and signals
infrastructure, and with the appointment of staff officers, adjutants-
general, quartermasters and directors of medical services. That day
Maxwell reported that he had an Australian brigade prepared for
overseas service but no word from Carden as to where to send
them. The next day he was asking for help with numerous shortages
in the Anzac line of communication units which Egypt could not
meet.

Carden had decided that he wanted to land 10,000 men at Sedd-
el-Bahr 'if such a step is found necessary' and hold the tip of the
peninsula. Naval intelligence had already estimated the Turkish
defenders at some 40,000 men. Kitchener clearly needed a more
balanced military analysis of the problem and he sent orders to
Birdwood, via Maxwell, for his trusted old staff officer to meet with
Carden and report on his opinions concerning the combined
operations necessary for forcing the Dardanelles: on whether troops
would need to storm the forts from the land; whether the Bulair
lines would need to be held; and whether operations on the Asiatic
shore were necessary or advisable. Maxwell was requesting more
artillery and rifle ammunition for the Anzacs, as London was asking
Egypt to increase its hospital provision for the same force. Early
concerns were being expressed about hospital space in Egypt,
Cyprus and Malta, and for the evacuation of 'excess' patients back
to the United Kingdom. But at this stage accommodation for up to
5 per cent of Birdwood's force was all that was being requested.

On 24 February Kitchener stressed to Maxwell that the troops
were auxiliary to Carden's efforts. There was no question of landing
10,000 men in the face of 40,000. It was expected that a naval
breakthrough into the Bosphorus, to 'overawe Constantinople',
would make the Turkish defence of the peninsula untenable. The
Australian brigade was to proceed to Lemnos and Birdwood was to
see Carden and report privately to Kitchener as to whether he

thought the Navy could subdue the forts or whether the army would be required for that task.

Maxwell cabled on 24 February with the entirely reasonable request to see the General Staff studies of the strategic problem posed by the Dardanelles. He was not to know that Callwell's 1906 report was a classified state secret, and would not reappear until long after the battle had been joined. Maxwell reported that besides 40,000 Turks on the peninsula, a further 30,000 were close by in Asia Minor. He discounted an attack on the Bulair lines because of the immense strength of the position and favoured a landing in Besika Bay and an advance up the weaker Asiatic shore. He found Carden's plan concerning the use of troops so helpless that the military authorities ought to take the initiative at once. Kitchener's reply restated strongly that it was the Navy's job to silence the guns and destroy the forts with their gunfire. He was clearly worrying about the extent to which he was being drawn ever deeper into large-scale military operations against his better judgement. The War Office rejected the request for more ammunition – the Anzacs had sufficient shells for their field guns and 550 rounds per rifle would be more than enough for the small-scale operations envisaged. Maxwell responded with a warning that his hospital services, especially the provision of hospital ships, could not stand a sudden increase in usage. British intelligence reported the large increase in German personnel in the forts. The French expressed their preference for avoiding the peninsula and fighting along the Asiatic shore and clearing the forts, batteries and minefields from that side.

On 25 February the naval attack was resumed and in a sustained effort the outer forts were battered into submission. The minesweepers were able to enter the Dardanelles for the first time and the enormity of their problem revealed itself. These trawlers usually worked at about nine knots, but now they were in pairs linked by their sweeping gear and were running against a current of some three knots, which reduced their forward motion to barely three or four knots. Unarmoured, slow and manned by brave but helpless civilian crews, they became sitting targets, not for the great guns of the forts, but for the many Turkish field artillery and howitzer batteries of the defending force, which could move freely and at will to bring their fire to bear on shipping in the straits. Did no one in the Admiralty make the simple connection between the speed of these little ships and the speed of the current flowing out of the Dardanelles?

Over the next couple of days the capital ships took up the bombardment of the Inner Forts. Of great significance, and showing what might have been achieved if serious military force had been provided immediately, was the huge success of landing parties of marines and naval ratings in landing at the outer forts and totally destroying all their guns. On 26 February Kitchener was telling Birdwood that the main task for troops was now to land and silence the howitzer batteries that were proving so elusive to the ships' guns, but in the same breath he was warning him not to get involved in landings in the face of a strong enemy. While he could draw on reinforcements up to the full strength of his corps, he should only use the single brigade that had done a lot of embarkation/disembarkation training on being deployed forward to Lemnos. He stated yet again that he expected the Navy to force the Turks to evacuate the peninsula all the way past Bulair and his main concern was whether his projected force of 64,000 men would be enough to occupy Constantinople after the fleet had broken through.

There was already some concern over lax security. It had not helped that the first field post office address issued had been for the Constantinople Expeditionary Force, thus telling the enemy exactly where these troops were bound for. The change to the Mediterranean Expeditionary Force (MEF) was too late. The War Office had warned that the number of troops deployed at Lemnos should not be disclosed but Maxwell had to reply (1 March) that the Admiral, Dardanelles, had 'let the cat out of the bag' by giving the ration strength to a meat contractor. In a rare display of wit Kitchener cabled back, 'Do your best by dangling a canard to recapture the Admiral's escaped feline.'[3]

Birdwood's demands on Egypt for material assistance continued to grow; he needed mules, horse transport, night flares, wood for constructing jetties. By 2 March Birdwood had come to a provisional plan of operations if the Navy still needed military assistance after his maximum troop concentration timed for about 18

March. His plan closely resembled that finally adopted by Hamilton, with a naval demonstration and empty transports manoeuvring off Bulair, another off Smyrna and the real assault going in at Cape Helles, with a drive up the peninsula to deal with all the forts and batteries as far as Nagara Point before moving troops across the straits to clear the Asiatic shore. He confirmed in a follow-up cable that any landing at all would have to be carried out with the maximum strength of his corps (less the mounted brigades remaining in Egypt) as there were plenty of Turkish troops in the vicinity to protect their mobile batteries. He also vowed not to get sucked into extended operations on the Asiatic side as he could see his troops being swallowed up in the 'big country' there. He was as confident as everyone else that the Navy would win through and compel the Turkish surrender. Shortages continued to bedevil his force and he put in a plea for a single observation balloon to assist both military and naval reconnaissance.

On 4 March Kitchener was able to state that the Navy would have forced the Dardanelles by 20 March, by which time Birdwood would have 65,000 men available at Lemnos: his Anzacs, the Royal Naval Division and a division of French infantry under General d'Amade. This latter force, raised in a spectacularly short time in North Africa, was present as much out of French fears for excessive British interest in this highly sensitive region as out of solidarity. The introduction of the senior French general into the operation raised new problems for Kitchener concerning the overall command of the expedition. If the Navy had not won through, then it was recognized that this force would not be sufficient to assault the peninsula and more troops would be sent. If the Navy did win through and sink the Turkish fleet as expected, then a corps of 40,000 Russian troops would accompany the Russian fleet into the Bosphorus and be available for co-operation in subsequent operations.

Every night the Navy was escorting trawlers in their efforts to sweep the minefields, but they were driven back by Turkish gunfire. Changing the civilian crews for naval volunteers made no difference. The naval dilemma was simply stated: battleships could not wipe out the defences until the trawlers had cleared the mines; the trawlers could not sweep the mines until the defences had been destroyed. On 4 March the Navy tried more large-scale landings to demolish shore installations, but this time Turkish resistance was very determined and the landings failed with heavy losses. The opportunity for landing virtually as and when they pleased had passed for the British forces. On that day Birdwood confirmed that he did not think the Navy would ever get through as they faced ferocious fire every time they entered the Dardanelles. The army would need to wait for more assured better weather before it could attack. When Carden suggested moving the attack to the narrow Bulair isthmus, Birdwood countered with the four principal objections that would always apply to this scheme, so much favoured by the harshest critics of the campaign: landing there would not get the Navy past the forts and batteries of the Dardanelles; the assault would go straight into the teeth of defences especially prepared for just that eventuality; troops and ships attacking side by side from south to north could support each other; troops landed at Bulair would face attack from both Thrace and Gallipoli. He set for his objective the line Khilid Bahr plateau – Gaba Tepe – after which the Navy should be free to enter the Sea of Marmora and Bulair would be an irrelevance.

On the night of 7 March the little German-built minelayer *Nusrat* slipped out of Chanak and laid a line of twenty mines in Eren Keui bay. The mines were laid deep enough for small ships to pass over them in safety; their target was much larger. Instead of laying them across the straits they had been laid fore and aft in a line along the widest part of the bay, where great ships might get a good turning circle after a run at the forts at the Narrows.

Cables flew back and forth between London and Cairo addressing the problems of water supply, of medical facilities, especially hospital ships, of forage for an extra 30,000 animals and of how Egypt was to cope as the base for a new expeditionary force. To give some idea of the expected scale of the fighting, there was discussion about creating a training depot for rehabilitating some 1,000 sick men and handling some 10,000 Anzac reinforcements. Maxwell, seeing his command being totally subordinated to the new requirements, began to express his fears of the 'strong undercurrent of disaffection' amongst the Moslems of the Middle East and how Egypt would require a strong garrison at all times. He firmly resisted the request to send an Indian brigade to Basra.

On 10 March Kitchener finally released the 29th Division for service overseas and it began to sail on 16 March. Before then he had made the decision to appoint Sir Ian Hamilton as the Commander-in-Chief of the Mediterranean Expeditionary Force. Initially he had been quite happy for Birdwood, whom he knew and trusted, to command the force, which was to be entirely auxiliary to the Royal Navy. Then the French selected the senior d'Amade to command their troops and this required the appointment of a still more senior British general to command the overall expedition. His first choice might have been Sir Leslie Rundle, who had served with him in the Sudan and South Africa. There were other forces at play, advancing the claims of even more senior officers. In his *Gallipoli Diary*, published in 1920, Hamilton tells a marvellous story of how he was marched into Kitchener's office in Whitehall on the morning of 12 March 1915 and was simply told, 'We are sending a military force to support the fleet now at the Dardanelles and you are to have command.' Kitchener returned to his paperwork as if Hamilton would repeat his South African adventures and just ride off to the field forthwith. It didn't happen quite like that.

It was Winston Churchill who had been lobbying hard for Hamilton to be appointed to this important command. Asquith had some reservations; once, after a dinner party in Hamilton's company, he had disclosed to his mistress, Venetia Stanley, that he thought the general had 'too much feather in his brain'. Having said that, the Prime Minister also recognized him as a 'sanguine, enthusiastic person, with ... much experience of warfare'[4] and was a strong advocate for him once he was chosen. Churchill, of course, had known the fighting and intellectual qualities of Hamilton for more than twenty years and argued forcefully for his selection, once he had heard Kitchener remark that Hamilton was the only man available of sufficient rank and reputation. On 5 March 1915 Hamilton was writing to Churchill that he so admired the 2nd London Territorial Division that it was only their lack of modern artillery pieces that prevented him taking it to Gallipoli rather than the 29th Division. A week ahead of his meeting with Kitchener he was discussing the composition of his force. He concluded, 'No human soul has been told of your news regarding myself – I have allayed some curiosity on the part of the ADCs who knew you had sent for me by fixing up engagements for the next fortnight.' On 10 March he wrote to Churchill: 'K[itchener] has just seen me and told me he intends me to go to the Dardanelles. I have no instructions yet or staff, but I mean to be off to Marseilles as soon as possible. For this I feel myself everlastingly in your debt.'[5]

On 12 March Hamilton had a three-hour meeting with Kitchener at which the scope of the campaign was sketched out. It was stressed that the military force was in a supporting role to the Royal Navy and that ideally it would have no task before it save occupying the conquered forts and proceeding to the investment of Constantinople, where it would be joined by a Russian corps. If the peninsula had to be attacked then it would be necessary to await the arrival of all available forces, and the planning would have to be of the most careful nature. A defeat had to be avoided at all costs, as much for its political ramifications in the Middle East as for military reasons. Hamilton was told that he was not to get embroiled in fighting on the Asiatic shore. The Turks were present in force and it would involve hard fighting to shift them, but Kitchener spent more time discussing future developments once they had been driven from the peninsula. He apparently held the Turks in low esteem, even suggesting that the appearance of new Allied submarines in the Dardanelles would see the Turks abandon their positions in some panic. When the Director of Military Operations, Sir Charles Callwell, was called into the meeting he briefed Hamilton on the Dardanelles situation, drawing from memory of his 1906 report for the War Office. Even the author was not allowed to see this document now that it was a 'state secret'. When Callwell said he had estimated the ideal attack force at 150,000 men, at a time when a good deal of help was expected from the Greeks, Kitchener interrupted and insisted that 75,000 men were more than sufficient for the task ahead, this just happening to be the number of 'rifles' at Hamilton's disposal. He also told Hamilton that the 29th Division was only 'on loan' to him and could be withdrawn at any time. Kitchener exacted from his subordinate a promise that he would only correspond with himself concerning the campaign. This was to put a real block on how freely Hamilton could discuss the campaign as it unfolded. After their service together in South Africa, there can be no doubt that Hamilton had a deep sense of loyalty to Kitchener and he was always obedient to his wishes.

At this point Hamilton was introduced to his chief of staff, Sir Walter Braithwaite. Hamilton had asked if his current chief, Gerald Ellison, could come out in that capacity, but Kitchener denied the request and gave him Braithwaite. Braithwaite was a thoroughly competent staff officer, and we should remember that he was at Camberley when Aston was developing the notion of military/naval co-operation and combined operations and was as well qualified as any man for the upcoming campaign, but there were to be a few occasions when Hamilton could have relied on Ellison, who knew so well the workings of his mind, to back him in some of his decisions where the more orthodox Braithwaite opposed him. It must be stressed. however, that Hamilton found Braithwaite a tower of strength in every other way and he never spoke ill of him at any time.

It was at this same meeting that Braithwaite made the reasonable, forward-looking request for more aircraft to be provided for the expeditionary force. Kitchener reportedly pounded his fist on his desk and shouted, 'Not one!' He was already reluctant to provide the military forces that had been committed so far; he quickly stamped on any further requests. Thus we should take seriously Hamilton's point that he often refrained from asking Kitchener for reinforcement, however desperately needed, because he had seen commanders in South Africa have such requests rewarded by having troops withdrawn from them to teach them a lesson. This was clearly still a transitional phase between Britain's long history of colonial expeditions and the greatest, bloodiest conflict she had ever seen.

The British army's *Manual of Combined Naval and Military Operations* stated that:

> '. . . when operations oversea are contemplated by the Govern-
> ment, it will be necessary for the naval and military authorities
> to advise as to the forces to be employed for the attainment of
> the object, having regard to the information available concerning

the enemy, the topography and resources of the proposed
theatre of operations, the anchorages, landing places and har-
bours, and the districts inland. A detailed scheme will also be
required for the organization and mobilization of the expedition;
and plans must be prepared for its embarkation and disembar-
kation and, as far as possible, subsequent operations.'

Elsewhere it pointed out that

'the complicated duties of embarking and landing troops and
stores can only be carried out successfully so long as perfect
harmony and co-operation exist between the naval and military authorities and commanders, and when the staff duties
devolving on both services have been carefully organized and
adjusted.'[6]

What exactly was Hamilton presented with in March 1915 when he
accepted his command? He later commented that had he been a
German general the Great General Staff would have handed him
meticulously detailed plans, prepared long in advance and kept for
such an eventuality. What he received from the War Office was a
1912 handbook on the Turkish army, a sort of tourist guide to the
area with a thoroughly defective map and the single sheet of
general instructions from Kitchener. His group of nine general
staff officers, assembled in two days and of whom he only knew
Braithwaite personally, were not given access to Callwell's 1906
report or to the valuable reports on the Dardanelles by the British
military attaché, Lieutenant-Colonel Cunnliffe-Owen, a keen amateur yachtsman who had sailed the area while on leave from his
Constantinople duties. The troops available were the untried
Anzacs, the marines and 'surplus' sailors of the naval division,
a French division of startlingly recent creation and the fine battalions of the 29th Division, who had only been together since
late January 1915. None of them had any experience of amphibious operations and any special training would take place in
the three or four weeks before the assault itself. The transport
officers at the War Office and the Admiralty had no idea that the
troops were required to make a major attack on a defended coast
and so the ships carrying troops to the eastern Mediterranean

were sensibly loaded with a view to the maximum saving of space. Everything would have to be unloaded at a suitable port, reorganized and reloaded before proceeding to the theatre of operations.

Hamilton dashed off a letter to Churchill on the evening of 12 March chafing that he had not been able to leave that very day for the Dardanelles. He said that he had asked specifically for Churchill's brother, Jack, as the naval liaison officer on his staff – the only man he dare ask for to be released from service in France for the new campaign. Jack Churchill was the only member of the staff with first-hand experience of the new conditions of war in 1915. Hamilton also foresaw some of the political difficulties he would face:

> I must not in loyalty tell you too much of my W[ar] O[ffice] conversation but I see I shall need some courage in stating my opinions as well as in attacking the enemy; also that the Cabinet will not be quite eye to eye whatever I may have to say!![7]

The next day he and his General Staff had crossed the Channel and taken a train to Marseilles, where they would board a destroyer for a fast passage to the Dardanelles. To emphasize the ad hoc nature of this staff, the cypher officer, Orlo Williams, had been a House of Commons clerk just two days before. In forty-eight hours he was commissioned into the army and despatched to the front. On the boat Hamilton was reading the latest novel by Compton Mackenzie when someone mentioned that the author was seeking a commission to take part in the campaign. Hamilton immediately appointed him to his intelligence staff, where he did a useful job in the line of espionage and counter-espionage. Hamilton also tried to encourage the poet Rupert Brooke, serving with the RND, to join his staff, undoubtedly with a view to preserving this gifted young man from harm. That gallant officer wanted to stay with his battalion for the fight, and met a tragic death from an infected insect bite and disease before the assault took place. Such was the nature of the British Army at this stage of the war; still highly personalized in its command structure and displaying that hint of amateurism that gives fuel to its critics.

More seriously, though Braithwaite had begun the task of appointing the other vitally important supply and personnel staff officers, the Adjutant-General and Quartermaster-General and their respective staffs. Hamilton's group left before this was complete. It would be a week into April before the 'A and Q' staff came out to Alexandria, just as the general staff was leaving for Mudros. It was well after the landings had begun before the whole staff began working together in the proper way.

Meanwhile Maxwell was thinking ahead and clearing Alexandria as a possible future base. When he heard that both the French and 29th Divisions were on their way to Mudros, he foresaw impossible congestion there and so he kept back part of Birdwood's force rather than adding to it. At this time it was thought prudent to add a second hospital to Birdwood's force.

Hamilton's ship dropped anchor at Tenedos island at 3.15 p.m. on 17 March and he immediately visited the new naval commander, Vice-Admiral De Robeck, who had replaced the ailing Carden that very day. They were joined in conference by Admirals Wemyss and Guepratte, Generals d'Amade and Braithwaite and De Robeck's tough and battle-hungry chief of staff, Commodore Keyes. De Robeck spoke bluntly about the impossibility of clearing the mine-fields because of the Turkish field artillery, and described how the peninsula's defences grew stronger with every passing day. Hamilton was impressed by the Navy's determination to make one more great attack, scheduled for the next day, before definitely calling for military assistance.

Early on 18 March Hamilton had already decided to relieve the congestion at Mudros by redirecting the French, 29th and Royal Naval Divisions to Egypt, leaving only McLagan's Australian brigade at Lemnos for emergency use by the fleet. He made a reconnaissance of the peninsula in HMS *Phaeton*, exploring the coast and the defended landing places and even venturing inside the Dardanelles, where he experienced that fury of Turkish artillery fire that forced them to beat a hasty withdrawal.

That afternoon a total of sixteen British and French capital ships, with their escorts, began a series of attacks on the forts inside the Dardanelles towards the Narrows. A fierce fire fight developed, with the Turks putting up a terrific resistance that masked the fact that they were running desperately short of ammunition. Some of the main forts were down to their last four shells. Then a series of disasters struck the attackers. As the ships completed their attack runs and began to turn in the wide Eren Keui Bay, they got amongst the mines laid by the *Nusrat*. Three battleships were sunk; three more were crippled, requiring months of repair work. The attack, which had not completely silenced any of the forts, was called off.

The next real tragedy of the campaign unfolded. If De Robeck had kept his nerve and ordered a renewed attack the next day, the Turks would have been powerless to resist. They would have been out of ammunition and the ships could have battered all the forts into submission, leaving the minesweepers to sweep a clear passage through the Narrows. The wisdom of hindsight was not available to the fleet and the prospect of losing ships at that rate, even if 'surplus to requirements', was more than the Admiral could contemplate, even when the home authorities ordered three more battleships out as immediate replacements. The amazement and relief of the enemy at the respite granted to them is recorded by the American ambassador, Morgenthau, and a German journalist working in Constantinople. On 19 March Hamilton, who had personally witnessed the naval assault, had to report to Kitchener that he:

> was being most reluctantly driven towards the conclusion that the Dardanelles are less likely to be forced by battleships than at one time seemed probable and that if the Army is to participate, its operations will not assume the subsidiary form anticipated. The Army's share will not be a case of landing parties for the destruction of forts etc., but rather a case of a deliberate and progressive military operation carried out in force to make good the passage of the Navy.[8]

Kitchener replied within a couple of hours restating his view that 'those operations must be undertaken after careful consideration of the local defences and must be carried through'.[9]

Hamilton turned his thoughts to the military problem facing him, though it should be stressed that no final decision had been made at this stage about the abandonment of the naval attack. Churchill certainly kept up the pressure on De Robeck to renew the attack as soon as possible. The Prime Minister expected this sooner rather than later. Commodore Keyes took the initiative and organized a flotilla of destroyers as minesweepers. Fast, protected by armour, carrying some firepower and manned by servicemen, these would have dealt with the minefields quickly and efficiently; it is another tragedy that they were never used in that role.

The administrative details and equipment shortages were a constant source of concern for the army. Arrangements were put in hand to get the more badly wounded Australians and New Zealanders back to their home countries. Hamilton put in a request to the War Office for more engineers and their specialist equipment, for more hand grenades, trench mortars and bombs, periscopes, even for some lighting equipment for headquarters' use on campaign. The special difficulties of coalition warfare soon manifested themselves. The simple decision to move the French division from Lemnos to Alexandria apparently could not be made by d'Amade or his 'commander', Ian Hamilton. Still worse, d'Amade, through some 'fantastic point of honour', as Hamilton described it, would not ask for permission to leave the island and Hamilton had to cable Kitchener to cable Paris to cable d'Amade with new orders! All this added to the delays.[10]

When Hamilton advised that 14 April would be the earliest possible start date for operations, Kitchener, the great procrastinator, cabled that he considered such a postponement was far too long.[11] He clearly had no idea of the problems facing the MEF and its need to unload the transports, all packed according to peacetime and space-saving routines, and re-embark the entire force in the proper sequence for an assault landing. In replying to Kitchener's worries about the date, Hamilton pointed out that even leaving Lemnos for Alexandria was far from easy as bad weather allowed only one day in an entire week in which to re-embark men already ashore there. It was a contrite Kitchener who replied, 'I can, I know, implicitly trust you not to waste time, and I have no wish in any way to rush the situation so long as it is being pushed along by you and the Admiral with all despatch to a final conclusion.'[12] It is worth remembering that from Hamilton and his staff leaving London with the task of supporting the Navy to the carrying-out of large-scale assault landings, just forty-three days elapsed. Far from criticizing their performance, we should be astounded at their achievement in such a short time.

It was on 22 March that the momentous decision to ask the army to assault the Gallipoli peninsula, clear the Turkish defenders and their troublesome artillery from the area and allow the Navy to pass through the Dardanelles and into the Sea of Marmora was taken. Hamilton and his staff were joined by Birdwood and his staff in a conference with the naval chiefs on board HMS *Queen Elizabeth*. Hamilton, Birdwood and Braithwaite had agreed to let the Navy have the final say as to whether the army went in or not, though all were agreed that such a development was inevitable. What they didn't know was that the two naval commanders, British and French, had already met and agreed to discontinue their attacks until the army had cleared the way. Thus when De Robeck opened the conference by saying that he could not get through without the help of all Hamilton's troops, there was little need for further discussion. De Robeck's first report to the Admiralty simply stated that the next 'decisive effort' would be in mid-April. His next cable gave details of the preparations for a combined operation 'having conferred with the general and heard his proposals'. This has been seized upon by Hamilton's detractors to suggest that Hamilton had argued for a land campaign as a solution to the naval deadlock and that he 'enticed de Robeck away from the naval attack'. This is absolutely not the case. Hamilton, 'chivalrous to a fault' as Churchill described him, may have been glad to come to the aid of the sister, and 'senior', service, but at no time did he or any of his comrades not expect the Navy to renew its attack on the Dardanelles. All the planning premises were based on the army and the Navy storming forward together. Churchill certainly assumed this would happen. Roger Keyes was astounded when his chief told him that the Navy would await the outcome of the land attack before resuming its campaign. Keyes's flotilla of minesweeping destroyers was ready from 4 April and he has placed on record his unshakeable certainty that they could have cleared the way at any time after that.

Hamilton cabled Kitchener with the news on 23 March, saying that the main features of his campaign plan were already in place but that he would not disclose them just yet for security reasons. It was, of course, the proper duty of a general staff to prepare for the eventuality of a landing ahead of the final decision and, as we have

observed, Birdwood's staff had already come to the same conclusions of the plan, dictated as much by geography and transport
availability as anything else. In a supplementary cable Hamilton
stressed the importance of getting the maximum number of troops
ashore in one go when under fire, and requested twenty or thirty
of the Admiralty's new large, armoured lighters, each capable of
carrying 400 to 500 men. These 'beetles' had been developed by
Fisher as part of his scheme for attacking the Germans in the Baltic.
They were not sent out until the Suvla Bay landings in August.

Hamilton was now wrestling in earnest with his force requirements for the attack and the severe shortages he faced. Birdwood's
corps was weak in artillery; the RND had no mobile guns of any
description; he was trying to obtain a brigade of Gurkhas, 'admirably suited to the terrain', from Egypt. This led to the first real bit
of obstructionism from an otherwise helpful Maxwell. There simply
was no all-Gurkha brigade amongst the Indian troops in Egypt.
The 29th Indian Brigade had been alerted for service but no move
was made to replace its non-Gurkha battalions. Hamilton was told
there was no such brigade as the one he was requesting.

The War Office was already complaining about the amount of
shipping being used by the expedition, ninety ships plus another
twenty-five carrying a mounted division to replenish Egypt's garrison. It asked for some ships back by name, plus any Australian
ships as 'the trade of this country is seriously affected by the loss of
this number of ships'. We might ask whether this expedition was
being treated seriously as a major strategic operation or was it just
a colossal nuisance? Maxwell's reply was brief and to the point. 'No
ships can be spared from here.'[13]

Meanwhile, on 25 March, General Liman von Sanders had been
promoted from corps commander to commander of the Turkish
5th Army tasked with defending the Dardanelles. He had six
divisions on hand and large reinforcements available as needed. He
welcomed the sight of the Allied forces steaming away from Lemnos
for Egypt and completely reorganized the peninsula's defences.
Light covering forces defended every likely landing place; strong
reserves were kept back for counter-attacking once the Allies had
shown their hand. He rehearsed his troops in deploying rapidly to

the various beaches, and spent a good deal of effort improving the roads on the peninsula for that purpose. He also arranged for barbed wire to be positioned below the water line at the most obvious beaches. It was his great good fortune to be given an uninterrupted four weeks to complete his preparations. He still expected, and indeed hoped, that the main attack would come at the narrow Bulair isthmus; he deployed two divisions in the vicinity. Another two divisions were kept on the Asian side in case the attack developed there first. The other two divisions defended the peninsula itself – one in the region of Cape Helles and Krithia; the other covering Gaba Tepe and the northern region.

Once at Alexandria, Hamilton's staff, together with naval staff officers, proceeded with the detailed planning of the landings. The Gallipoli peninsula, besides offering so few useful landing places, presented real problems of water supply and poor communications, making movement difficult once inland. The army staff had to make special provision for both of these problems early in the landing schedules, sometimes at the expense of food and ammunition supply. By working double shifts they were able to report that the Anzacs and 29th Division had been made ready for embarkation for Lemnos by 4 and 6 April respectively, and that the RND and the French would be ready to follow soon after. Kitchener was able to confirm to Hamilton on 1 April that he had heard, via the Foreign Office, that the Russians had assembled at Odessa a complete army corps under General Istomine for operations against Constantinople. The joint naval and military force was under Admiral Eberhardt, who was liaising with the British and French admirals and would order his force forward once the Allied fleet had entered the Sea of Marmora. This news was a real morale booster for Hamilton, who was under few illusions about the difficulty of his task and considered Russian participation in the campaign to be of the highest importance.

Hamilton asked Kitchener not to forget his force if any new device for dealing with barbed wire should be approved. Kitchener replied that only shrapnel and high explosive shells seemed to work. Hamilton was desperately short of the former and utterly devoid of the latter. Hamilton used this reply to begin pressing his claims for more ammunition of all types. He pointedly remarked that the 500 rounds per rifle allowed for the 29th Division was little enough when they were so far from home.

The Director of Medical Services, MEF, arrived in Alexandria on 1 April to find a considerable number of British, Australian and French general and stationary hospitals already established, with nearly 5,000 beds available and four complete hospital ships on hand. Hamilton had also asked his old colleagues in Malta to mobilize the base hospital there, giving another 500 beds and a further 3,000 places if personnel, equipment and supplies were sent out from Britain. When the Director-General of Medical Services at the War Office requested details of the hospital arrangements and medical personnel available for the Gallipoli peninsula, the DMS, MEF, was able to report on an apparently adequate system of hospitals in Egypt and on Lemnos, besides the Casualty Clearing Stations ready for the peninsula itself. The reply was perfectly measured; there was no hint of any friction between the General Staff's early arrangements and the subsequent work of the DMS under the direction of the Adjutant-General. It is important to make this clear as, when the horrific losses incurred on 25 April threatened to overwhelm the medical arrangements, it became great sport for the enemies of the campaign to pour scorn on the early efforts of the General Staff and to accuse them of causing much unnecessary suffering. Nobody at the time had any idea how many casualties would occur during an amphibious assault. The only modern study of medical arrangements available to them was of the battle of Mons in 1914. There two divisions engaged had lost a total of some 1,500 (7.5 per cent) of the men engaged. The General Staff, working under great pressure, had allowed for some 3,000 (10 per cent) wounded in the three divisions they were using in their attack. Once again the wisdom of hindsight has been allowed to cloud the judgement of later commentators.

On 6 April an extremely important cable went from Kitchener to Maxwell:

You should supply any troops in Egypt that can be spared, or even selected officers or men, that Sir Ian Hamilton may want for Gallipoli. You know that Peyton's Mounted Division is

leaving for Egypt. This telegram should be communicated by
you to Sir Ian Hamilton.[14]

Now this seems a slightly cavalier approach to a matter of the
highest importance. The problem is that this order was not seen by
Hamilton at the time and, indeed, he knew nothing of it until he
read it in the preparatory drafts of the official history in the 1920s.
It was the occasion then of some bad feeling as Sir John Maxwell
was known as something of a 'Hamilton-hater' by then and there
were faint hints that he might have failed to copy it to Hamilton. A
simple administrative error was (hopefully) a much more likely
explanation, but it was a grievous one. If Hamilton had known, in
those first desperate days after the landings, when the attacking
divisions were exhausted, that he could have prepared in advance
and drawn upon fresh troops from Egypt, what a difference it
might have made.

Logistical problems still beset the force. Crucially, two ships
containing all the ammunition and other vital stores for 29th
Division, arrived very much later than expected. Hamilton also had
to complain about the overly relaxed approach of the civilian
transports. 'Broadly speaking the delay is chiefly due to the fact that
everyone and everything connected with the Mercantile Marine
seems to work in arrears.' The French also seemed 'rather at sea on
the water' and were lagging far behind the rest of the force in their
preparations. In a typically gallant, and quite clever, touch, Hamilton gave d'Amade to understand 'that he is being regarded as
Napoleon's Old Guard and kept a little in reserve'.[15]

The supply officers still wrestled with shortages and uncertain-
ties. The force had risen to 86,000 men and 31,000 animals. Stores
were accumulated for some six weeks but already problems of
storage were arising. 'The only useful form of cheese is the small,
round Dutch. As packed at present, Cheddar cheese is useless owing
to rapid deterioration.'

After a reconnaissance on the *Queen Elizabeth* Hamilton
reported home that 'with reasonable luck we shall get ashore
without too great a loss'. Confidence in the power of the ships'
guns to cover the landings was high and much work was put in to
work out 'an effective observation system between the ships and

the land forces'. News that a Turkish army corps had moved to
Constantinople from the Caucasus was alarming. Hamilton asked
if the Russians could be induced to 'stir up' the Caucasus front, or
at least load their two divisions at Odessa onto their ships and
make something of a diversion.

It was not until 15 April that the weather improved enough for
good quality aerial photographs to be made available to headquarters to help in the final planning. They identified all the main
defences of the peninsula from Gaba Tepe to Cape Helles, but
could not distinguish between real and dummy positions. Bad
weather closed in again and caused further delay in the shipments
from Alexandria to Lemnos and, more seriously, saw the destruction at sea of some of the floating piers that were being towed
across. Morale for the expeditionary force could not have been
higher. One Australian colonel, asked by Hamilton what were his
main concerns, replied, 'What is worrying me is how to feed and
water the prisoners'.[16]

On 19 April, after a further conference with the admirals,
Hamilton set 23 April as the day for the assault, weather permitting.
GHQ, MEF urgently requested and received another hospital ship,
but always with the carping proviso – 'presumably the intention is
not to retain her permanently ferrying between Alexandria and the
sphere of operations'[17] – that reveals a reluctance to get drawn
further into the commitment of already scarce resources. More bad
weather set in on 21 April, halting any movement at sea that day.
Kitchener sent his final message of good cheer on 23 April, directed
at the Navy, the French and Hamilton and all his troops. 'The task
they have to perform will need all the grit Britishers have never
failed to show.'[18] He was never famous as an orator!

It is difficult now to imagine the enormity of the task facing Sir
Ian Hamilton and his soldiers as the fleet slipped out of Mudros
harbour on the evening of 24 April. Quite simply, never before in
human history had troops assaulted a beach defended by the
modern, quick-firing weapons of war. We are used to seeing film
of assault landings involving epecially designed fast, powered,
armed and armoured landing craft. Hamilton's men would have
been seated in ships' cutters and towed towards the shore by the
Navy's steam pinnaces before being cut loose to row onto the

beaches. There was, in the words of the official history, 'a great deal of misplaced confidence as to the effect . . . of the fire of some 200 naval guns'.[19] While bitter fighting was expected during the landings, all were confident that the leading troops could get ashore and quickly put the defenders to flight, clearing the way for the main body to land without difficulty.

The chief problem was the paucity of suitable landing places and the limited number of vessels to carry the men. The *Manual of Combined Naval and Military Operations* called for a covering force to be thrown ashore that would secure a large enough area to permit the main force to land without interference from serious artillery fire. The admirals arranged that these leading waves would be carried by capital warships and destroyers to within sight of land, and the men would then climb down the side-netting into the boats (the only aspect of the attack they had been able to practise a little at Mudros) and commence their perilous approach. The regulars of 29th Division were selected for the hardest task, the storming of Cape Helles, where two relatively extensive beaches, code-named 'V' and 'W', would be attacked by men of the Fusilier Brigade, while a further two battalions would be put ashore at two smaller beaches, 'S', just inside the Dardanelles in Morto Bay, and 'X', which was a little further up the coast on the seaward side. The divisional commander, Major-General Hunter-Weston, together with Vice-Admiral Wemyss, had executive control of these landings. Late in the planning process Hamilton, based on his personal reconnaissance and anxious to get the maximum number of troops ashore in the first wave, made the bold suggestion that a further two battalions could be put ashore at a place designated 'Y' Beach. It was little more than a goat track up a steep cliff and for this very reason Hamilton surmised, correctly, that the Turks would not guard its summit. It has to be said that Hunter-Weston was not best pleased with this late addition to his task and that, after issuing the basic orders for that landing, took no further interest in it whatsoever. This very serious need to get men ashore quickly also led to the imaginative suggestion that an old collier, the *River Clyde*, could be run ashore below Sedd-el-Bahr castle carrying a further 2,100 men to add to the 4,900 being rowed ashore in the ships' cutters. The collier would also have a battery of machine-guns firing from a sandbag 'redoubt' on its forecastle. The covering force was to clear the southern tip of the peninsula, linking up with 'S', 'X' and 'Y' Beaches, before the main body landed to carry the advance through Krithia and up on to the summit of Achi Baba, the large hill that dominated the southern peninsula.

Further north, just above the Gaba Tepe promontory, was a broad expanse of sandy beach, called Brighton Beach by the Anzacs and 'Z' Beach by the planners. Here 1,500 men of the 1st Australian Division would be rowed ashore and another 2,500 in the boats of eight destroyers would go in close behind them. These men were to sweep to their left and clear all the southern spurs of the Sari Bair ridge before the rest of the two divisions were landed to complete the capture of the highest peaks and thrust across country as far as Mal Tepe, almost cutting the peninsula in two.

Two brilliantly effective diversions completed the plan. The French were to put a brigade ashore on the Asiatic side, to take Kum Kale and Yeni Shehr. This threat to the Asian side would pin down the two Turkish divisions there. Meanwhile most of the Royal Naval Division would sail into the bay off the Bulair isthmus and make as if to attack there. A volunteer swimmer, the remarkable New Zealander Bernard Freyberg, would go ashore to light various flares and generally make it look as if something was happening and this, too, would immobilize two enemy divisions for the crucial period of the assault landings.

It was agreed that the Anzacs would approach the coast by stealth and land in darkness. Hamilton favoured the same technique at Cape Helles, but Hunter-Weston objected that this would create a good deal of confusion and disorder as the troops tried to move inland over wholly unfamiliar country. He preferred to trust the guns of the fleet to suppress the enemy's fire in daylight. Naval opinion decided the issue when they pointed out that the strong outflow current from the Dardanelles would make it impossible to guarantee that the boats would be put ashore at their correct beaches. The time of 5.30 a.m. was agreed, with a full thirty minutes of naval bombardment to clear the way before the boats headed for the shore.

On that evening of 24 April there were many anxious prayers offered up for the success of Hamilton's force. Maurice Hankey had always feared the very worst for the landings; as late as 6 April he had tried to get the whole expedition cancelled rather than risk such difficult landings. (On a visit to Sir Douglas Haig in France a few days before, Hankey had described the operation as being 'run like an American Cinema Show, meaning the wide advertisement which had been given to every step long before anything had actually been done'.)[20] Kitchener related that he went to bed that night with a heart full of foreboding. Charles Callwell later wrote:

> Soldiers who had examined carefully into the factors likely to govern a disembarkation in force in face of an enemy who was fully prepared, were unanimous in viewing such an operation as a somewhat desperate enterprise. There was no modern precedent for an undertaking of the kind. One dreaded some grave disaster, feared that the troops might entirely fail to gain a footing on shore, and pictured them as driven off after suffering overwhelming losses.[21]

Hamilton and his staff, together with the naval staff working under Roger Keyes, had done as much as was possible to plan for this, the most hazardous operation of war. Modern readers are used to accounts of assault landings, based on countless examples from the Second World War in Africa, Europe and the Pacific, the Korean War and other conflicts up to and including the Falklands War of 1982. A great deal of specialist equipment and specialized training went into these operations, planned by men who had years to study previous battles and campaign analyses. With all this experience, things could and did still go wrong for them. An account of the (unopposed) landings in San Carlos Water reveal all the same anxieties and potential for disorganization and even disaster as faced by the men of April 1915. Someone had to be first, planning it all with no practical examples to guide them.[22]

For Hamilton the personal strain must have been enormous. The assault, to be made by troops with minimal training and no experience, was in every sense a leap into the dark. In the absence of artillery support everything depended on the weight of naval gunfire to suppress the enemy defences, which were known to be powerful. For the period of the landings themselves, the admirals were in command. This is standard procedure for all amphibious assaults. The generals only resumed command of their troops after the landings were deemed to have succeeded, or once the troops were established above the high-water mark on the beaches. Hamilton then knew he had to proceed into unknown country, with a force short of every kind of military stores and ammunition. Whereas divisions proceeding to France took with them a battle reserve of an extra 10 per cent of their strength, none of the divisions at Gallipoli had this immediate reinforcement available. He was also acutely aware of the difficulty commanders in the First World War had in directing their troops once they were committed to battle. This was an age before the ubiquitous portable radio familiar to later soldiers. Hamilton once wrote that a rifleman might as well try to direct the flight of a bullet as a modern general direct his troops once they had launched an attack. How much more true was this when the men were struggling ashore from open boats and their commanders were incarcerated in battleships engaged in bombardment duties. Kitchener, with his dire warnings about the effect of a defeat on the British Empire in the Middle and Far East, must have added to the stress. But Hamilton was as battle-hardened as any general in the British service; his warrior spirit welcomed the opportunity to fight; he had repeatedly put his reputation and even his life at hazard when the stakes were high. He was ready to face his greatest test.

As it happened the landings on 25 April 1915 came as close to disaster as many had feared. As the boats carrying three battalions of 3rd Australian Brigade left the battleships that had carried them thus far, it was an inky black night. The young naval officers and midshipmen in command of the steam pinnaces towing the lines of boats were obliged to steer by compass; there was inevitable bunching together. As the coast loomed ahead and some light began to emerge, the boats that should have been using the promontory of Gaba Tepe as a guide began slowly and impercep-tibly to turn towards that of Ari Burnu, with perhaps the feature called 'The Sphinx' behind it adding to the confusion. The south to north current along the coast, not as severe as some thought, added to this drift and the soldiers found themselves deposited on a beach nearly a mile north of the one they were expecting. It should be stressed that this is not uncommon in amphibious operations – the

Allies managed to miss Utah Beach in Normandy by over 2,000 yards on 6 June 1944, after months of preparation.

Now officers and men who had made some study of maps and pictures of the sandy expanse of Brighton Beach found themselves dumped on a narrow beach at the foot of a steep cliff, just as the Turkish defenders became alert and opened a withering fire on the beach and the approaching boats. The Australians plunged ahead and soon dislodged the immediate enemy. As more men got ashore and disappeared into wholly unfamiliar country all semblance of command and control disintegrated. In a day of desperate and courageous fighting these troops, fit and keen to distinguish themselves in their first real test of combat, battled their way onto the first ridge (Plugge's Plateau, Russel's Top, Walker's Ridge and the Nek), and onto the second ridge (400 Plateau), with small parties making it onto Baby 700 at the foot of the Sari Bair Ridge and the third ridge, known as Gun Ridge. While it later transpired that this accidental landing in what became famous as Anzac Cove may have saved them from facing extremely powerful machine-gun and artillery defences at Gaba Tepe, it was the worst of bad luck that the Turkish commander of their 19th Division had selected this very day to mobilize his whole force for an anti-landing exercise. Mustafa Kemal Bey (Kemal Ataturk), a particularly fine soldier, was soon directing a series of counter-attacks that struck the disorganized and inexperienced Anzacs and sent them reeling back towards the coast. Stragglers and wounded tended to spread some alarm in the rear, but the soldiers in the forward positions stuck to a series of defensive positions covering the landing beaches and solidified the perimeter by nightfall.

Late in the night of 25 April, Hamilton was awakened from his sleep aboard HMS *Queen Elizabeth* by Braithwaite and handed an alarming message from Birdwood:

Both my Divisional Generals and Brigadiers have represented to me that they fear their men are thoroughly demoralized by shrapnel fire to which they have been subjected all day after exhaustion and gallant work in morning. Numbers have dribbled back from firing line and cannot be collected in this difficult country. Even New Zealand Brigade which has been only recently engaged lost heavily and is somewhat demoralized. If troops are subjected to shell fire again tomorrow morning there is likely to be a fiasco, as I have no fresh troops with which to replace those in firing line. I know my representation is most serious but if we are to re-embark it must be at once.[23]

This serious collapse of confidence by the generals had first been related to Admiral Thursby, who personally conveyed it to the *Queen Elizabeth*. While it is true that the officers and men of the Anzacs had stabilized the perilous situation to some extent by the time the message reached Hamilton, there can be little doubt that his famous and inspirational message did much to stabilize their commanders. Having heard Thursby estimate it would take three days and huge losses to get the Anzacs away, he sent the following to Birdwood:

Your news is serious indeed. But there is nothing for it but to dig yourselves right in and stick it out. It would take two days to re-embark you as Admiral Thursby will explain. Meanwhile, the Australian submarine has got up the Narrows and has torpedoed a gunboat at Chanak. Hunter-Weston, despite his heavy losses, will be advancing tomorrow which should divert pressure from you. Make a personal appeal to your men and Godley's to make a supreme effort to hold their ground.

PS You have got through the difficult business, now you have only to dig, dig, dig, until you are safe.[24]

It had already been a bad enough day for Hamilton before he received the news from Anzac. The direct assault on the two beaches at the tip of Cape Helles had been as bloody as most had feared. Despite the mighty salvoes of the enormous guns of the fleet, the Turkish machine guns, which waited until the last moment before opening fire, took a terrible toll of the attacking infantry.

At 'W' Beach the 1st Lancashire Fusiliers leapt out of thirty-two cutters into waist-deep water and became thoroughly held up in uncut and submerged barbed wire as machine-guns scythed through them. By sheer dogged courage the men forced their way onto the beach. They were to be awarded six Victoria Crosses as a recognition of the prodigies of valour displayed on this day.

Brigadier-General Hare, the overall commander of the covering force, was accompanying them and discovered a calmer spot whereby he was able to lead a party ashore and turn the Turks out of their defences. He was severely wounded soon after. As the Lancashire Fusiliers fought their way inland, naval and military beach personnel began the preparations for introducing the main body into the area.

Things went very badly at 'V' Beach. Well-placed machine-guns and pom-pom guns decimated the leading waves of the 1st Royal Dublin Fusiliers in the open boats. Those that made it to the beach at all could only cower under the slight shelter of a small sandbank and were pinned there all day. As the *River Clyde* ran in and began to disgorge its complement of 1st Royal Munster Fusiliers and 2nd Hampshires the narrow gangplanks along which the men had to disembark became death traps. The sea around the ship ran red with the blood of the hapless infantry. The senior army officer on the ship ordered the futile attempt to get more men ashore be abandoned. Eyewitnesses reported seeing battleships direct massive salvoes at identified machine-gun nests, which disappeared under great clouds of smoke and debris, only to hear the dreadful rat-a-tat-tat resume once the dust had settled. Brigadier-General Napier and his brigade-major were killed as they came ashore; the colonel who replaced the general was killed a few hours later. Losses like this among the senior commanders played havoc with troop cohesion and complicated the task of the division immeasurably. No further progress was made that day, apart from small handfuls of exhausted soldiers worming their way along the beach and around the base of the castle to join those men ashore at the Camber, a small piece of dead ground below Sedd-el-Bahr village.

At 'S' Beach, in Morto Bay, the 2nd South Wales Borderers got ashore secretly and efficiently and were poised to storm De Tott's battery when a misunderstanding neutralized them completely. They took prisoners and demanded to know from one of them how many Turks were in the vicinity. His reply of about 2,000 left the battalion thinking it was about to be overwhelmed in its perilously exposed position and they dug a defensive perimeter. The prisoner had spoken the truth but had meant there were only 2,000 Turks in the whole of the southern peninsula. At 'X' Beach

2nd Royal Fusiliers had got ashore after the lightest of resistance but then fell prey to that sheer lack of experience and tendency in the British army of the day to wait for further orders. They lost a good deal of precious time before beginning to edge towards the fierce battle going on at 'W' Beach.

At 'Y' Beach, the 'impossible' landing place chosen by Hamilton himself, things went very well at first. Two full battalions got ashore unopposed – 1st King's Own Scottish Borderers and the Plymouth Battalion of Royal Marine Light Infantry. They were not discovered by the enemy for some eleven hours and it is small wonder that Hamilton, in his diary, imagined that he had 2,000 infantry loose in the enemy's rear doing who knew what damage there to the great advantage of the landings. Instead the force was paralysed by confusion and indecision. Colonel Koe of the KOSBs thought he was in command; Colonel Matthews of the Royal Marines was actually senior to him and had been told, at a conference missed by Koe through ill health, that he was in command. Neither displayed any great initiative and simply dug in to await the approach of the covering force storming ashore to the south. It was the greatest lost opportunity of the day and a real tragedy, especially as the Turks finally reacted and threw heavy attacks against the confused soldiers and marines, which eventually induced them to abandon the position entirely, being taken off by ships' boats early the next day.

It was a sorry tale of inadequate orders and uninspired leadership; a classic illustration of the great von Moltke's dictum that no plan survives first contact with the enemy. What made the failure so frustrating was that Hamilton had tried to use the early success to his advantage. Having witnessed from the sea the terrible struggle at 'W' Beach and then reconnoitred towards 'Y' and seen men and supplies streaming ashore in safety, he had tried to organize the further movement of troops there to exploit the success. As troops destined for 'V' were already being diverted to 'W', Hamilton signalled to Hunter-Weston, 'Would you like to get some more men ashore on Y Beach? If so, trawlers are available.' The signal elicited no reply and had to be repeated. This hardly seems a decisive use of his command function, but we have to remember that the orthodoxy of the day demanded that the executive commander of the battle, in this case Hunter-Weston, had control and he should not be 'interfered with' by higher command. Though Roger Keyes was all on for the shift and encouraged Hamilton, Braithwaite, that most studious of Camberley-trained staff officers, insisted that the matter be referred correctly to Hunter-Weston and, more importantly, to the relevant naval commander, Wemyss, who duly advised Hunter-Weston not to do anything to alter existing landing arrangements and cause confusion and delay. This is one occasion when the presence of Hamilton's old friend, Gerald Ellison, as his chief of staff might have encouraged him to insist on a bolder solution to the problem. As it was orthodoxy prevailed and the friction of war took its course.

It is also worth considering the conditions in which the battle commanders had to operate. Hunter-Weston was on board HMS *Euryalus*, his office a few yards from a 9.2-inch gun turret. As the ship carried out its bombardment duties, Hunter-Weston and his staff were deafened every five minutes or so by the roar of the guns, and one witness reported that the various signals and paperwork were sent flying about the room. Once again, those reading the events with hindsight must try and think themselves back into the real events as they unfolded at the time, in all their manifest complexities.

The day ended with troops getting ashore through 'W' Beach in increasing numbers. It was hoped the next day would see a big push to clear the tip of the peninsula. The smooth evacuation of the wounded, in much greater numbers than had ever been envisaged, had been greatly hampered by the loss of small boats to ferry them. Many boats had been shot to pieces; many crewmen had themselves been killed and wounded; others had seized rifles and plunged into the thick of the fighting. All this made the smooth transfer of men and stores ashore, and wounded back to the ships, an ongoing problem for some days.

The French had landed at Kum Kale and been somewhat pinned there by a spirited Turkish defence but it had the desired effect of confusing the enemy and preventing the early movement of two divisions towards Gallipoli. According to plan the French held on there into the 26 April, when the Turks began to break before them and there were large-scale surrenders. As they followed the pre-scribed schedule of withdrawal, to be rerouted through 'W' Beach,

De Robeck, backed by Braithwaite, suddenly urged that they be allowed to stay in place for another day to prevent Turkish artillery fire from harassing 'V' Beach. This decision came too late as the embarkation was already in full swing.

As he went to bed that night, Hamilton must have been disappointed that more progress had not been made. Far from occupying the height of Achi Baba, his force was clinging desperately to the beaches of Cape Helles, but he remained sanguine and expected a brisk advance the next day. The news from Anzac Cove was an added shock but did not materially alter his appreciation of the situation. As Callwell was to comment later, 'The message announcing that a large part of the army had been safely disembarked came as an immense relief.'[25]

10

Stalemate at Gallipoli,

1915

On 26 April things did not go along as quickly as had been hoped. While 'W' and 'X' Beaches were able to link up and consolidate their grip in that corner of Cape Helles, the fighting to clear the village of Sedd-el-Bahr and Hill 141 behind it was very severe indeed. A staff officer, Colonel Doughty-Wyllie, became an inspiration to the men of the Dublin and Munster Fusiliers and the village and hill were stormed, with the colonel falling mortally wounded at the moment of victory. By mid-afternoon the attackers were exhausted and no further progress was attempted until after the relatively fresh French troops had begun to come ashore that evening. The Turks were equally shattered by their experience up to that time and it was a mutual fatigue that overcame the combatants.

On 27 April the battered regiments of 29th Division, with some French units, pushed forward over ground recently evacuated by the Turks, which gave them some sense of achievement. They then prepared for what they thought would be the big push to get them through Krithia and into a position to clear Achi Baba. Only twenty-eight British and French field guns had been got ashore and the attack on 28 April, the First Battle of Krithia, went in with a very meagre bombardment preceding it. The Turks had been reinforced by troops brought down from the Bulair lines and the attack was comprehensively defeated. The 29th Division had been fought to a standstill and reinforcements would be needed before any new attempt was made to advance.

At Anzac these early days passed in improving the defences at the head of the valleys leading up from Anzac Cove and in sorting out the confusion into which the attacking units had fallen in the hectic first day. Repeated Turkish attacks were defeated and the guns of the fleet meted out such severe punishment to the Turkish infantry that they soon lost all desire for making daytime attacks. On 28 and 29 April, to give some help to the exhausted Anzacs, Hamilton sent in four battalions of the RND to relieve some of their units in the front line.

What was Hamilton to do? He is greatly criticized for not making the early failure more explicit in his reports. In his first cable after the landing he did speak of the heavy fighting and the severe losses, but was in no position to give casualty figures, which were still being counted. Next day (27 April) he explained that some of the attacking battalions had had 25 per cent casualties and that rifle ammunition was seriously depleted, but still remained optimistic that 29th Division and the French would break through in their attack of the following day. On that day Churchill was able to tell Kitchener that he had heard from Admiral De Robeck just how badly things had gone during the landings and Kitchener immediately cabled Hamilton: 'If you want more troops from Egypt, Peyton's transports ought to be available, and Maxwell will give you any supports from Egyptian garrison you may require.'[1] This message, which Kitchener must have considered a reminder, must have come as a revelation to Hamilton who, we must remember, had never seen that vital communication of 6 April that placed the whole garrison of Egypt at his disposal.

Meanwhile another warning message had arrived at the War Office, this time from the French admiral, Guepratte, and forwarded by GOC, Malta. It expressed admiration for the gallant manner of the troops getting ashore at all but stated bluntly 'it is of the utmost importance to reinforce immediately the Expeditionary Force which is insufficient for such extensive operations, in order to ensure continued success'.[2] This cable also estimated casualties at 5,000, which was the first intimation that the medical arrangements that had allowed for 3,000 wounded might be in difficulty.

On 28 April, before the failed attack of that day, Hamilton still told Kitchener that 'thanks to the weather and the wonderfully fine spirit of our troops, all continues to go well'.[3] This kind of optimistic message is used to damn the general who sent it but it may be understood in three ways: in terms of the sheer relief at getting most of the troops ashore at all, which was universally at the time regarded as a great achievement in itself; in terms of the reluctance to admit that he needed more men to a chief he had promised faithfully he would not pester for more troops; and in terms of the fact that Hamilton and his staff were still confined to the *Queen Elizabeth* until more headway had been made inland and were not as fully briefed on the front-line situation as they might be. Nevertheless Hamilton did conclude this cable with the request: 'May I have a call on the East Lancashire Territorial Division in case I should need them? . . . You may be perfectly sure that I shall not call up a man unless I really need him.'[4]

Before receiving the above message Kitchener had already cabled Maxwell, relating the Guepratte/Malta signal and expressing some surprise that 'Hamilton has not made any mention of this to me'.[5] (He, of course, did not know that Hamilton knew nothing of the 6 April order and was constrained from asking for more men as a result of that.) Kitchener expressed his hope to Maxwell that he was keeping all his troops ready to embark and presumed that he was keeping in close touch with Hamilton on such matters. Maxwell was by now more concerned about the depletion of the Egyptian garrison. In common with Kitchener, he had wider concerns, fearing that 'any failure on the part of Hamilton would bring about a critical situation all over the Moslem world'.[6]

Kitchener ordered the immediate embarkation of the East Lancashire division. Hamilton, grateful for the men, had to point out that the congestion in the narrow beach heads made it necessary to receive the division a brigade at a time. Large drafts of reinforcements were also on their way for Birdwood and Godley; the 29th Indian Brigade was ready to land at any time; d'Amade informed Hamilton that the French government had offered a second division for the expeditionary force. In a pattern to be repeated during the campaign, large-scale reinforcements were being made available just that little bit too late for them to be of decisive use. The official history was to make the point: 'What a single division could do today might need a corps tomorrow.'[7] As the East Lancashires were preparing for embarkation they were found to be short of machine guns, transport and their divisional ammunition columns. Meanwhile Turkish reinforcements flowed freely onto the peninsula from Constantinople and Asia Minor, through the little port of Gallipoli. While Hamilton's force remained at his original fifty-three battalions, the Turkish forces rose from fifty-seven to seventy-five battalions.

Hamilton visited Birdwood at Anzac and found the men 'cheery and self-confident'. Their early propensity to waste ammunition in wild fire-fights had been restrained and they were now efficiently defeating the repeated Turkish counter-attacks and taking every opportunity to improve their own positions. At Cape Helles, 29th Division's artillery was finally ashore and the division was 'visibly recovering from moral and physical exhaustion'. The fact that Hamilton had to ask the War Office for a reinforcement of 900 regimental officers reveals how heavy the losses had been to date and also adds to our understanding of the confusion of the early days and the difficulties of reporting the situation accurately. Kitchener had 200 immediately available in England and asked Maxwell to supply as many as he could from Egypt. He was now badgering Maxwell to send every man available, regardless of whether their equipment was complete; he wanted men in the firing line at all possible speed.

Liman von Sanders had received a peremptory order from Enver Pasha to 'drive the invaders into the sea'. So began a series of massive counter-attacks made by Turkish infantry with empty rifle magazines; reliance on the bayonet alone was meant to increase their fervour. On the night of 1 May any small inroads they made into the British and French positions were swiftly eliminated and their losses were simply tremendous. The French thought to profit by the repulse and made a hasty night attack, which made some small gain but at grievous loss (over 2,000). Turkish attacks were defeated again the next night, though it was noted they were made with much less enthusiasm. Eight fresh Turkish battalions landed on the peninsula on 3 May and were rushed into the attack that night. They were shot to pieces and rendered unfit for further service for a week or more.

This must have encouraged Hamilton and his men as they prepared for their next big effort to break the deadlock on the Cape Helles front. Cox's 29th Indian Brigade was landed, and the first of the Territorial brigades was to follow them. He would then bring down two brigades of Anzacs from the relatively quiet northern sector and put all his resources into a major attack on Krithia and Achi Baba. The Australian official history entirely supports Hamilton in his concentration of effort:

> The support of the naval artillery, upon which Hamilton was intended by the Government, the War Office, and the Admiralty to rely, had not yet been fully tested. Helles was the obvious field for it, and, until that method proved insufficiently effective, Hamilton was justified in making his main thrust there.[8]

The War Office had despatched more artillery and rifle ammunition to the Dardanelles. That they could report 'we are sending you eleven spare-parts boxes for machine-guns' gives us some idea of the shortages facing the British army in general and how these scarce resources had to be eked out. On 4 May the headquarters of the MEF reported 'the supply of ammunition is becoming a very serious matter, owing to the continuous fighting which has occurred since 25 April'.[9] This drew the first of a series of goading messages from the War Office. 'The ammunition supply for your force was never calculated on the basis of a prolonged occupation of the Gallipoli Peninsula. It is important to push on.'[10] That last, fatuous, addition to the message, coming from men safely ensconced in London offices, must have been galling to Hamilton's staff. It was followed by demands for details of all ammunition expenditure to date and future requirements.

The Expeditionary Force required a major reorganization for the ensuing battle. All the battalions of the battered 29th Division were grouped into two brigades and were joined by the newly arrived 125th Brigade (four battalions of Lancashire Fusiliers) and the Indian Brigade (reduced by a quarter by the decision to leave out of the fighting its four Muslim companies). Major-General Paris of the RND had just two battalions of his Royal Marines under command and four Australian and four New Zealand battalions. The twelve battalions of the 1st French Division, who were feeling the strain of some particularly vicious fighting on their sector and whose Senegalese troops were proving very fragile, were reinforced by a British naval brigade of three battalions. Some 25,000 rifles were available for the attack, with 72 British and 33

French guns, and no reserves to speak of. In the absence of aerial reconnaissance and the difficulty of patrolling in the face of Turkish attacks, the knowledge of the enemy's defences was abysmally low. There was not even any certainty as to the location of the enemy's main line of resistance, which made artillery bombardment a matter of pure chance. The estimate of 20,000 as the number of Turks in the line was commendably, if worryingly, accurate. On the Western Front the army was learning the painful lesson that attacking without adequate artillery preparation merely provided targets for hidden enemy machine-guns. All too aware that a similar fate awaited his men, Hamilton suggested to Hunter-Weston, once again the executive commander for the battle, that the attack should begin at least one hour before daybreak, so that the men might approach the enemy positions under the cover of darkness. Given the severe losses amongst the company officers, Hunter-Weston was not prepared to allow even the 29th Division to risk an opposed advance in the dark, let alone the other formations who were either equally short of officers or wholly unfamiliar with the terrain. We know from his writings that Hamilton was a keen advocate of night fighting, but he was way ahead of most of his contemporaries in these opinions. The command orthodoxy of the day deprecated senior commanders interfering in the conduct of a battle (in much the same way as, over a year later, Haig would only advise Rawlinson on how to prosecute his attack on the first day of the Somme). Yes, it would have been better if Hamilton had imposed his will upon Hunter-Weston, but that is simply not how the British army conducted itself at that stage in its history. With Hamilton, based offshore on the *Arcadian* but with full cable communications with his subordinates, acting as an overall army commander, Hunter-Weston was the equivalent of a corps commander; even he had to hand 29th Division to his senior brigadier. The official history comments, with a rare hint of criticism, 'it was plain that Sir Ian Hamilton would be able to exercise little or no influence on the coming battle. His last remaining reserve had been handed over in advance to his subordinate commander on shore, and all that was left to him of the high office of Commander-in-Chief was its load of responsibility.'[11]

The Second Battle of Krithia was another deep disappointment for the Allies. 'Even the Great War furnishes few examples of a series of offensive operations being entered upon with troops so worn out by continuous fighting and lack of sleep as those who took part in the Second Battle of Krithia.'[12] The attack was opened on 6 May by 125th and 88th Brigades and the French. They were only able to push a few hundred yards through the enemy outpost lines before being halted everywhere by machine-gun fire. There was a mournful comment in Hamilton's diary of events to the effect that 'I still think we might have done as well at much less cost by creeping up these 200 or 300 yards by night'.[13] Ironically the 125th Brigade was halted before the position above 'Y' Beach that had been so tragically and unnecessarily evacuated on 26 April. It was in the middle of this desperate fighting that the War Office cable telling them to 'push on' reached the headquarters staff. Hamilton says he prayed to God to give him patience.

As casualties had been relatively light, and another Territorial brigade was landing, Hamilton decided, after consultation with Hunter-Weston and d'Amade, to renew the attack on 7 May. What he could not know was that Liman von Sanders had sacked the German commander of his southern group of forces and replaced him with another who promptly recommended (request denied) a deep withdrawal to strengthen his weak position. Once again the presence of a fresh division on the Allied side might have made all the difference. There were exhortations to the troops to make another supreme effort. A large supply of high-explosive shells would have been more welcome. After another weak bombardment the same troops attacked and were brought to a halt after a few hundred yards. That afternoon the 87th Brigade was fed into the battle, and the New Zealand brigade was brought up in support, to little or no avail. Still casualties had not been excessive and there were three brigades not yet engaged, so it was agreed that the battle would continue into its third day.

On 8 May every available naval and army gun 'made a further heavy inroad on their slender stocks of ammunition' and the 29th Division and the New Zealanders attacked again and were again forced to go to ground after a slight advance. The terrible strain on the infantry showed itself when, for the first time, the French attackers failed to leave their trenches at all. Late that afternoon the last effort was made. Every available gun fired for all it was worth, regardless of vanishing stocks of ammunition, but so little was known of the enemy positions that much of it must have been wasted. The French charged with drum and bugle to no avail. The Australian brigade prepared to advance steadily over open ground and was destroyed as it rose from its trenches. The tough veterans of 29th Division called these Australian soldiers 'White Gurkhas'; high praise indeed from British regulars. The attack failed everywhere and the final losses (6,500 men, or some 30 per cent of the attackers) left Hamilton with only eight territorial and four Indian battalions in any condition to conduct operations. The official historian surmised that the men were being asked to do too much with such limited resources. The 18,500 rounds fired at the second battle of Krithia would have made little impact on the Western Front, but if the 80,000 rounds fired at the same time during the failed attack on Aubers Ridge and two of the three divisions engaged there had been thrown in at Gallipoli, it might have carried Sir Ian Hamilton to the Narrows and the fleet to Constantinople.

During the course of the battle, in response to the staff exchanges about ammunition, Hamilton sent a stiff cable to Kitchener pointing out that the BEF in France was but twenty-four hours from the shell-producing factories at home whereas 'we are distant a fortnight. I consider that 4.5 inch, 18 pounder and other ammunition . . . should now be despatched here at once via Marseilles'.[14] He received a reply so banal that he seriously doubted whether Kitchener had ever seen it, let alone written it, despite it coming out in his name. 'It is difficult to judge the situation unless you can send me your expenditure of ammunition for which we have repeatedly asked. The case is not affected by the other considerations you mention.'[15] Was this meant as a slap on the wrist or was the War Office blind to the problems of operating at such a distance from the home base? Hamilton's response was to send the bluntest report he had written to date.

I might represent the battle as a victory, as the enemy's advanced positions were driven in, but actually the result has been a failure, as the main object remains unachieved. The fortifications and their machine-guns were too scientific and too strongly held to be rushed, although I had every available man in today. Our troops have done all that flesh and blood can do against semi-permanent works, and they are not able to carry them. More and more munitions will be needed to do so. I fear that this is a very unpalatable conclusion, but I see no way out of it.[16]

He went on to estimate that his 37,000 rifles in all, with only one brigade still to arrive, were now faced by some 60,000 Turks.

That day the War Office ordered the BEF in France to prepare 22,000 shells to be sent to the Dardanelles via Marseilles. (This would greatly add to the furore in the British press about the scandalous shell shortages and the government would soon find itself fighting for its life.) This heightened sense of urgency also prompted a desperately worded message from Kitchener. He said he could not understand the reports of the number of troops Hamilton had under command and wanted to know where the second French division had got to. The whole situation gave him anxiety, especially with regard to the number of transport ships tied up by the expedition. He asked for Hamilton's opinion as to how the operation would develop in the future; expressed disappointment that naval artillery had not been more effective against the enemy's fixed positions, and trusted that Hamilton and the Admiral would consult and devise some means of clearing the way through. To this Hamilton had to explain that, valuable as the ships' guns were to a force so weak in artillery, the southern peninsula was spoon-shaped and the guns were only effective in firing at its outer rim. More aerial reconnaissance, even by balloon, was essential. In this message Hamilton promised 'to hammer away until the enemy gets demoralised' and to keep up the pressure on Achi Baba by night advances. Then he asked for two fresh divisions organized as a corps to enable him to push on with good prospects of success, 'otherwise I am afraid it will degenerate into trench warfare with its resultant slowness'.[17]

Kitchener was not able to comply with the request immediately but cabled to say he was sending out the 52nd (Lowland) Division (TF), though shipping constraints meant they couldn't bring out all three of their artillery brigades. On 12 May Hamilton expressed his gratitude for the reinforcement and displayed another flash of prescience based on his extensive knowledge of the pre-war army, this time concerning the new division's commander. 'Please take stock of Egerton. In peace time he is an excellent commander and a strict disciplinarian, but at Malta I found him to be highly strung and apt to be excitable under distress. Calm imperturbability is above all things required in these operations by the commander.'[18] He suggested that he check with Sir Lesley Rundle, who knew Egerton well. Concerning the guns, Hamilton would settle for a brigade each of field guns and howitzers but reminded the War Office that two such brigades belonging to 42nd (East Lancashire) Division were still in England and that these might be sent out instead, and thus save on the need to send artillery headquarters personnel.

Meanwhile on 10 May another short cable from the War Office to Maxwell signalled more anxieties for the MEF and its staff. 'Representations made here regarding inadequacy of arrangements for wounded in ships. Insufficient doctors, nurses and dressings.'[19] Given that we have recorded the careful preparation of hospital facilities throughout the Mediterranean before the assault, and the terrible difficulties arising from that day, it is understandable that Maxwell fired back a strongly worded rebuttal.

Will you please state the source of representations, which I believe to be unfounded. The rush of wounded could not be dealt with in fitted hospital ships, well supplied with everything, and therefore we had to use and will have to use ordinary transports. Under most difficult circumstances the best possible surgical arrangements were made. Of course, as troops had to disembark and the wounded embark on the same day, the transports could not be cleaned. More than 11,000 cases have been brought from the Dardanelles, all with their wounds dressed. With the exception of 2,000 sent to Malta, all of these were made comfortable in hospital and within eighty hours of being wounded they were all attended to. The wounded arrived under circumstances well attended to, according to the reports of the surgeons in all the hospitals.[20]

Maxwell had further occasion to strenuously deny other detrimental stories about the medical arrangements forwarded to him by the War Office. Tittle-tattle about the Gallipoli campaign was already gaining ground in London.

Thus it was that Callwell found himself at a meeting of the War Council where criticism of Hamilton was freely expressed. He wrote:

> At another meeting, at which Lord Kitchener likewise was not present, a marked and disagreeable tendency to criticise Sir Ian Hamilton for his ill-success made itself apparent. I was the only representative of the army present, and it was manifestly impossible for an officer miles junior to Sir Ian to butt into a discussion of that kind. But Mr Churchill spoke up manfully and with excellent effect. The gist of his observations amounted to this: If you commit a military commander to the undertaking of an awkward enterprise and then refuse him the support that he requires, you have no business to abuse him behind his back if he fails. That seemed to me to fit the situation like a glove; it did not leave much more to be said on the point, and no more was said, thanks to the First Lord's timely remonstrance.[21]

When Churchill was dismissed as First Lord of the Admiralty in May, following the resignation of Admiral Fisher as First Sea Lord and the Unionists' ultimatum for creating a coalition government, Hamilton was to lose his stoutest defender in the Cabinet. Churchill's continuance as the Chancellor of the Duchy of Lancaster was a marked loss of prestige and influence and, before the year was out, he would prefer service in the trenches on the Western Front.

Hamilton's daily reports chronicled the relief of the desperately weak 29th Division for the first time since it landed, with its place in the line taken by the 42nd Division; the arrival of the second French division; the defeat of Turkish counter-attacks; and the excellent work of Gurkha infantry in scaling precipitous sea cliffs to seize a strong Turkish position and greatly improve the Allied position on the left (henceforth known as 'Gurkha Bluff').

Then came the momentous 'Private and secret' cable of 14 May: 'The War Council would like to know what force you consider would be necessary to carry through the operations upon which you are engaged. You should base this estimate on the supposition that I have adequate forces to be placed at your disposal.'[22] Those responsible for the higher direction of the war had finally realized that the venture on which they had embarked so casually was in critical need of more resources.

Three days later Hamilton's carefully considered reply spelled out the real dilemma of operating in such cramped conditions so far from the home base.

On the one hand, there are present on the Peninsula as many troops as the available space and water supply can accommodate. On the other hand, to break through the strong opposition on my front will require more troops. I am, therefore, in a quandary because, although more troops are wanted, there is at present no room for them. Moreover, the difficulty in answering your question is accentuated by the fact that my answer must depend on whether Turkey will continue to be left undisturbed in other parts and therefore free to make good the undoubtedly heavy losses incurred here by sending troops from Adrianople, Keshan, Constantinople and Asia; we now have direct evidence that the latter has been the case.

If the present condition of affairs in this respect were changed by the entry into the struggle of Bulgaria or Greece or by the landing of the Russians, my present force, kept up to strength by the necessary drafts, plus the army corps asked for ... would probably suffice to finish my task. If, however, the present situation remains unchanged and the Turks are still able to devote so much exclusive attention to us, I shall want an additional army corps, that is two army corps additional in all.

I could not land these reinforcements on the Peninsula until I can advance another 1,000 yards and so free the beaches from the shelling to which they are subjected from the western side and gain more space; but I could land them on the adjacent islands of Tenedos, Imbros and Lemnos and take them over later to the Peninsula for battle. This plan would surmount the difficulties of water and space on the Peninsula and would, perhaps, enable me to effect a surprise with the fresh divisions.

I believe I could advance with half the loss of life that is now

being reckoned upon, if I had a liberal supply of gun ammunition, especially of high explosive.[23]

This was swiftly followed by a request for a further 26,000 shells of
various calibres, as he either expected to attack again soon or be
attacked by the Turks, who had moved another army corps into
the theatre of war. Kitchener's reply on 18 May was far from
encouraging:

> I am quite certain that you fully realise what a serious disap-
> pointment it has been to me to discover that my preconceived
> views as to the conquest of positions necessary to dominate the
> forts on the Straits, with naval artillery to support our troops
> on land, and with the active help of naval bombardment, were
> miscalculated. A serious situation is created by the present
> check, and the calls for large reinforcements and an additional
> amount of ammunition that we can ill spare from France.
>
> From the standpoint of an early solution of our difficulties,
> your views, as stated, are not encouraging. The question
> whether we can long support two fields of operations draining
> on our resources requires grave consideration. I know that I can
> rely upon you to do your utmost to bring the present unfortu-
> nate state of affairs in the Dardanelles to as early a conclusion
> as possible, so that any consideration of a withdrawal, with all
> its dangers in the East, may be prevented from entering the
> field of possible solutions.[24]

We cannot be sure that Kitchener yet understood the real situation
when he suggested that Hamilton might be able to 'press forward'
with 4,500 Australian reinforcements that Maxwell was sending
him. Hamilton sent a 'Private and Personal' reply trying to cheer
up his old chief. 'You need not be despondent at anything in the
situation. Remember that you asked me to answer on the assumption that you had adequate forces at your disposal, and I did so.'[25]
Touché, mon général!

Much better news was soon to follow. At Anzac the defenders,
now organized into two divisions, were firmly ensconced in their
narrow bridgehead and had steadily improved their position and
defeated many counter-attacks. On 16 May Liman von Sanders,

under orders from Enver Pasha to achieve some notable success at ending the invasion, fed a fourth division into the lines against them. At 3.20 a.m. on 19 May the astonished Australians saw anything up to 40,000 Turks rise from their trenches and deliver a brutal, frontal assault across no-man's-land from Bolton's Ridge, the 400 Plateau and all the way up to the Nek. By 5 a.m. 10,000 Turks had been shot down and the attack comprehensively defeated. Birdwood's troops counted 3,000 dead lying before their trenches. Their own losses had not exceeded 600 all told.

While staying on a high state of alert, they were more worried by the health hazard of so many fly-blown corpses on their parapets. Birdwood asked Hamilton if he could arrange a truce to allow the Turks to bury their own dead and collect their wounded. Hamilton thought the Turks might make propaganda of the Allies suggesting a cessation of fire and preferred to wait until the Turks requested it. Birdwood replied that they were so callous towards the bodies of their soldiers that such a request might never come. The solution was to throw messages into the enemy trenches inviting them to collect their dead and wounded without formal discussion. In the meantime good-hearted Australian medical personnel had already been succouring wounded Turks and before long they were joined in the work by Turkish stretcher-bearers. A series of officer meetings culminated in a formal interview between Braithwaite and a Turkish envoy and an armistice on 24 May during which the 3,000 Turkish dead were removed for burial. This defensive victory, coupled with the defeat of the attacks at Cape Helles earlier in May, had inflicted enormous losses on the Turkish army and showed that both lodgements on the peninsula were there to stay. Intelligence reports soon after suggested that 'mutinous feeling has appeared among Turkish troops in Gallipoli' as their losses passed the 50,000 mark.[26] This is, of course, the sort of thing intelligence officers tend to say about the enemy. It must be stressed that 'Little Mehmet' (the Turkish equivalent of 'Tommy Atkins') fought with a steadfast courage to defend his homeland from the foreign invader. He would earn the hard-won respect of the Allied soldiers pitted against him.

Hamilton's force had now risen to over eight divisions and he could no longer liaise with separate divisional commanders at Cape

Helles. He asked Kitchener to promote Hunter-Weston to temporary Lieutenant-General to act as a British corps commander, which came into effect on 24 May. The MEF now operated as three corps and Hamilton established his headquarters on the island of Imbros, where he was equidistant from Anzac and Cape Helles and in permanent cable communication with both. Out of deference to the conditions endured by his soldiers, he kept a very Spartan camp, with no great flourish in the culinary department, much to the disgust of some staff officer types who expected better. He went a stage further and contracted the dysentery that was ravaging his force; his secretary, Mrs Shield, reminds us that it stayed with him until 1923 or 1924. A regular series of visits to all parts of the battle front kept him abreast of developments and he kept a special watch on the new formations as they arrived, doing everything he could in the cramped areas available to get them 'blooded' and acclimatized to the new routines of trench warfare on the peninsula.

His daily reports related the constant small-scale fighting that went on every night – a small advance here, a desperate defence there. At one notorious point at Anzac, Quinn's Post, only ten yards separated the two front lines, with a 200-foot vertical drop just behind the Australian position. There was very little chance of 'live and let live' arrangements developing anywhere at Gallipoli. Hamilton also forwarded details of prisoners taken from new Turkish formations flowing in from Syria and Smyrna and other areas.

Towards the end of May came the disappointing news that, because of the German offensives on the Eastern Front, the Russian divisions at Odessa had been sent to Galicia. He begged that the Russians be encouraged to stage a naval diversion in the Black Sea (a curious twist considering the origins of this whole campaign) or at least keep some second-line troops at Odessa to prevent the Turks from releasing still more men for Gallipoli. Hamilton told Kitchener that this development was so serious that it required a 'fresh appreciation of the situation'. From its very inception, Hamilton had always thought that the overall success of the campaign depended greatly on Russian and other nations' participation. If he is to be criticized for over-optimism, this factor should always be borne in mind.

The Russian 'defection', he argued, could release 100,000 Turks for service against him. As there were already 80,000 on the peninsula, 20,000 about to move down from the Bulgarian frontier, 10,000 in Asia and a further 65,000 under training in European Turkey, he was looking at the movement of a quarter of a million men in his direction. He was, in Churchill's' words, in danger of fighting the entire Turkish army in relays.[27] While they were not all of the best quality, they had German officers and advisers, which made them formidable. They lacked nothing in rifle ammunition and hand grenades, and the arrival of two hundred Krupps engineers at their Constantinople arsenals would soon solve their relative shortage of shells. Against this Hamilton had to cope with the curtailment of daytime support from the Royal Navy. German U-boats had arrived in the eastern Mediterranean and begun to torpedo British warships, which promptly vanished to the safety of Mudros harbour until better anti-submarine protection could be fitted. The loss of their gunfire was bad enough, but the moral blow to the soldiers ashore was considerable. The MEF urgently needed the support of a new ally in the theatre; the Greeks would be a particularly useful adjunct to his efforts. Hamilton couldn't know then that Britain's ally and the country for which much of this effort was ostensibly being made, Russia, had absolutely refused to countenance any Greek troops being allowed anywhere near Constantinople. At the very least the four British divisions he had theoretically asked for should have been made available immediately, though even that number had been requested while the Russians were still thought to be in the field.

Kitchener, drawing on the experience of the trench fighting in France, expressed doubts about the likelihood of early decisive success in the restricted ground at Gallipoli. He asked Hamilton if he was convinced, with the reinforcements asked for, that he 'could force the Khilid Bahr position and finish the Dardanelles operations'.[28] He was, in reality, unable to answer Hamilton's direct requests for help as Asquith's Liberal government had been forced to reorganize itself into a coalition of twelve Liberal and eight Tory ministers and was reforming the War Council as the Dardanelles Committee. All these changes delayed the decision-making process.

Hamilton deferred his reply because he was about to renew his assault on the Turks at Cape Helles. Being constantly urged by London to keep up the pressure on the enemy, and having spent some days gradually advancing his front line trenches closer to those of the enemy, and with his British and French corps commanders confident that their divisions were in good shape and ready for another battle, Hamilton accepted the limited objectives of some 800 yards set by them in this first truly trench-to-trench assault on the peninsula. 4 June would see the Third Battle of Krithia. Two British, one naval and one Indian brigade and the two French divisions were earmarked for the assault, with every available gun, two destroyers close in and three capital warships in support and even the machine-gun armoured cars operated by the Royal Naval Air Service committed to the attack. The planning was the first of that meticulous detail becoming a commonplace on the Western Front. There was even a *ruse de guerre* inserted into the plan whereby the guns would fire up to 11.20 a.m. and stop for ten minutes, during which the infantry would cheer and show their bayonets above the parapet. Once the Turks had crowded their firesteps and their batteries had opened fire, thus revealing hidden positions, the Allied artillery would resume an 'intense' bombardment for thirty minutes before the actual attack.

Of course, what passed for an intense bombardment on the peninsula would have been jeered with derision even in 1915 in France and Flanders. The British guns had only shrapnel shells, the effect of which was largely neutralized by the Turks having roofed in their trenches. Still worse, the French artillery, because the opposing lines on the right were only one hundred yards apart, had refrained from shelling the Turkish front line and concentrated on the support lines and the rear. This was only reported to Hamilton after the battle.

The French attack as a result was a complete failure, and led to some very harsh criticism of their performance in later reports. This, in turn, uncovered the right flank of the RND and the complete annihilation of the Collingwood Battalion by machine-guns firing in enfilade. The Manchester Brigade of 42nd Division, backed by French 75-millimetre guns liberally supplied with ammunition, drove a thousand yards into the enemy trenches and threw back a defensive flank where the RND had not been able to keep up. The 88th Brigade (of 29th Division) got into the enemy's first line but then ran into machine-guns firing from undamaged redoubts, which halted further progress. On their left the Indian Brigade attacked trenches at the head of Gully Ravine that were untouched by shellfire and were driven back to their start line. Both Hunter-Weston and Gouraud determined to renew the attack with their reserves and both essayed to try again where the attacks had broken down, rather than exploit the success already gained by 42nd Division. The official history excuses this as being the first experience either general had had in this sort of fighting.

In any event the French were so badly shaken that their second attack was cancelled, which at least spared the RND from having to go in again that day. Instead some seven battalions were fed into the battle on the left but neither the 88th nor Indian brigades could make any further advances. Then the Turkish reinforcements moved onto the field and heavily counter-attacked the Manchester Territorials, who had fought magnificently, and drove them back some distance. The battle closed with a British gain of some 250 to 500 yards over a mile of front in the centre; Allied losses of some 6,500; Turkish losses by their own admission of at least 9,000 men. Both Turkish and German accounts state that another British attack of such violence the next day would have ruptured their front line. Luckily for them it would be some time before the Allies were ready to try again.

As part of his reply to Kitchener's question about whether he could finish the job if reinforced, Hamilton expressed grave disappointment at the assistance rendered to him by the French corps. He praised their commanders, staff and artillery, 'but the infantry is composed mainly of Senegalese, who are unreliable under shell fire, and Algerian Jews and Martinique Eurasians who are quite hopeless. Too small a proportion of the French is thus left to leaven the lump.'[29] Their total failure on 4 June unhinged the entire attack. This, from a man who was famous for his gallantry and his admiration of good fighting men, was harsh and deeply felt criticism indeed. It was mirrored by the experience of Joe Murrray of the Hood Battalion, who recorded the Senegalese as being cheerful and steady in defence, but in attack they were rather excitable and prone to panic.[30]

The sense of hopeless stalemate was getting a grip and led to the exploration of other avenues. Hamilton's keenness to get another Allied power involved was expressly to open a 'second front' in theatre. He favoured putting new Allied troops ashore in the Bay of Enos, north of Bulair, an area known to be denuded of Turkish troops as the Turks poured into the Gallipoli peninsula. It has to be said that the admirals were dead set against any such extension of the fighting because the area lacked suitable anchorages and was widely exposed to the new U-boat menace.

It was at this point that Hamilton first revealed the new plans he had been developing with Birdwood and the staff at Anzac. Quite independently, they had begun to think along similar lines from about the end of May. The New Zealanders had been patrolling in the wild country north of the Anzac beachhead, finding it very lightly garrisoned, and checking out some of the steep pathways that might lead up onto the highest parts of the Sari Bair ridge. Hamilton had also been wondering whether the only way to break out of the deadlock at Anzac would be to secretly reinforce it and attack by night through the supposedly impassable country on the left flank. Now he told Kitchener that Birdwood thought he could do it with just four new brigades of infantry. Hamilton declared that he would give Birchwood all six brigades of one of the new army corps he had requested, and that the other two division corps would be used at Cape Helles to relieve the French and the RND in the line. 'No troops in existence can continue fighting night and day without respite.'[31]

The very next day Hamilton sent in a message confirming intelligence gathered by the Anzacs that another two Turkish divisions had arrived to replace two that had been severely battered in the recent fighting. These new divisions immediately launched heavy counter-attacks at Cape Helles, driving in the 88th Brigade, which was occupying some of the trenches captured on 4 June. In a day of desperate fighting much of the ground was regained, a hundred prisoners taken and heavy casualties inflicted by British machine-guns on an enemy increasingly reluctant to press home his attacks. It was clear that the recently appointed commander of 88th Brigade had failed to prepare the positions for defence and he was relieved of his command. Hamilton is often criticized for being too lenient with generals under his command but this culling of unsuitable commanders, down to battalion level, was a constant feature of the relentlessly demanding Gallipoli battle front. Hamilton used this proof of Turkish reinforcement, and details of the powerful nature of the Turkish defences he now faced, to press home his call for reinforcement. The first need was to take the pressure off the troops already in the line. They were being asked to do the impossible. They got no rest at all and were attacking gallantly and failing through sheer exhaustion. In so many of the battles to date, the immediate availability of a complete and fresh reinforcement would have made a decisive difference.

On 7 June Kitchener cabled some good news to Hamilton: 'Your difficulties are fully recognised by the Cabinet who are determined to support you. We are sending you three divisions of the New Army.'[32] Transport shortages meant that they would not all arrive until mid-July but by then the Royal Navy would have been reinforced with a good many units less vulnerable to submarine attack and it was expected that this would see a renewal of the naval attack. Kitchener closed with a call to keep steadily pressing the enemy in the meantime, without running any premature risks. Hamilton replied that this filled him with fresh confidence, and that he hoped the reinforcements would be accompanied by the two corps staffs required for them to operate in the field effectively. He kept up the pressure on London by pointing out that, while he had five divisions under his command, he only had the artillery of two divisions. Effectively each gun on the peninsula was doing the work that two and a half guns would do in Flanders. A calculation of how many shells per gun per day were available should have taken this shortfall into account. He was losing the artillery battle to the Turks, who were being reinforced by German gunners. While the fighting on the peninsula died down a little in mid-June, a sort of mutual exhaustion having settled over the combatants, the shelling of the Cape Helles beach head from the Asiatic shore by Turkish heavy artillery increased dramatically and became a serious burden on the southern front.

While Hamilton was wrestling with these problems, and planning what to do with the reinforcements for a new offensive, he and his staff had to cope with a parsimony emanating from the

War Office that was more tragic than farcical.[33] He had been asked if he could not organize the collection of rifles from the battlefield and from troops not in the fighting line so that drafts could be sent out from England unarmed. A much-needed 4.5-inch howitzer battery was offered by New Zealand but it had no ammunition and no possibility of replacing its personnel with further trained men. (Hamilton stated bluntly that if it were a charge on his existing stock of shells he would do without it.) He was told that ammunition would be sent allowing the expenditure of seventeen rounds per gun per day for his field artillery, when he had calculated that it would take at least thirty per day to break the Turkish lines. The offer of some 6-inch howitzers, the vital heavy guns he needed, came with the news that they would be supplied with no means of moving them once landed. Hamilton was reduced to accepting them gratefully and also asking for a handbook on using them (it was a wholly unfamiliar weapon to the gunners on the peninsula) and perhaps a tractor and crew to move them. He was probably not surprised to hear that of the three new divisions coming out, one would have old-fashioned 5-inch howitzers and the other two none at all. While their 18-pounders would be welcome, this failure to supply the vital howitzers necessary for fighting in such hilly country was especially regrettable. When a second battery of 6-inch howitzers was offered it was stated baldly that it would come with no ammunition at all and that, as the rate of shells being sent out would not increase, they didn't want to hear the staff of the MEF complaining about the small number of rounds per gun available. Perhaps the Navy could help with some 6-inch shells. That Hamilton himself should have to cable to accept this battery, even if they only use it to replace damaged guns already in action on the peninsula, shows to what a sad, almost beggarly, state the MEF had been reduced at a time when it was tasked with smashing the Turkish army and enabling the Royal Navy to put Turkey out of the war. The vexation felt by the general and his staff comes out in a cable describing the strength of the Turkish trenches. 'We realise for our part that in the matter of guns and ammunition it is no good crying for the moon, and for your part you must recognise that until howitzers and ammunition arrive it is no good crying for the Crescent.'[34]

We should, perhaps, pause to consider what the leaders of the expedition, Hamilton and Braithwaite, were trying to achieve with these constant requests for more guns and ammunition. In a very revealing personal letter to Hunter-Weston, Braithwaite explained how he and his commander had handled requests from Hunter-Weston and his chief of Royal Artillery for more artillery support for their attacks at Cape Helles:

> It was not that we were sticky, it was that, as I explained to Simpson-Baikie (when he was at General Headquarters) more than once, I personally knew for a fact that the ammunition for these howitzers did not exist, and that it was quite probable the howitzers themselves did not exist yet.
>
> I only left the War Office three months ago, and it was part of my work, when I was there, to keep an eye on this howitzer and ammunition question; and I have not studied the charts of futures in the way of both howitzers and ammunition, certainly weekly if not daily, for nothing ... you will see that it is no good asking for what does not exist.[35]

Both Hamilton and Braithwaite knew that Kitchener was facing impossible demands from all quarters for more of everything. With these persistent requests for a better provision for the MEF, they were trying to force him to make the larger strategic decision to elevate the Dardanelles expedition and its needs above the trench deadlock in France and Flanders. They were not to know that Kitchener was not drawing this problem to the attention of the Cabinet and that their cries for help were largely going unheard.

The new war cabinet had reorganized itself as the Dardanelles Committee, which at least suggested that it was taking the campaign seriously at last. Winston Churchill would argue convincingly for a greater effort to break the deadlock. It also meant that Hamilton suddenly found himself bombarded with cables asking his opinion on all sorts of strategic options that should properly have been considered before troops were ever committed to the region. 'Have you considered the advantage of landing troops on the Bulair Isthmus, thereby cutting off the Peninsula completely from the mainland and enabling us to send supplies overland to our submarines in the Sea of Marmora?'[36] This was asked on 11 June, seven weeks of hard fighting after the initial landings, and was followed the next day by questions about new Turkish coastal defences above the Narrows, whether Turkish communications could be cut north of Anzac or by attacking in any other direction, and whether it was true that the troops at Anzac were clinging to difficult cliffside positions. This level of ignorance emanating from London must have been quite depressing, especially as Hamilton had recently sent a detailed description of his positions on the peninsula at the request of the War Office. He had to patiently explain again all the reasons why the Royal Navy did not favour an attack at Bulair.

In a long reply he stressed that the cutting of the peninsula 'lay at the heart of my problem'. The original orders for the Anzac landings had made that an objective. Now he favoured an attack out of Anzac in a south-easterly direction as the best way to cut off all the defenders on the peninsula and prevent their further reinforcement and supply. This was how he intended to use the new divisions being sent out to him. He ended by making clear his reluctance to discuss the details of his plans. 'It is vitally important that future developments should be kept absolutely secret. I mention this because, although the date of our original landing was known to hardly anyone before the ships sailed, yet the date was cabled to the Turks from Vienna.'[37] Then came a baffling message from Kitchener asking for Hamilton's views on a diversion on the Asiatic side as part of the new operations, something he had expressly forbidden at the outset. Hamilton replied that he could see the advantage of clearing away the pestilential Turkish guns that were tormenting his troops and forcing the Turks to divert troops to a new sector, but concluded that it would require another full-scale assault landing against formidable defences and would use up a full two divisions that would be hard pressed to maintain themselves on that shore. The Royal Navy was not in favour of such a diversion of effort.

Hamilton next turned to the important question of commanders for the new forces being sent out. In his cables he again revealed his thorough understanding of the pressures of modern warfare on the minds as well as the bodies of men.

I should like to submit for your consideration the following views on the qualities necessary in an Army Corps Commander on the Gallipoli Peninsula. In that position only men of good stiff constitution and nerve will be able to do any good. Everything is at such close quarters that many men would be useless in the somewhat exposed headquarters they would have to occupy on this limited terrain, though they would do quite good work if moderately comfortable and away from constant shell fire. I can think of two men, Byng and Rawlinson. Both possess the requisite qualities and seniority; the latter does not seem very happy where he is, and the former would have more scope than a Cavalry Corps would give him in France.[38]

When we consider the debacle at Suvla Bay in August it would be well to remember these prophetic words of 15 June.

Kitchener had to reply that he could countenance no request for officers currently serving on the Western Front. Instead he raised the names of three senior lieutenant-generals available for service. The first was something of a problem for him, in that Lieutenant-General Sir Bryan Mahon was commanding the division raised by himself in 1914, the 10th (Irish), which would normally be the domain of a major-general. He tentatively suggested he might get the corps but Hamilton doubted his suitability for the post. 'I will give Mahon every support and encouragement, but remembering his condition when he disappointed you by returning to the Sudan when you offered him a Cavalry Brigade in South Africa, I fear he may not long stand the strain of this class of warfare.' The other generals available were Sir John Ewart and Sir Frederick Stopford. Hamilton turned down the former because he knew him to be very stout of girth. 'I greatly admire his character but he positively could not have made his way along the fire trenches I inspected yesterday. He has never approached troops for fifteen years although I have often implored him, as a friend, to do so.' Kitchener's firm resolve to stick to the precedence of the Army List, where Mahon had outranked both Julian Byng and Henry Rawlinson anyway, reduced Hamilton to a forlorn request. 'Would not Stopford be preferable to Ewart, even though he does not possess the latter's calm?'[39] Hamilton knew that Stopford was a very fine staff officer but he had never commanded troops in battle in his entire life. He had even turned down the command of a cavalry brigade in South

Africa, offered to him by Hamilton, preferring to return home with his old chief, Sir Redvers Buller. There is something of a plaintive air to Hamilton's remark to Kitchener that 'I will do my best with what you send me'. To his friend, Gerald Ellison, Hamilton would write on 10 July, about the imminent arrival of Stopford in a similar vein. 'He is undoubtedly the best man available who is at the same time senior to Mahon. In fact, if only his nerve stands the strain, I could not have a better, but, there's the rub. Only the stoutest nerves will stand this sort of racket for there is no getting away from these shells anywhere.'[40]

Another interesting exchange of views began on 21 June with Hamilton's request for an assessment of the three new divisions:

> If you would give me some indication regarding the merits of the 10th, 11th and 13th Divisions as disclosed in training reports, especially in regard to the training of infantry and officers, it would be a great help to me. On arrival, these divisions are likely to be employed at once, and the information I ask for would be of assistance to me in choosing for a suitable operation the best division.[41]

The reply by the War Office the next day was emphatic and should be given in full.

> The three divisions being sent to you are well trained with fine personnel. From the training point of view, there is not much to choose between them, but they might be placed in the following order: – 11th, 13th, 10th. The infantry is excellent and their shooting good; the artillery have fired well. The Royal Engineers, Royal Army Medical Corps and Army Service Corps are above the average. You will understand that the new officers' knowledge is not yet instinctive, and allowance should be made for this by the staff; if so, in a short time, there will be no finer troops in Europe. Upon the personality of the Commander, of course, will depend the choice of divisions for any particular operation.[42]

Kitchener announced that they would arrive in the eastern Mediterranean on 10, 18 and 28 July, and hinted that there might be a fourth division available but he doubted if Hamilton could find room for it, or ammunition to allow it to operate.

The Admiralty put in a detailed request for information concerning the water facilities on the peninsula and the estimated requirements for the new force. The question of the allocation of hospital ships was also raised. Surgeon-General Birrell had twelve at his disposal between Egypt and the Dardanelles, which seemed adequate. An added worry for the MEF was news that German gas warfare experts had arrived in Constantinople; the War Office sent out 60,000 gas helmets post haste, with more to follow.

Hamilton was able to report a success by the French corps on 22 June, when they had stormed the formidable Haricot Redoubt and its adjacent trenches; their losses of some 2,500 men were set against truly appalling losses for the Turks. Their attempt to counter-attack in mass formation had been annihilated by the French 75-millimetre cannon; their casualties were estimated at 7,000. Hamilton used this report to accept the offer of a fourth British division, which he said he would feed into the battle once the new offensive had cleared the way for it. He was resigned to the idea that he would get no extra ammunition to fight this new formation effectively. But then he was told that, while the cabinet had not fully decided if the fourth division would be sent, he might be offered a fifth division if he could say how it might usefully be deployed. This came with a quite generous promise of artillery ammunition, including high explosives. Hamilton took a few days before replying (on 29 June) to this important development. He was tempted (naval considerations permitting) to put all five new divisions, and one or two from the Peninsula, ashore in the Gulf of Saros for a direct march by Rodosto on Constantinople. This he had to reject because the fourth and fifth divisions would be late arriving. If the reinforcements were to arrive in echelon, he would use them in echelon. The first three divisions would be used to break out around the enemy's right and secure the line from Gaba Tepe to Maidos. He was quite frank in his estimation that the next two divisions might be needed to reinforce a non-success on this wing. If those operations were successful, the extra troops would be deployed at Cape Helles or against Chanak on the Asiatic shore, where they would be reinforced from Gallipoli.

In the midst of all this serious operational planning came some less welcome interference from London. A former Medical Director-General RN, Sir James Porter was suddenly appointed as a Hospital Transport Officer for the Mediterranean, charged with organizing the movements of all sick and wounded men by sea. All naval and military medical officers were to report their requirements to him and he would arrange the necessary shipping. It was obvious that those early enquiries about the provision for wounded men, which had so angered Sir John Maxwell with its implied slur on the medical services, had generated this new posting. It certainly suggested a lack of confidence in the medical officers serving in theatre, where the word of their critics had been clearly elevated above the reports of the services themselves. Hamilton cabled by return: 'I hope you realise that this creates one more link of possible friction which I will try to avert to the best of my powers.' He had complete confidence in Surgeon-General Babtie, 'a most capable man', who had worked out a complete scheme of evacuation of sick and wounded by land and sea and who knew nothing of this new appointment. 'Who is to be "boss"?' Hamilton asked.[43] The War Office insisted that no friction would be caused and that Porter would be invaluable in procuring the Navy's assistance in every way, which was yet another implied slur on the previous work accomplished. They blithely held that Porter and Babtie could work independently ('neither is boss') and that the high-water mark was the boundary between their spheres of activity.[44] Hamilton was not at all happy with this complacency and told London that he knew a good deal more about high-water marks than they did! They were storing up trouble by this complication of arrangements, 'even presupposing seraphic dispositions on either side ... Either Babtie must order up the ships when and where he wants them, or Porter must order the wounded down when he is ready for them'.[45] The proper disposition of the wounded was the responsibility of the Surgeon-Generals working under the Adjutant-General at GHQ. In response to their exasperated questioning of Porter over his intentions, the new Hospital Transport Officer simply accepted en bloc all the arrangements already in place. This provoked one of Hamilton's angriest cables to the War Office, wondering why he had been appointed in the first place, in direct contravention of Field

Service Regulations, and stating that he and his staff would take no responsibility in the future for how the evacuation of wounded men was conducted while Porter remained in charge. The War Office refused to back down on their appointment.

Meanwhile Hunter-Weston had organized and fought another battle on the Cape Helles front, which showed what could be done when powerful artillery support could be laid on. A total of 77 guns, including nine French 155-millimetre howitzers, fired over 16,000 rounds in support of an attack up the Gully Ravine and the spurs either side of it. De Lisle's 29th Division, Cox's 29th Indian Brigade and 156th Brigade (52nd Division) were used in the attack. The line was pushed forward over half a mile along the ravine and Gully Spur, putting a great strain on the Turkish position. A great tragedy overwhelmed the Scottish Territorials of 156th Brigade, who were mown down from Turkish defences unaffected by artillery fire; their commander, Brigadier-General Scott-Moncrieff was killed leading a renewed effort to no avail. Frantic Turkish counterattacks went on for two days, and were met with devastating fire from British artillery and warships. A last great effort on 5 July was equally unsuccessful and the Turks admitted to over 14,000 casualties on this sector alone. Once again thousands of enemy dead before the British and French lines threatened to become a health hazard. The Turks requested a burial truce but this time the Allied commanders decided that a no-man's-land choked with Turkish dead would be a useful deterrent to further attacks and the request was denied. Captured documents revealed that the Turkish high command was issuing dire threats to officers who lost trenches or failed to recapture them immediately, regardless of the cost. Summary execution of reluctant attackers was called for.

Despite these tactical successes, Hamilton still had to spell out some home truths for the authorities in London, reminding them again of the special problems of the Gallipoli expedition when compared to the BEF in France and Flanders. He was now completely devoid of drafts to replace the losses of his British divisions, all of which were so reduced in numbers that he must stand down active operations on the Helles front for a month, which would allow the Turks to make good all their recent reverses. Divisions in France all went to war with a battle reserve and received a steady flow of replacements. He needed major drafts of men kept available in Egypt so that he could replace battle losses quickly and he shouldn't need to make special requests for that type of reinforcement, which could take a month to come out from the home country.

The Turkish artillery fire from the Asiatic shore increased significantly early in July, just as Hamilton had to report that the 15-pounder guns that had come out with the Territorials were so unserviceable that an entire brigade could provide only one and a half batteries for effective use. On one day the Turks poured 5,000 shells into the French sector and launched heavy counter-attacks at their junction with the RND, and at other parts of the Helles lines. All these attacks, which usually took place just after fresh Turkish units had arrived to 'drive the invaders into the sea', were bloodily defeated at minimal loss to the defenders.

To show how the wider strategic picture had to be handled by the theatre commander, Hamilton cabled to the British ambassador in Athens to ask if he could land one of the new divisions temporarily on the island of Mitylene, where it and some deliberately misleading signals traffic could usefully pose a feint threat to the Turks in and around Smyrna. The ambassador replied that asking the Greek government for permission might lead to difficulties so he suggested that they do it anyway, presenting them with a fait accompli. There was a precedent set by the Royal Navy using the island quite freely.

On 13 July the staff of MEF alerted the War Office to the need for increased medical facilities. They estimated that, with 80,000 rifles in the firing line for the upcoming battle, they should make provision for 20,000 casualties. 'Though the figure seems alarming when put down in cold blood, it is not an extravagant proportion when calculated on the basis of Dardanelles fighting up to date.'[46] This is a far cry from the possible 10 per cent losses estimated in April. They asked for 200 extra medical officers, with nurses, other personnel, tents and equipment in proportion. This began a long exchange of messages with the War Office, trying to get Egypt, Malta and Gibraltar to shoulder more of the extra burden. All these places were in a high state of readiness and were evacuating many wounded men back to Britain, Australia and New Zealand to free up hospital beds. The usual carping followed about the excessive number of hospital ships already on station and how more would be needed, if only temporarily. Again Hamilton's staff had to point out some home truths to London:

> No demand has been made on Egypt or Malta as they will require all the available personnel for themselves. I am aware that it is not usual to make extensive preparations for a specified battle, but the circumstances here are altogether exceptional, as the only means of removing men from shell fire is to place them on board ship.[47]

Once again it is clear that these men had absorbed the lessons of the April landings and were doing everything possible to be better prepared in August.

In similar vein Hamilton wrote to point out the huge new burden this large reinforcement would place on the port facilities at Mudros and how the Navy would be stretched to the limit to man all the landing craft and supply boats required for the new operations. In the event of army success the Navy would be withdrawing many of these crews to renew its attack on the Narrows. All this had to be thought through now. In a suggestion typical of his advanced pre-war thinking, Hamilton suggested sending out some civilian experts from one of the great shipping companies to take over the complex burden of organizing the shipping with maximum productivity, leaving the Navy to concentrate on its fighting ships.

Hamilton then put in a bold request for huge monthly supplies of artillery ammunition (300,000 rounds of 18-pounder; 30,000 of 4.5-inch, and so on), half of it to be high explosive, together with new batteries of field and heavy howitzers. He based his request on the fact that operations in France seemed to have been stood down during the summer, and that recent fighting on the peninsula had shown what could be achieved with the liberal use of artillery fire. (The French and the 52nd Division, supported by the RND, had seized more of the Turkish trench system before Krithia and Achi Baba in hard fighting in mid-July. It was during this fighting that Hamilton's warning about Egerton's fitness was proved correct. Hunter-Weston replaced him as GOC 52nd Division during the battle. Because he had not followed proper procedure, Hamilton insisted that Egerton be reinstated, only for Egerton to admit that he was not up to the job and ask to be relieved. Hamilton then found him a job in Egypt, as a base commander, where he performed excellently for the rest of the war. To his critics, this was Hamilton being soft on his old friends. (But it can also be seen as an example of good man-management, finding a posting where Egerton could make a valuable contribution to his country's war effort, rather than sending him home in ill-deserved disgrace.)

Hamilton stressed that he only required this level of munitions support for two months, during which he could achieve decisive success before offensive operations were resumed in France. The War Office swiftly replied that ammunition sent to the Dardanelles on this scale would require the complete cessation of all operations on the Western Front, which was, of course, out of the question. Rather they were concerned as to whether they could keep up the supply at the rate already promised. Hamilton was not impressed with this reply and answered bitterly that his forces were not being kept fully informed of what ammunition was being sent out, which added greatly to their anxieties.

A great help to Hamilton was the appointment of Lieutenant-General E. A. Altham as Inspector-General of Communications, whose deputy was none other than Hamilton's good friend, Gerald Ellison. While the front-line troops never went without their basic requirements of food and ammunition, there is no doubt that the complex demands of routing men, munitions and supplies from Britain, Australia and New Zealand through Egypt and Mudros and on to the peninsula had thrown up some serious disorganization along the lines of communications. Inevitably there were some staff officers more concerned with their own comfort than with the proper support of the fighting men. The soldiers, never slow in complaining about the staff in general, spoke of 'Imbros, Mudros, Chaos'. It has to be said that the officer responsible for much of this disorder had been an old Indian army acquaintance of Kitchener's who appointed him, despite warnings of the man's inadequacy for the important task ahead of him. Altham and Ellison, both excellent and clear-headed organizers, swept through the lines of communication and rapidly put things on a better footing. Altham promptly commissioned four gentlemen working in shipping export offices and utilized their skills (just as Hamilton had suggested earlier) and pointed out to the War Office that much of the chaos in the Mediterranean, bound to be complicated by so much transhipment of supplies at so many bases, came about because ships arrived from the home country without proper manifests of their cargo. Officers simply did not know which ships carried which supplies, a truly disgraceful situation that could not be blamed on the staff in theatre. Thus, when the ammunition column of 13th Division arrived it had only 6,000 shells with it, much less than half that expected, and nobody knew where the balance was. Another supply of shells arrived without their fuses, which were reported to be on another ship but were missing from it completely. A supply of new artillery fuses arrived on 10 July but the keys vital to their operation were not even despatched from Britain until 15 July. What was already a shell shortage was gravely exaggerated by such failings at home. Armed with the new clarity provided by Altham's reforms, Hamilton was able to point out just how bad the supply situation was, ruthlessly exposing incident after incident of careless despatching from Britain.

The French put in a request that some of the new reinforcements be used via Besika Bay to clear the Turkish artillery off the Asiatic shore. Kitchener duly asked Hamilton for his views. He replied that Besika Bay was now a formidably fortified place and that he, and the Navy, could not contemplate a diversion from the main operations at this late stage, however desirable the new front might be. He did point out to Kitchener that, because of the tight secrecy he was maintaining around the new plans, he had not told the French of the destined use of the new divisions.

On 28 July Kitchener sent a long message to Hamilton, meant to encourage him in the forthcoming struggle but effectively adding to his confusion. He began with praise of Hamilton and his troops for their efforts to date and then listed the forces sent out since May: three divisions of the New Army; six batteries of heavy artillery; the 53rd (Welsh) and 54th (East Anglian) Territorial Divisions (without a single artillery piece between them); the promise of two further heavy batteries to follow; a total of 15,300 drafts for the regular and Territorial divisions (a breathtakingly inadequate number, leaving them all very weak); and a total of 221,000 shells, with some 60,000 more in the last week of July (which made no allowance for those fired off during the two months under review and left the MEF with meagre reserves). In addition Kitchener listed 8,500 cavalry, 11,500 Indian troops and all the artillery in Egypt as being available to Hamilton if he needed them. With the troops en route Kitchener reckoned Hamilton had 185,000 men, with another 20,000 in Egypt. The message closed with an extraordinary paragraph:

> We should like to hear from you after considering your plans whether there is anything further in the way of personnel, guns or ammunition we can send you, as we are most anxious to give you everything you can possibly require and use. You will realise that as regards ammunition we have had to stop supplying France to give you the full output, which will be continued as long as possible; in the short time available before the bad weather intervenes the Dardanelles operations are now of the highest importance.[48]

In a coda to this Kitchener admitted that the BEF in France actually interfered with the rail transport of shells destined for Gallipoli and that if Hamilton wanted to speed up the supply he himself should send a ship to Marseilles to collect them.

Hamilton's reply the next day set the record straight on a number of points. He had several times in the recent past stated exactly what his men and munitions requirements were for assured success, and it was a surprise to hear that London had ceased supplying shells to the BEF in favour of the MEF, having been told a few days before that such a consideration was quite impossible. Kitchener's idea that Hamilton had 185,000 men to hand was wide of the mark, in that it included casualties in hospital and other non-effectives, as well as the 53rd and 54th Divisions, which would not arrive until after the new offensive had begun. Hamilton reckoned his strength at 120,000 men in total. He again expressed amazement that all the troops in Egypt were at his unreserved disposal; still no one had realized that he had been denied all knowledge of that vital cable of 6 April. He explained that he was labouring the point about numbers as he wanted the true facts placed on the record, displaying an understanding of how the argument might go if his new attack should fail.[49] He closed with a renewed appeal for more high explosives and howitzers.

Kitchener's reply again reveals that he wasn't really thinking through the difficulties faced by the MEF.[50] He expressed astonishment that the 53rd and 54th Divisions, both due at Mudros before 8 August, could not be considered as available for the new operations. Did he really think that these totally untried divisions, arriving a couple of days before the new offensive without artillery, could be regarded as effective reinforcements? He did promise a further 10,000 shells from France to be collected by Hamilton's ship at Marseilles, together with two batteries of 4.5-inch howitzers, but the latter would have no gun teams at all to move them. Hamilton thanked him for all these extra efforts and said he would allow his gunners to fire freely, secure in the knowledge that more ammunition was on its way. Kitchener must have thought about Hamilton's remarks concerning Egypt as he cabled Maxwell in fairly strong terms:

Egypt is, perhaps, more than anywhere else concerned in the success of operations at the Dardanelles, and I feel sure that I can rely on you to give all possible assistance in the event of more troops being required, even if it should involve risk in Egypt. Your troops will not be long absent, the operations being only of a temporary nature. Secrecy is essential for success. Make arrangements with Hamilton and give him all possible help with your best fighting men.[51]

Maxwell was at the end of his tether as regards the constant drain on his resources posed by the Dardanelles force. He had already refused to send any more officers to Cox's Indian brigade at the expense of his own Indian brigades, instead calling for Cox's force to be returned to Egypt. Now he told Kitchener that the Senussi, a Western Desert tribe, had been called to revolt by Islamic leaders and he couldn't release another man from his garrison. Hamilton would later pour scorn on the idea that this insignificant foe could apparently threaten the fabric of the British Empire whenever Egypt was asked to reinforce the MEF.

Sir Frederick Stopford had arrived in theatre on 11 July and had been sent to the Cape Helles front to familiarize himself with the fighting conditions on the peninsula. In his first meeting with Sir Ian Hamilton, Stopford had to pass on some annoyingly patronizing advice from Kitchener about the importance of surprise in the attack and the need to feed in reserves, ending with that goading for results with which the leaders of the MEF were, by now, depressingly familiar: 'It is not intended however that Sir Ian should do nothing in the meantime, and if he gets a really good opportunity he is to seize it.'[52] In a similar manner, Kitchener sent a message out with Gerald Ellison when he was finally appointed to Hamilton's staff, that Hamilton was to attack with the three New Army divisions and not wait for the two Territorial divisions on their way out. For a week Stopford actually commanded the Cape Helles sector, as on 17 July Lieutenant-General Hunter-Weston, GOC VIII Corps, was invalided home suffering from sunstroke. Sir Francis Davies, formerly GOC 8th Division in France, was sent out to replace him as corps commander. Things grew quieter on the southern front after Hunter-Weston's departure. He had always been a fierce driver of his men and, though he remains one of the most controversial generals of the First World War, he would be sorely missed in the weeks ahead.

The whole of 13th (Western) Division had reached Gallipoli by 17 July and went into the trenches at Cape Helles, thereby allowing all the 29th and part of 42nd Divisions to take a well-earned rest on the islands and giving the new division valuable battle experience that would show in their efforts during the August fighting. The final plans for the offensive were being laid.

11

Defeat at Gallipoli,

1915

Since the middle of May Hamilton and Birdwood had been exchanging ideas about breaking out of the Anzac position. Birdwood thought that the addition of Cox's Indian brigade was all he needed to begin the advance, with a full division of three brigades to hold the expanded lodgement. Hamilton knew that, even if Achi Baba was captured, the Turks were too strong in the south and so he reverted to the original intention of the Anzac landings, to get clear across the peninsula and cut off the Turkish troops below them. In June the government had offered him three divisions of the New Army, to be joined by two Territorial divisions. This decision was already late as far as the campaign was concerned. Shipping shortages would make sure that the troops would not all be available until the second week in August. To put such large reinforcements to use in such a cramped theatre of war required a major revision of plans.

Consideration was given to the other possible landing places – Bulair, the Gulf of Enos, Asia Minor – but all these had been massively reinforced and fortified by the Turks. The Royal Navy was also absolutely opposed to this sort of diversion of effort, especially as the open waters were vulnerable to enemy submarines.

It was decided to reinforce Anzac with the maximum number of troops that could be squeezed into that crowded sector (five brigades) and put the balance of the new forces ashore at Suvla Bay to the north. Here the broad Suvla plain stretched for some four miles inland, surrounded on three sides by ridges – the Kiretch Tepe to the north, Tekke Tepe to the east and the Anafarta Spur to the south. The Turks were tightly packed in around the Anzac positions and did not occupy the Suvla area in any great strength.

They occasionally based artillery there to shell Anzac and several positions were prepared for defence but not fully occupied. New Zealand patrols confirmed all this in June. The Royal Navy warmly accepted this option as anti-submarine nets could make Suvla Bay quite safe for its ships. A great bonus was the provision by the Admiralty of the specialized landing-craft, with landing ramps, capable of carrying 500 troops at a time. These had been denied to Hamilton in April but could now ensure the rapid build-up of troops ashore.

Besides Cox's Indian brigade, brought up from Cape Helles for its hill-fighting abilities, Anzac was reinforced by the whole of the 13th Division and a brigade of the 10th Division. It is one of the great feats of staff work that these reinforcements, some 25,000 men with extra animals, vehicles, guns, ammunition, stores and supplies, were introduced into the bridgehead over the three nights before 6 August without the enemy's knowledge. Camouflaged terraces and new dug-outs had been prepared for them, as well as elaborate new measures to ensure a good water supply. Together with the Australian and New Zealand troops already in place, these forces were to break out to the left and seize the whole of the Sari Bair Ridge in an overnight *coup de main*. Simultaneously the 11th Division was to land at Suvla Bay and push rapidly inland to secure the high ground overlooking the Suvla Plain. It would be reinforced by the two brigades of 10th Division. The 53rd Division would be a general reserve, to be joined by 54th Division as soon as possible.

If the new troops had come out sooner and could have been acclimatized in the trenches at Cape Helles, Hamilton would have taken the opportunity to rest and refit the 29th Division and use it to make the Suvla landing, but it was in far too weak a state to consider such a move in August. Instead the 11th Division was chosen for what should have been a fairly straightforward task. The division had been lavishly praised by the War Office and Braithwaite had engaged its commander, Major-General Hammersley, in a discussion about its suitability for an important, if still secret, mission. Hammersley was absolutely adamant that no other force in the British army had left the United Kingdom after such long training as a full division and that it could be relied on to achieve anything asked of it. With that sort of confidence in the troops, the general staff went ahead with its plans. It was 22 July when Hamilton visited Stopford at Cape Helles to tell him for the first time of the August offensive and his part in it. It was stressed from the start that if the leading troops pressed forward resolutely they would sweep aside light Turkish resistance and achieve their main objectives before break of day, when reinforcements would join them and secure the area. Lieutenant-Colonel Aspinall of the General Staff was tasked to brief Stopford on the details and the Corps Commander expressed complete agreement with the plan. He even claimed to have thought of something similar himself on his way out from England, was sure of its success and offered his congratulations to those who had framed the plan. Next day he had been joined by his own chief of staff at IX Corps, Brigadier-General H. L. Reed, VC. He brought with him all the orthodoxy of a gunner officer from the Western Front and denounced the plan as unfeasible because troops could not be expected to attack enemy positions without artillery preparation, which would have to wait until daylight on 7 August at the earliest. In his later writings Hamilton would comment that even the holders of the highest awards for bravery in battle could still manifest signs of moral cowardice. Without naming names, he clearly meant Reed.

General Headquarters, their hands full with the planning of the larger operation, assured Stopford that once his troops were ashore they would find little enough resistance and would make good progress. But they did allow a gentle and persistent watering down of the instructions for the IX Corps, from a definite instruction to seize the Chocolate and W Hills (which dominated Suvla Plain inland) during the night, to a desire to gain these hills at an early period during the attack. When Stopford visited Anzac to view the future battlefield, Birdwood explained the plan to him again and stressed the need to push forward vigorously against light opposition. Hamilton must have taken some comfort from Stopford's letter to him of 31 July in which the latter said he realized that his security depended on securing the Tekke Tepe Ridge quickly and that he must try for the Chocolate and W Hills immediately. 'The capture of these hills by a *coup de main* at night would have such far-reaching effects that I have decided to attempt it.'[1] He went on to tell Hamilton that he had decided, contrary to the original plan to land on the outer beaches at Suvla, to land one brigade inside Suvla Bay in order to secure the smaller hills of Lala Baba and Hill 10 and develop the attack on the Chocolate and W Hills from that direction, before making his troops available to support the attack by Birdwood on Hill 971, the highest peak on the Sari Bair Ridge. With these reassurances Hamilton apparently turned his full attention to the main attack out of Anzac. He failed to notice that all the subsequent orders issued by IX Corps failed to give any sense of urgency. The words 'if possible' became the theme and the overall objective was reduced to securing the Suvla Bay beaches as a base of supply and for the debarkation of the 10th Division.

It should be realized that the Suvla landings, though pregnant with possibilities, were only ever an adjunct to the main effort – the attack on the Sari Bair Ridge from the Anzac bridgehead. Major-General Godley, long in command of the left-hand sector at Anzac, was given the executive command of the battle. Two covering forces were to march off to the left and seize the Turkish positions covering the approaches to the ridge. Then two main assault columns were to pass through: the Right Assaulting Column to push straight up Rhododendron Spur to Chunuk Bair; the Left Assaulting Column to march along the coast to the Aghyl Dere, swing to the right and push inland before dividing, with Cox's 29th Indian Brigade moving up Damakjelik Spur to Hill Q, and Monash's 4th Australian Brigade using the Abdul Rahman Spur to advance on the main height, Koja Chemen Tepe (Hill 971). Diversionary attacks would be carried out both at Cape Helles and on the right of Anzac.

These were very ambitious plans and their surprise effect was meant to compensate for the many violations of regulations included in them. All the troops, and indeed most of the officers, involved were informed at the very last moment of what was expected of them. The 'open secret' of the April landings was replaced by incredibly tight secrecy surrounding these operations. Rather than alert the Turks in Allied interest in the area, a scaling down of the patrolling of the routes to be used was ordered. Medical services had been organized to deal with between 20,000 and 30,000 casualties; an unusually thorough preparation for what was clearly expected to be a bloody fight. The provision of water

had also exercised all the staffs involved and elaborate plans had
been laid to get water containers ashore early at Suvla, together
with the mules to carry them, including extra provision for the Left
Assaulting Column to be supplied from Suvla. In addition, the
Royal Navy was on hand to land pumping equipment and pipelines.
After four months fighting on the peninsula, the importance of
these things was perfectly clear.

Hamilton was keen to operate from a forward battle headquarters. He first considered Anzac, and then thought he would be
more useful at Suvla itself. All his advisers insisted that he remain
at GHQ Imbros, where he was in cable contact with all the
battlefronts and could see how the operation developed in full. His
natural fighting instinct was once again worn down by the requirements of the new industrialized warfare.

On the afternoon of 6 August the 88th Brigade, 29th Division
launched the first of the diversionary attacks – a frontal assault on
trenches before the village of Krithia. General Davies, fresh from
command on the Western Front, expressed his horror at the
inadequacy of the artillery preparation for the attack; the British
infantry at Gallipoli were entirely unfamiliar with the scenario. The
attack was comprehensively defeated, with nearly 2,000 of the 3,000
attackers becoming casualties. An attack by the 42nd Division the
next morning was equally costly and equally unsuccessful. These
brave efforts to assist their comrades in the north failed to divert
any Turkish troops from that decisive sector, but did provoke
the local Turkish commander to consider abandoning the entire
southern front, including Achi Baba. Liman von Sanders had him
replaced immediately and the front held.

At 5.30 p.m. on 6 August three battalions of 1st Australian
Brigade suddenly erupted from tunnels dug out into no-man's-land
and smashed their way into the powerful Turkish defences on Lone
Pine. Reinforcements were fed in as the Turks kept up bombing-
party counter-attacks for the best part of two days. The Australians
consolidated their positions and seven Victoria Crosses were
awarded to recognize their remarkable achievement. They posed
such a threat to the Turkish flank that two regiments were ordered
up from Gaba Tepe to secure the position and these, unfortunately,
were thus available to join the fighting for the Sari Bair Ridge.

Soon after dark on 6 August 2,000 New Zealanders of the Right Covering Force swarmed over the Turkish positions just to the north of Anzac as far as Bauchop's Hill. There was some stiff fighting to clear four enemy strongpoints, 200 prisoners were taken and all objectives achieved, if some two hours or so behind schedule. The Left Covering Force – two battalions and some engineers of the 13th Division – pushed along the coast and secured the head of the Aghyl Dere, capturing Damakjelik Bair and two hundred prisoners, clearing the way for the main assault force. This was an excellent performance by these New Army troops, who had clearly benefited from their stint in the trenches at Cape Helles.

The Right Assaulting Column was formed by the New Zealand Infantry Brigade under Brigadier-General Johnston, with some Indian mountain guns and New Zealand engineers. He should have moved rapidly up the Rhododendron Spur to secure Chunuk Bair by daybreak. Unaccountably, he delayed his start by nearly an hour because he could hear firing on Bauchop's Hill close to where his troops would pass by. As this was being cleared by the covering force, it is hard to understand the delay. As the Otago Battalion approached the feature known as the Table Top they were delayed by having to accept the surrender of a large number of Turks who had evaded the covering force but were keen to throw in the towel. On a clear moonlit night the column moved along the spur to a spot where they were supposed to meet the Canterbury Battalion before covering the last 1,000 yards to the top of the ridge. Tragically, the Canterbury Battalion had taken a wrong turn up a gully leading to a totally impassable cliff face. The order to retrace their steps was misunderstood and they returned all the way to their start line before trying again. Daylight, at about 4.30 a.m. on 7 August, found Johnston awaiting their arrival at the first rendez-vous instead of digging in on Chunuk Bair. The perils of night operations, even with veteran troops, were manifesting themselves.

The Left Assaulting Column, under Brigadier-General Cox, had a great deal further to travel, over ground much less well known. It was to work its way up the Aghyl Dere, with its left protected by the New Army battalions on Damakjelik Bair. Two Australian battalions (of Monash's 4th Brigade) were to extend the left flank protection; two battalions of Gurkhas were to proceed directly towards Hill Q, while the remaining four battalions (two Australian, one Gurkha, one Sikh) were to push along the Abdul Rahman Spur to be in position by about 2 a.m. to make the final assault on Hill 971. Allowing three and a half hours to cover three miles of very difficult country at night was to prove woefully inadequate.

Because the column lost some time by running into the rear elements of the Left Covering Column, the excellent Major Overton, New Zealand Rifles, took the advice of a native guide to move off the main track and take the 'short cut' through Taylor's Gap. This was one of those defining tragic moments in a campaign full of tragedies. A few Turkish pickets sniped at the column, causing delay as troops deployed to see them off. But then the gap itself, little used for months, was found to be almost closed by prickly undergrowth. The New Zealand engineers were required to clear a path; the column stood in nervous idleness for hours. Monash's men, in common with most of the Anzacs, were not in the peak of condition after their long ordeal since landing; their fighting effectiveness was gravely affected by the delay. It was fully three hours before they even reached the head of the Aghyl Dere. Perfectly good battalions were now confused and disorientated; each had to be led forward by brigade staff officers to be got moving again. The moonlight saw increased Turkish sniper fire and more delays. Dawn found the area very quiet but all the troops tired and drained. The Australians dug in where they stood; the Indian brigade pressed on, some in the wrong direction and ending up on the flank of the New Zealanders on the Rhododendron Spur. It was 9 a.m. before 1/6th Gurkhas finally dug in still 1,000 yards short of Hill Q.

Unaware that the timetable of the operation was fatally compromised, the Australian 3rd Light Horse Brigade went ahead with its planned assault on the Turkish positions at the Nek, covering the fortress hill, Baby 700. The attack should have gone in as the main assault was opening up all along the Sari Bair Ridge and would have been a valuable adjunct to that operation. Instead wave after wave of gallant young men were shot down by Turkish machineguns in one of the most terrible incidents of the entire campaign.

To complete this sorry tale, things had gone badly at Suvla. Landing-craft and destroyers were available to land the entire three brigades (10,300 infantry) of the 11th Division in one sweep, assisted by highly experienced Beach Masters, Military Landing Officers and the men of the RND's Anson Battalion. These would be rapidly followed by another 7,000 men of the 10th Division, 56 guns, hundreds of mules, water provision and stores. Hamilton and his staff were firmly convinced that they would face minimal opposition and that their weight of numbers alone would sweep them across the Suvla Plain and into the hills surrounding it.

If ever a general can be said to have been defeated in his mind before a shot had been fired, Sir Frederick Stopford was such a one. With both Mahon and Reed telling him that he faced powerful enemy defences, which would require much daylight preparation to attack, his anxiety was acute. Instead of waiting at Imbros as GHQ desired, he took his staff onto the naval sloop *Jonquil* and accompanied the attack. Having sprained his knee on the morning of 6 August, he was deeply depressed when a GHQ staff officer visited him that evening.

> I want you to tell Sir Ian Hamilton that I am going to do my best, and that I hope to be successful. But he must realize that if the enemy proves to be holding a strong line of continuous entrenchments I shall be unable to dislodge him till more guns are landed. All the teaching of the campaign in France proves that continuous trenches cannot be attacked without the assistance of large numbers of howitzers.[2]

That last sentence was word for word what Reed had told him when he came out as IX Corps Chief of Staff. The staff officer assured him that no such continuous lines existed at Suvla but his words fell on deaf ears. The staff of IX Corps then declared that there was no room for the GHQ liaison officer to accompany them on the *Jonquil* and this staff captain instead went ashore at Anzac. The fact that he was able to walk from there to Suvla the next day shows how complete was the MEF's grip along the coast.

The attacking formations only received their orders the day before embarkation began. The troops themselves were only informed as they prepared to get into the boats; many of them later confessed they had no idea where they were or where they were going. Most were suffering the after-effects of inoculations against tropical diseases.

By 10.00 p.m. on 6 August, in pitch darkness, the first four battalions were ashore on the outer beaches without a single casualty. Two battalions of 33rd Brigade swung to the right and formed a flank guard. The other two, of 32nd Brigade, advanced directly on Lala Baba, which was taken after a stiff fight, with particularly heavy casualties amongst the officers, all leading by example from the front. The loss of a colonel and a major this early on a dark night in a strange place was an ordeal for new troops who had already been on their feet for seventeen hours without a rest. A message sent back to brigade reporting the first success never reached its destination; the runner was killed. (To add to the tragedy the note he was carrying was a wrong page torn from a field message book in the dark and confusion; it would have been meaningless if delivered. Of such little mishaps is the true history of a battle made.) The troops were expecting to be joined by 34th Brigade, landing inside Suvla Bay, for the advance inland via Hill 10 and they waited for them accordingly.

Things did not go well for 34th Brigade. Their boats got confused in the approach and the first two battalions were put ashore out of place and sequence; some boats running onto reefs in the unfamiliar bay added to the confusion. As they formed up they came under heavy rifle fire. The 11th Manchesters did exactly what was asked of them and pushed along the beach to their left and got up onto the Kiretch Tepe Ridge, pushing Turkish pickets aside. The boating confusion meant that Brigadier-General Sitwell and his other two battalions were still not ashore by 3 a.m.; more and more boats were running onto reefs, some getting stuck fast, and the push inland just wasn't happening at all. Meanwhile the rest of 32nd and 33rd Brigades landed smoothly and six battalions were massed around Lala Baba, waiting for someone to tell them what to do. When Sitwell did get ashore he organized a movement towards Hill 10 but in the early morning gloom a low hummock nearby was attacked instead and Turkish fire forced the confused attackers to go to ground.

Daybreak, rather than seeing the 11th Division closing on the Tekke Teppe Ridge, found it clinging to the beach with its two flanks pushed somewhat further forward. Hammersley and the divisional staff were ashore trying to work out where the various

units were. Nobody thought to inform GHQ of the situation. One
telegraphist sent a private message to a fellow operator at Imbros:
'A little shelling at A now ceased. All quiet at B.'[3] But for the
anxious staff at Imbros it meant that the landing had been made
good. Braithwaite said to himself: 'The thing is done.'

Thus, by early on 7 August, every aspect of the operation except
the storming of Lone Pine had gone awry. Yet the Turks had again
been taken completely by surprise. Liman von Sanders was at a loss
to know whether this was the start of a new offensive or the
diversion for some other enterprise. He again ordered the Bulair
Lines to be placed in a high state of readiness. The Sari Bair Ridge
was still but thinly held and it was still possible for 7 August to
prove the decisive day of action. The official historian would later
write:

> A study of the Turkish records for 6 and 7 August suffices to
> show that a very small turn of Fortune's wheel would have
> steered it through to success. This, however, is no uncommon
> phenomenon. In many a hard-fought battle, when the issue
> trembles in the balance, a tiny mischance will tip the scales
> from overwhelming victory to irretrievable defeat. A slight error
> of judgement by a subordinate, the mistake of a guide, or the
> failure of an order to reach its destination, may prove the
> deciding factor; and many a well-laid plan will be classed as an
> illegitimate gamble which, in the hands of a luckier general,
> would have led to resounding success and be acclaimed the
> mark of his genius.[4]

Sir Ian Hamilton's luck was not with him that August.

At 6.30 a.m. on 7 August, Johnston gave up waiting on the
Rhododendron Spur for the missing battalion and ordered two
battalions to push on towards the summit. Five hundred yards
short of the crest they came under accurate fire and went to
ground. The men were so tired that their officers preferred to wait
and see the outcome of other fighting along the ridge before
organizing a new advance. We now know that the German Colonel
Kannengiesser had ordered a mere twenty Turkish riflemen, the
escort to two guns in the area, to oppose the oncoming New
Zealanders. General Birdwood had personally addressed all the

senior officers of the division to impress upon them the importance of bold and decisive leadership in the forthcoming operation; everyone had to press on to their objective regardless of their flanks. Yet the perfectly capable Johnston, commanding excellent, if tired, New Zealand infantry, could not bring himself to order them forward to make one last great effort to take the crest so tantalizingly near. When two companies of 2/10th Gurkhas appeared on his flank, eager for a fight, Johnston ordered them and three companies of the Auckland Battalion to resume the attack at 10.30 a.m., after a fifteen-minute artillery and naval bombardment. By then two companies of Mustafa Kemal's infantry had taken their places on the crest and, although the now wounded Kannengiesser could not keep them in place when the attack developed, he was greeted by the sight of his two regiments from Gaba Tepe deploying in good time to comprehensively defeat the pitifully few attackers.

On the left General Cox, in overall command of the column, accepted that Monash's brigade was too exhausted to make any further effort against the distant Hill 971. Seeing his own Indian brigade widely scattered over the hills before the ridge, he requested the use of 39th Brigade (13th Division) from Godley's reserve to renew the attack. Seeing that the Rhododendron Spur offered an easier path up to the crest he directed 39th Brigade, at about 11 a.m., to take that route. Brigadier-General Cayley led off and soon saw that the New Zealanders were still on the Spur and so he tried to redirect his brigade back into the Aghyl Dere for a different approach. One battalion could not be found and fetched up with the New Zealanders later in the day. The others were confused and exhausted by the counter-marching and ended the day in the gully, but not much further forward than any troops had been that morning. The entire day had been lost.

Chaos developed at Suvla. As six battalions of 10th Division sailed into Suvla Bay, scheduled to land at A Beach, they were hailed by a IX Corps staff officer and redirected to C Beach, where they were to support 11th Division in any way they could. At that moment the admirable Commodore Keyes appeared with news that he had detected a suitable landing place close to the Kiretch Tepe Ridge, the true objective of 10th Division. General Stopford, supported by Admiral Christian, argued that Brigadier-General Hill had been given his orders and that to change them again so soon would create more difficulty than it solved. Hammersley promptly ordered Hill off to the right towards the Chocolate Hills with five battalions that should have been marching for Kiretch Tepe. One battalion had become detached from his command already and did move off to the left. It would be several days before 10th Division recovered any semblance of order. When Mahon landed he had exactly three battalions of infantry, one of pioneers, some Royal Engineers (and no artillery at all) to take a ridge originally assigned as the objective of two brigades.

Large numbers of infantry were available ashore. They were tired but had not been subjected to any great exertion yet. Hammersley was trying to get some forward movement, but at least one of his brigadiers (Sitwell) had adopted a very defensive attitude. All were awaiting the reinforcement of Hill's command. The staff work of IX Corps collapsed. A succession of orders and counter-orders threw everything into confusion. One entire brigade was regularly left out of the orders altogether. Stopford had decided that he could not land the mules on schedule, and especially not send a goodly number of them off carrying water to Anzac, as planned. We already know that a staff officer had walked up from Anzac and there was absolutely nothing to prevent a smooth passage along the coastal paths except the nightmares in the mind of Stopford. This failure to land the mules added greatly to the rising problem of water shortage ashore.

A telephone line was run from Anzac to 11th Division headquarters and Birdwood was able to tell Hammersley that from the heights they could see the Turks retreating across the Suvla Plain. General Hill of the Irish Division was chafing at the lack of action but the brigadiers of 11th Division seemed paralysed with indecision. One of them was wounded by shellfire; a shell-burst at divisional headquarters had also done some damage and rattled Hammersley considerably. The more combative officers were demanding to be allowed to press their attack on the hills in the plain; all around them the men were getting more and more tired, confused and thirsty. By the time a forward movement was got under way, light was fading. It was getting dark when British and Irish troops finally stormed the Chocolate Hills and Green Hill. On the left, Mahon's troops were hardly able to progress at all along the Kiretch Tepe Ridge. If we add to this the failure of the Royal Navy to land many guns on 7 August, and the failure to land mules and water, leading to serious shortages for the men ashore, we see that there had been another day of complete failure to progress.

Hamilton was largely in ignorance of this, having received only few and very misleading messages from the front, which he duly cabled back to London late on 7 August, giving a fairly inaccurate picture of progress against a surprised and weakened enemy. The 11th Division, for instance, complained that a muddy foreshore had delayed their advance inland. Stopford's message, timed at 7.30 a.m. and giving a truthfully gloomy picture, was not received at GHQ until the afternoon, by which time it was known that 10th Division was ashore and things were thought to be going on well.

Meanwhile the Turks were still weak on the Sari Bair Ridge, where their numbers had risen from some 2,000 rifles in the morning to 5,000 by dusk. Tiny forces were in place on the Suvla Plain; 1,100 men and five guns covering a 3,000-yard front. But two divisions had been ordered south from Bulair towards Suvla; two divisions were ordered north from Cape Helles with all speed. The door was still ajar; it was soon to be slammed shut.

Godley ordered a renewed general offensive against the Sari Bair Ridge for 8 August. Johnston was to use his New Zealand brigade, plus reinforcing units (over three battalions), to attack Chunuk Bair. Cox was to use fully three brigades (4th Australian, 39th and 29th Indian) to take Hill Q and Hill 971. One of Johnston's New Zealand battalions had been severely shot up as it moved into position the night before, so he attacked with one New Zealand and two new British battalions. They got forward expecting a severe fight and, to their amazement, walked onto the crest and captured the sleeping crew of a single machine-gun. The Turkish infantry had gone! The exhilaration of an easy triumph soon passed. From the dominating heights of Hill Q to the left and Battleship Hill to the right a terrible enfilading fire was soon cutting the attackers down and driving them into cover. No reinforcements could get along the Rhododendron Spur. The three leading battalions were shattered but they were still on the crest at nightfall, when the Otago Battalion and two squadrons of Wellington Mounted Rifles crept up to relieve them in that bloody position. Cox's force, much dispersed but for Monash's brigade, was organized into four columns and ordered to be in place for an assault at daybreak. Once again these orders were issued without the knowledge that the troops were some half a mile further back than the staff realized. In the early morning gloom the leading Australian troops missed the Abdul Rahman Spur and began climbing the spur behind Hill 60, where they ran into stiff resistance and lost heavily to machine-gun fire. Two of the other columns were so lost in the gullies and ravines before the main ridge that they made very little headway all day. Alone, Major Allanson's 1/6th Gurkhas climbed boldly up the ridge towards Hill Q. Three hundred yards short they were pinned down by heavy fire. Allanson went back and collected some lost British troops to reinforce his men and, after dark, this force crept to within one hundred feet of the crest and dug in.

Daybreak at Suvla on 8 August saw a cloudless sky, promising a hot and thirsty day, but not a sound of military activity, British or Turkish. Still neither Stopford or Reed had left the *Jonquil* to see what was going on ashore. Paralysis still gripped 11th Division; it was quite junior staff officers who were going about trying to get the mass of unused troops away from the beaches. Mahon gave no instructions to his troops on Kiretch Tepe, so they dug in where they stood. Even the active General Hill was finding his men lethargic for want of sleep, water and food. We know that the Tekke Tepe Ridge was absolutely bare of Turkish troops at this time. The firing from the W Hills sufficed to pin the British in place, and Stopford warned his generals not to risk any attack without artillery preparation. Stagnation all along the front was the result. In a serious breakdown of discipline thirst-maddened troops were seen to attack water pipelines with their bayonets, temporarily slaking their own needs but ruining the overall arrangements for water supply.

Hamilton had become alerted to the lack of news from Suvla and ordered Lieutenant-Colonel Aspinall to go over and report on the situation. His run of bad luck persisted as the destroyer on hand for just such an eventuality developed boiler trouble and hours were lost before Aspinall, and the visiting Maurice Hankey, could hitch a ride on a trawler to Suvla. Before they arrived

Hamilton had finally realized how dilatory had been Stopford's performance and he determined to go himself to get things moving. He too was delayed by the provision of transport, not boarding the *Triad* until 4.30 p.m. and entering Suvla Bay after six o'clock. Aspinall and Hankey had already found the area so peaceful they were sure their troops must be in complete command of all the high ground. Hammersley soon disabused them of that notion. They rushed to see Stopford, meeting irate officers (especially gunners) along the way demanding some action. Reaching him at 3 p.m., they found him in high spirits that his splendid men had got ashore. Having urged him to get his men forward, Aspinall got to De Robeck's flagship and sent the famous message back to GHQ:

> Just been ashore, where I found all quiet. No rifle fire, no artillery fire, and apparently no Turks. IX Corps resting. Feel confident that golden opportunities are being lost and look upon the situation as serious.[5]

Stopford did finally go ashore and try to get Hammersley to go forward. He also heard that Hamilton was sending him two brigades of 53rd Division as a reinforcement. When the Commander-in-Chief arrived, with Keyes and Aspinall, Stopford still insisted on resting his men overnight and landing more guns before resuming the attack on 9 August. Hamilton immediately left to consult Hammersley on the spot, who was every bit as reluctant to move with any celerity. Hamilton persisted and badgered Hammersley into ordering his forward units of 32nd Brigade to pushing troops forward that very evening so that at least one battalion was on the Tekke Tepe Ridge by daybreak. The brigade commander simply did not know that two of his battalions were well forward, one already on Scimitar Hill and one almost at the foot of the ridge. He sent runners out with orders to concentrate the whole brigade at Sulajik – another tragic error. It was many hours before the forward troops were located and had to reluctantly abandon their positions in order to lead the attack to retake them. It was nearly 3.30 a.m. on 9 August before the attack began, just as the Turkish troops hurrying down from Bulair deployed in strength on the Tekke Tepe Ridge. The attack was defeated; by the narrowest of margins the Turks had won the race for the high ground. Activity had triumphed over lethargy.

The attack on Sari Bair Ridge was renewed on 9 August, with the British New Army troops taking up more of the strain. But the day is famous for the achievement of Allanson's Gurkhas in storming up onto Hill Q and starting down the other side, putting the Turks there to flight. At the moment of their triumph they were struck by heavy artillery fire and their attack was ruined. At first it was thought that Royal Navy gunfire from offshore had struck them; Hamilton's report to this effect caused very great offence to the Senior Service. Later it was thought that artillery firing from within the old Anzac perimeter had mistaken the Gurkhas for Turks; either way it was probably one of those tragic incidents of 'friendly fire' that sealed the fate of the attack. The British troops met tremendous resistance from the rapidly reinforcing Turks and soon they were under increasing pressure from Turkish counter-attacks. These were shot down bloodily but the last hope of winning the high ground was gone forever. Before Chunuk Bair, Johnston's brigade was shot to pieces and his men were pulled out and replaced by British troops. At Suvla, IX Corps lurched into activity just as its last real opportunity had passed it by. Destroyer gunfire helped the Irish forward on the Kiretch Tepe Ridge but down in the plain all attacks were delivered in inconceivable chaos, thanks to some very, very bad staff work. The 53rd Division had been landed and was already scattered to the four winds and was almost useless as a reinforcement. Hamilton himself made reconnaissances close to the firing line, but could make nothing of the situation. When Braithwaite arrived at Suvla, Hamilton left him to watch over things there and proceeded to Anzac for a closer look at the situation there.

Over the next few days, the enemy resisted all further attacks at Suvla and increased its counter-attacks along the Sari Bair Ridge; the whole line was under the able command of Mustafa Kemal. Soon the leading British battalions were overwhelmed by wave after wave of Turkish infantry and it took desperate fighting to steady the line and bring the Turkish attacks to a halt. Hamilton had offered the 54th Division to Birdwood but he had to refuse as it could not be accommodated at Anzac. It was duly landed at Suvla where it was drawn into the general failure of operations there. By 14 August Hamilton realized that his efforts to goad Stopford's IX Corps into decisive action was in vain. The whole force needed a complete rest and reorganization.

On 10 August he had sent a frank cable to Kitchener reporting the disappointment of IX Corps's performance: 'Just as no man puts new wine into old bottles, so the combination of new troops and old generals seems to be proving unsuitable except in the case of the 13th Division.'[6] Next day he elaborated on the theme. Insisting that all their carefully laid plans had meant that the attack came as a complete surprise to the Turks and that they had trebled the area of the old Anzac lodgement, he reminded London that he would have done things differently if he had had the reinforcements earlier:

> The new troops undoubtedly have much to contend against, and the conditions under which they are fighting are entirely novel, but I feel that had I been able to mix them up with any regular formation, they might have been able to advance with dash and rapidity. In some cases I watch the fighting of the new troops quite near at hand. I was much impressed by the superior spirit and dash of the 13th Division over the 10th and 11th, which was due in part to the fact that General Birdwood is a fount of energy to those under him, and in part, perhaps, to the fact that the 13th Division had been previously employed against the Turks in trenches by the side of the 29th Division.[7]

Kitchener expressed his disappointment at the failure of 10th and 11th Divisions, hoped that they could be 'gingered up' and announced reinforcements of a dismounted yeomanry division and five battalions of the London Regiment (TF) soon to be relieved at Malta. Hamilton, entirely in keeping with his character, scaled down his criticism of the troops, reserving his scorn for their generals: 'My impatience with the New Army troops is now somewhat lessened, seeing that the conditions under which they fight are quite foreign to their training and, moreover, there are no Regulars to set them a standard, and the country is covered with jungle and very big.'[8]

When Hamilton cabled on 14 August that Stopford and his divisional generals were not fit for further offensive action,

Kitchener sent an immediate and astounding reply asking if Hamilton had generals on hand to replace Stopford, Mahon and Hammersley. 'This is a young man's war, and we must have commanding officers that will take full advantage of opportunities which occur but seldom ... Any generals I have available I will send you.'[9] This is precisely the warning that Hamilton had given Kitchener in such good time before the operations had begun. Now Kitchener was asking Sir John French to supply a corps commander and two divisional commanders from France – the very men that Hamilton had asked for by name and had been refused. Julian Byng was to come out to command IX Corps; with Stopford relieved of command on 15 August, Hamilton brought De Lisle (29th Division) up from Cape Helles to assume temporary command. He specifically asked Sir Bryan Mahon if he would forgo his seniority and serve under De Lisle but Mahon took this as an insult and promptly resigned his command in the middle of the battle and took himself off immediately. The splendid Hill took command of the 10th Division but Hamilton, whose warnings about Mahon's temperamental unsuitability to high command had been proven true, asked Mahon to consider his personal honour as a soldier and persuaded him to resume command of his formation by 23 August.

Major-General Lindley voluntarily resigned as GOC 53rd Division, recognizing that he had not done well under the strain of battle. Lawrence of 127th Brigade, 42nd Division replaced him. Major-General E. Fanshawe came out from France to relieve Hammersley of command of the 11th Division.

This culling of the generals was basically too late. Turkish divisions flowed into the area, making further attacks against them doomed to failure. The arrival of 5,000 men of the 2nd Yeomanry Division and the transfer of the 'incomparable' 29th Division, reinforced by fresh units of the London Regiment, from Cape Helles to Suvla was not enough to redress the balance. There were now 75,000 Turkish rifles containing the 50,000 within the Anzac–Suvla area. Later attacks in August against Scimitar Hill and Hill 60 failed; there really was no prospect of success without another massive reinforcement from the home country.

In his lengthy report of 17 August Hamilton gave Kitchener a full description of the failed operations. After estimating that some

110,000 Turks with all the advantage of position now faced his total force of 95,000 he even admitted that 'the Turks have temporarily gained the moral ascendancy over some of our new troops'.[10] In another telling phrase he related that, in his attempt to deploy it as a reinforcement, 'unfortunately, the 54th Division broke in my hand, leaving me like a fencer with rapier broken'. He foresaw a very difficult winter and hard attritional fighting, requiring 45,000 drafts to bring existing units up to strength and a further 50,000 in new formations, which should restore the superiority of the attacking Allies, unless the Turks were themselves heavily reinforced. He was clearly thrusting the decision for the future of the campaign firmly back to the authorities in London. He stressed how well things could have gone:

> I hope you will realize how nearly this operation was a success complete beyond anticipation. The surprise was complete, and the army was thrown ashore in record time, practically without loss, and a little more push on the part of IX Corps would have relieved the pressure on Anzac, facilitated the retention of Chunuk Bair, secured Suvla Bay as a port, and threatened the enemy's right in a way that would have enabled Anzac to turn a success into a great victory.[11]

Kitchener's reply stressed that grave news of German success against the Russians meant some victory was urgently required 'either in France or at the Dardanelles'. Given that a large offensive was being prepared on the Western Front for September, he looked to Hamilton 'to do what is possible, without incurring undue risk of a serious setback or heavy losses without corresponding advantages'.[12] Some drafts were on their way but there would be no large-scale reinforcement possible because of the autumn offensive in France. Hamilton's reply was a gloomy tale of further failure at Suvla, of rising rates of sickness sweeping through his formations and of a declining effectiveness in the face of a steadily reinforced enemy. Soon telegrams were being exchanged, querying the numbers of drafts said by London to have been sent or to be on their way compared to those that had actually arrived. It was almost as if the 'record was being set straight' by both sides to meet any future investigation of the events.

Things were turning against Hamilton in London. When Stopford returned there, utterly unrepentant and certain that his troops had done everything they could possibly have done, he began making his opinions very freely known throughout military and political society. Lloyd George, Bonar Law and Carson on the Dardanelles Committee were convinced that there was no future for the operations. Before long Lloyd George would be pushing for his preferred scheme of landing Allied troops at Salonika to keep the Serbians, under mounting pressure from Austria, in the war. Bonar Law, at a committee meeting on 19 August, coined the damning phrase that Hamilton was a general who 'was always nearly winning'. Hamilton had sent one of his staff officers, Major Guy Dawnay, to London to convey fuller information of the difficulties at Gallipoli than could be conveyed in the telegrams and to answer questions at the War Office. Though he had been one of the first to suggest the evacuation of the Suvla position, Hamilton still endorsed Dawnay as 'one of the most sound and reliable officers I have struck'. Maurice Hankey, during his visit to Gallipoli, had found Dawnay 'disagreeable and too big for his boots'.[13] Over some weeks in London in September, Dawnay was first interviewed by Kitchener, together with the CIGS and Callwell, the DMO, at the War Office. He was a firm believer in shutting the campaign down completely but stuck to his honourable resolve to answer only questions put to him truthfully, hoping that the dismal facts would speak for themselves. Privately to Kitchener and Callwell he was able to freely state his case for evacuation. Before long he was being seen by the King, Asquith, Churchill, Lloyd George, Bonar Law, Carson, Grey and others, making sure that all these influential people were given his less than encouraging appreciation of the situation.

This coincided with an intervention by two discontented journalists that had a fatal impact on Hamilton's career. Ellis Ashmead-Bartlett, a fairly experienced war correspondent with the *Daily Telegraph*, was a heavily indebted bankrupt when he secured a lucrative posting as representative of the Newspaper Proprietors' Association to serve as special correspondent with the Royal Navy at Gallipoli. He was warmly received by Hamilton who, unlike Kitchener, greatly approved of press correspondents being able to convey war news to the public, and Ashmead-Bartlett made early promises to abide by the rules of wartime press censorship. He was utterly obsessed with the idea that the peninsula should have been attacked at Bulair and it was noted that he seemed to think he knew better than all the military authorities about how the campaign should be conducted. His early frustrations at the slowness of getting his reports back to London soon degenerated into an open hostility to the whole campaign that led to repeated clashes with the military authorities. Having once received permission to visit Malta, he absconded back to London and began his campaign of vilification of the campaign, gaining access to the Prime Minister in the process. Hamilton asked that he be kept in London and not be allowed to return as he was such a pessimist and a bad influence on all around him. But the powerful NPA insisted on sending him back to Gallipoli, whereupon Hamilton cleverly obtained the enlargement of the press corps (to include his old friend from South Africa days, Henry Nevinson) and its further subordination to the military censors.

Ashmead-Bartlett, from his luxurious encampment near GHQ on Imbros, was now openly at war with Hamilton's staff. He boasted that he would 'break' Braithwaite and see a new Commander-in-Chief within two months. Despite giving his word of honour as a gentleman that he would not infringe the regulations again, his blatantly defeatist reports were routinely suppressed. Then late in August the Australian journalist, Keith Murdoch, working in Egypt, asked if he could come out to make a short visit before proceeding to London. He picked up some very pessimistic gossip at Anzac and was thus very receptive to Ashmead-Bartlett's views when they met on 7 September. It was Murdoch who encouraged him to write everything in one damning report which he offered to convey to London in secret. A fellow journalist, ashamed at this betrayal of the trust accorded to the war correspondent, reported the plot to GHQ and Murdoch was detained at Marseilles and the letter confiscated. The original has disappeared – it was probably read, in horror, at the War Office and destroyed – but Ashmead-Bartlett had been dismissed from Gallipoli and was able to reproduce the whole report when he returned to London. Murdoch promptly wrote an excoriating attack on the whole campaign, full of comment on things of which he could have had no first-hand knowledge, and sent it to the Australian Prime Minister, Andrew Fisher. Thanks to Lloyd George the letter was soon in the hands of the British Prime Minister who, to his credit, considered the contents to be 'gossip and second-hand statements', but it was circulated as a cabinet paper without Hamilton ever having the chance to see it or comment upon it. The damage was done.[14]

Despite some last-minute efforts to revive the campaign, things were rapidly drawing to a head. The French offered to send four more divisions out, but this was a ruse to find employment for the senior general, Sarrail, who was at odds with their high command at home. Hamilton's spirits lifted as he began to discuss their possible use in Asia Minor to extend the Turkish front and ease pressure on the peninsula. He selflessly offered to be subordinated to Sarrail if this would guarantee the French support. Then came the mobilization of Bulgaria on the side of the Central Powers and a renewed assault on Serbia. The 10th (Irish) Division from Suvla and a French division from Helles were ordered to Salonika. The fate of the Gallipoli campaign was sealed, especially as the weather took a turn for the worse and storms severely damaged the landing stages all around the peninsula. Kitchener tried to warn Hamilton about the rising tide of criticism at home, drawing particular attention to complaints about the staff work. He offered to recall Braithwaite and replace him with Sir Lawrence Kiggell (later chief of staff to Sir Douglas Haig) but Hamilton refused to sacrifice his friend, 'the man who stood by me like a rock during those first ghastly ten days'.[15]

On 11 October, at the behest of the Dardanelles Committee, Kitchener cabled Hamilton to ask, 'What is your estimate of the probable losses which would be entailed to your force if the evacuation of the Gallipoli Peninsula was decided on and carried out in the most careful manner?'[16] Next day Hamilton replied along lines that would have been agreed with by most military men of the day. He thought losses would reach half of all the men involved. With luck it could be less but it could also been even worse, 'We might have a veritable catastrophe'.[17]

On 15 October the axe fell:

Secret and personal. It was decided at a War Council held last night that, although the Government fully appreciate your work and the gallant manner in which you have personally endeavoured to make the operations a success in spite of the great difficulties you have had to contend with, they consider it advisable to make a change in command, which will also give them an opportunity of seeing you. General Monro has been selected to go out to relieve you with a Chief of Staff, so Braithwaite should also return ... General Birdwood should replace you pending the arrival of Monro.[18]

Lord Esher confided in his diary: 'Ian Hamilton has been made the scapegoat in Gallipoli. He has been recalled and is on his way home. Monro has been appointed to succeed him. The Government cannot deprive him of the honour of having carried out the most difficult and splendid landing operation ever planned. But they can plan to deprive him of everything else, and they evidently mean to do so.'[19]

Charles Bean, Australia's distinguished official historian, left a sensitive portrait of Hamilton as he left for London:

The poor old chap looked to me very haggard – almost broken up; so were some of the staff . . . I am honestly very sorry to see Hamilton go. He is a gentleman, and has always been courteous and considerate to us. The British Army has never believed in him, but he is a good friend to the civilians, and has breadth of mind which the Army does not in general possess.[20]

But he thought him fatally weakened by his inability to control his subordinates and his staff. Bean respected Braithwaite's staff brain but savagely criticized the influence he had over Hamilton and accused him of disloyalty to his chief. Hamilton would not have agreed with this line of argument and soon he and Braithwaite would be locked into a new battle to preserve the fame of Gallipoli for posterity.

After some weeks, during which terrible winter weather struck the peninsula and non-combat losses soared, Lord Kitchener finally visited the theatre to assess the situation. He was fearful of the effect that defeat would have on the British Empire and he was buoyed up by a newly aggressive stance by the Royal Navy, where

Wemyss and Keyes were strongly in favour of a renewed naval attack on the Narrows. Kitchener at last saw the conditions on the peninsula and could appreciate what a great achievement it had been to effect the landings and hold on in the face of such difficulties. But the politicians at home were planning his demise, removing many of his powers as Secretary of State to the revitalized office of Chief of the Imperial General Staff. Birdwood was originally keen to renew the fighting and was soon putting in requests for more artillery ammunition that made Hamilton's look positively modest. But General Monro was of that school of thought that saw France as the main theatre of war and everything else a diversion of effort. He threw his weight behind the calls for evacuation and soon it was so decreed. He too expected to lose anything from 30 to 40 per cent of his force in the process.

In December 1915 the Suvla and Anzac areas were evacuated and in January 1916 Cape Helles was abandoned, much to the chagrin of the Royal Navy, who had hoped that it would be retained to keep the Dardanelles closed. Despite the sad need to slaughter all the animals ashore and the destruction of vast quantities of supplies and stores, not one man was lost in the process. The deception plans and stealth of the whole proceedings remain among the greatest achievements in military history. It had all been planned and executed by those same staff officers who had been, and were still being, reviled and despised by the journalists and politicians at home. Lest we think that Hamilton's gloomy prediction of serious loss tells against him, we have this from the lips of Kitchener himself:

> My head aches badly tonight. I have not slept for three nights, because I have a picture before my eyes the whole time of those poor men being drowned and massacred on the beaches of Gallipoli. What a relief it is to me to know that they are safely off.

12

The Dardanelles Commission,
1915–18

Hamilton and Braithwaite were back in London by 22 October and soon involved in meetings to discuss what had gone wrong to date and how the campaign might unfold. Ian and Jean both felt themselves more isolated in society, with certain 'friends' falling away. One man avoiding him was Lloyd George, but when Hamilton finally ran him to ground he was told that one of the most damaging charges against him was that he tried to blame Stopford for all the failings at Suvla and they thought Hamilton had sought him out for the appointment because they were old friends from South Africa. Apparently Kitchener had never told the Cabinet of Hamilton's first request for vigorous young officers and they only knew of his forlorn choice between Stopford and Ewart. Lloyd George expressed his amazement at this and it is said to have fatally shaken his confidence in Kitchener as Secretary of State for War. Clearly Stopford's report was doing as much damage in London as 'Murdoch's lying letter'.

Hamilton had been sent a copy of Murdoch's letter of 23 September to the Australian Prime Minister only a day or two before he was recalled. He now took the opportunity to reply to it in detail, ruthlessly exposing it as having been instigated and informed by Ashmead-Bartlett.[1] For a man who confessed repeatedly that he had no military experience whatsoever, Murdoch made the most sweeping observations about the strategy, operations and administration of the campaign, of which he actually saw very little in person. He never once set foot on Cape Helles, though frequently invited to do so by a staff that took his promises to abide by press censorship rules at face value. The factual errors were numerous and all designed to put the high command in the worst possible light: 90,000 men had been put ashore at Suvla and still failed (the figure was actually 30,000); they had been kept on board ship for two weeks before the landing (totally untrue); they were put ashore with no water but what they carried in their personal water-bottles (it was the responsibility of IX Corps staff to handle the extensive arrangements that had been made for supplying water); 'there were many deaths from thirst' (not one such death was ever recorded). Reserving high praise for all things Australian, Murdoch heaped abuse on the British troops, especially the Kitchener and Territorial Divisions sent out in August. 'They were merely a lot of childlike youths, without strength to endure or brains to improve their conditions.' Hamilton wondered aloud if the authorities in London would accept this as a fair description of the troops that they sent to him to carry out a decisive attack in the Dardanelles. Every act of the staff – and he consistently confused the duties of the general and the administrative staffs – was 'wretched' or 'deplorable'. Hamilton sardonically replied that Murdoch had heard the time-honoured 'grousing' of front-line troops about the staff and had elevated it to the level of sedition.

Murdoch was only getting warmed up on the subject of British (not Australian) staff officers. 'The conceit and self-complacency of the red-feather men are equalled only by their incapacity . . . What can you expect from men who have never worked seriously, who have lived for their appearance and for social distinction and self-satisfaction, and who are now called on to conduct a gigantic war?' Hamilton vigorously defended the courage and integrity of his staff officers, who were working in highly dangerous and difficult conditions, and we have already seen how the usual abuse of staff officers is given the lie by the many remarkable achievements of those same officers. Murdoch singled out for attack the staff on the luxurious ship *Aragon*, the medical arrangements of Sir John Porter, the base arrangements in Egypt and, of course, Hamilton and Braithwaite personally, who were held up to be detested more than Enver Pasha. His appeal for a new, younger and more vigorous commander to be sent out ended with the odd warning that Sir Horace Smith-Dorrien would not be acceptable. Hamilton asked what Murdoch knew of Smith-Dorrien, and how did he even get hold of his name? It is one of the more obvious interventions by

Ashmead-Bartlett in this letter. Hamilton, of course, reminded London officialdom how he had opposed the unnecessary appointment of Porter and of his predictions of administrative difficulties arising from it. He actually agreed that the *Aragon* was a source of discord and that he would have preferred its work (that of the Inspector General of Communications) to be conducted ashore. It was the Royal Navy that absolutely insisted that the naval and military officers live and work together on the ship, well appointed with wireless communications as it was. The work done there was particularly poor until Altham and Ellison came out and set everything in that department to rights. Hamilton stoically accepted the personal abuse from Murdoch, but gently exposed his errors (that Hamilton had never set foot at Anzac) and his foolishness (he misinterpreted a gallant remark by the French commander comparing Hamilton to Achilles 'coming here from your island' as meaning that Hamilton never left his island headquarters!). Hamilton ended with a complaint that this document, an affront to his personal honour and a libel on his troops, had been elevated to the rank of a state paper and circulated without him seeing it first. He found the opinions in it vilifying the British army to be common gossip in London society.

In December 1915 Hamilton was arguing passionately with Kitchener, who had just returned from his somewhat belated visit to Gallipoli, not to evacuate the peninsula; he also, quite naturally, was asking what was to happen to him next. Kitchener said that he personally would welcome a quiet month or two on half pay but Hamilton replied indignantly that, as a soldier, he considered it a mortal insult to be unemployed whilst his country was at war. He bluntly asked Kitchener if he was truly a friend of his; whether he was inspired by friendly sentiments towards him. The affirmative reply seemed somewhat grudging and can have been of little comfort.

At the end of 1915 Hamilton again had to confront Kitchener and defend his record at Gallipoli. A friendly meeting on 31 December, during which Kitchener expressed an interest in sending Hamilton as an official representative to the Russian headquarters, which would have suited Sir Ian very well, ended with a request that Hamilton speak to the Adjutant-General, Sclater, about his

Final Despatch from Gallipoli, soon to be published. After one or two small, mutually agreed alterations, Sclater asked Hamilton to exclude reference to his divisions being 45,000 men below strength in August, or to insert the words 'on the peninsula', implying that the shortage was only local and that there were reinforcements in theatre to make up the numbers. As this implied that his staff had, in some way, 'mislaid' the reinforcements he was asking for, he naturally refused, despite Kitchener's insistence that he comply. His days of being a compliant servant of his old chief were definitely over. From a paper by Sclater, Hamilton could now see that the War Office was trying to argue that the two Territorial divisions (53rd and 54th) that had been sent out in August, stripped of everything but their infantry battalions, had really been meant as 20,000 drafts to fill up the ranks of the existing divisions. This was news to Hamilton and further served to warn him that certain elements in London were preparing a case, if not against him, then certainly putting their own actions in the most favourable light.[2]

Nothing came of the Russian appointment. Hamilton was sounded out as a possible Governor-General of Ireland in March 1916, which he declined; a blessed relief, given that a rebellion would blaze forth at Easter 1916 in Dublin. These remained dark days for both Ian and Jean. They were being 'cut' in the street by people they had thought of as friends, though many others saw Sir Ian as scapegoat and rallied to them. It is just as well that he did not overhear the conversation at a dinner party recorded by the young Foreign Office civil servant, Duff Cooper. He was dining with the Prime Minister, Lord Crewe and Lord Robert Cecil, and the politicians were having great fun at the expense of their generals and 'the miscalculations of military experts ... Crewe said, and the PM agreed, that the failure of the Dardanelles expedition was entirely the fault of one man – Ian Hamilton'.[3] This must surely rank as the single most ridiculous remark ever made about such an important phase in the military history of the United Kingdom. For these men – who had failed utterly to give or seek any true sense of leadership during the whole sorry affair from January 1915 onwards – to say that everything that had gone wrong, be it naval, military, political or diplomatic, was the fault of one man should make us all tremble at the level of political leadership on offer in 1915.

Hamilton must have taken special comfort from a letter to mark the first anniversary of the landings sent to him on 18 April by a Bombardier Clarke of the Australian Field Artillery and thirteen other Australian soldiers in training near Weymouth. It is interesting if only in showing how immediate was the impact of Gallipoli in giving Australians a sense of nationhood. 'The day draws near that marks Australia's first birthday. With you on the 25th of April last year we laid firmly the foundation of our Military History and in a few days we hope to celebrate a glorious anniversary.'[4] The letter then gave a complete declaration of the soldiers' confidence in and loyalty towards Hamilton. They acknowledged the difficulty of his task, admired his courage in pressing on with his duty and saw the lack of interest in the London authorities and their inability to send timely reinforcement as the true cause of their failure. Eddie Marsh, Churchill's private secretary, later reported to Jean that he had met some Anzacs in London in September 1916 who said that 'Sir Ian was far the best general they had served under, and that I might ask any Anzac I pleased, they would all say the same of him'.[5] They put down the failure entirely to want of reinforcements, and wanted it known that they had told their commander, Birdwood, the same!

Both the new CIGS, 'Wully' Robertson, and Sir John French, C-in-C Home Forces, were determined to see Hamilton re-employed as soon as possible; according to French, Robertson thought it a loss to the Empire to keep Ian unemployed. In May 1916 the Eastern Command became vacant and they both lobbied the Prime Minister to secure it for Hamilton. While not a fighting command, it was at least an active one and would suffice until something else came along.

But in a secret session of Parliament there was such a storm of protest about the handling of the Gallipoli campaign at all levels that Asquith lost his nerve and, fearful of the reaction of the popular press, declined to make the promised appointment. Lord French was so upset at this that he asked Jean to tell Sir Ian as he could not bring himself to do so. Churchill was back in London and, seeing himself a target of much criticism in the press, he began to demand that all the state papers relating to the campaign be published. Leaving aside that this request to reveal secrets of strategic thinking, military organization and operational performance is truly astounding while a world war was in progress, the government had its own reasons for not revealing too much about the muddled origins of the campaign. On 1 June Churchill did force through a note to have the papers published, but Maurice Hankey was immediately tasked with drawing up a report pointing out the dangers of such a move.

On 6 June Hamilton was dining with Churchill, revealing for the first time how Kitchener never showed the stream of cables requesting reinforcements, guns and ammunition to the Cabinet, when the news came of the drowning at sea of Lord Kitchener and his entourage, who had been en route for an official visit to Russia. The death of Kitchener, at a moment when an unanswerable case against his direction of the campaign was being prepared, enormously complicated the process. General Callwell, DMO, was gathering the relevant papers and wrote to Hamilton that the evidence was so damning that it would be impossible to publish it so soon after the death of the nation's hero. Hamilton agreed, and asked Churchill to relax his efforts, especially as the great Somme offensive had just opened in France and he did not want the government distracted on his account. On 14 July Maurice Hankey, writing as Secretary of the Committee of Imperial Defence, told Hamilton that he favoured his re-employment at the earliest possible date. 'To treat you as the Government has done, when you have successfully accomplished one of the greatest feats in the history of the world and only failed to achieve complete success for lack of proper support, is simply to discourage initiative in the whole corps of General Officers.'[6] It is worth reminding ourselves that getting troops ashore in an opposed assault landing really did rate as 'one of the greatest feats in the history of the world' to military men in 1915 and 1916.

A mounting tide of criticism over the British disaster in Mesopotamia, where 13,000 troops besieged at Kut-al-Amara had surrendered after costly failures to relieve them, pushed the government into ordering Commissions of Enquiry to investigate the defeats in both the Dardanelles and Mesopotamia. The second major reverse provoked the enquiry into the first and both were seen as ways of placating the press and public and making sure that state papers were kept out of the public arena.

The Dardanelles Commission was chaired by Lord Cromer (succeeded on his death by Mr Justice Pickford) and its secretary was Grimwood Mears. The services were represented by Admiral Sir William May and Field Marshal Lord Nicholson; the Dominions by Australia's ex-Prime Minister, Andrew Fisher, and New Zealand's Sir Thomas Mackenzie. The MPs Captain Stephen Gwynne and Walter Roch served throughout; T. Clyde and F. Cawley served until they took up other government duties. Hamilton only commented on two of the appointees. Officially, he pointed out that Fisher was likely to be biased against him as Keith Murdoch was his principal informant. In his usual gallant manner, Hamilton said that if Fisher declared his mind to be open, then he would accept the assurance with confidence. Privately, he was aghast at the appointment of Nicholson, who had been a venomous enemy for some years. His prediction that 'Old Nick', known to be hostile to the whole campaign, would make trouble was entirely justified. His fears were shared by Birdwood, who also denounced Nicholson as a wholly destructive influence. Churchill even advised Hamilton to seek out legal counsel to represent him at the Commission, and Hamilton was also shocked to hear that the government had appointed the Attorney-General, F. E. Smith (later Lord Birkenhead), as counsel for the deceased Kitchener. Clearly if the evidence was going to go heavily against Kitchener, the government would be equally open to censure, and they were taking steps to head off that difficulty. At a dinner party F. E. Smith had offered his brother's services to Hamilton, insisting that Hamilton's whole case lay in attacking Kitchener and that he must defend him rigorously. Hamilton angrily replied that he had no intention of attacking his old chief and that all legal deals were off. Smith warned him that he might be sorry.

When the Commission convened on 23 August 1916, promptly adjourning for twenty-three days to allow Hankey to prepare the papers of the War Council, Hamilton could not have known that nearly two years of his life would be spent defending his own reputation and those of the officers and men of his expeditionary force. The first enquiry was into the origins and inception of the campaign and the First Report, dated 12 February, was published in March 1917.

The report exposed the failure to seek adequate advice from

naval experts about the effectiveness of a purely naval attack on the Dardanelles forts and revealed the haste in organizing the naval attack and the delays in providing military support, which merely gave the enemy all the time in the world to organize his defences. It condemned the failure of the War Council to hold any meetings at all between 19 March and 14 May 1915, when the fate of the expedition was effectively sealed as it degenerated into trench stalemate. Inevitably, if gently, one man was singled out for blame:

> We are of the opinion that Lord Kitchener did not sufficiently avail himself of the services of his General Staff, with the result that more work was undertaken by him than was possible for one man to do, and confusion and want of efficiency resulted.[7]

The concluding paragraph damned the campaign with faint praise. 'We think that, although the main object was not attained, certain important political advantages ... were secured by the Dardanelles expedition. Whether those advantages were worth the loss of life and treasure involved is, and must always remain, a matter of opinion.'[8]

Fisher dissented from the notion that military and naval advisers to ministers should have been allowed to express their disagreements with their chiefs before the War Council. He felt this would have been subversive of democratic government. Walter Roch, who would prove to be one of the most effective commissioners, wrote a long memorandum to the report making telling points about: the failure of Lord Kitchener to place the original campaign more fully within the war-making potential of Britain in 1915; Churchill's failure to fully explain to the War Council the naval objections to a ships-only attack; and Ian Hamilton leaving at such short notice for the Dardanelles that 'he was assisted by no staff preparations and no preliminary scheme of operations of any kind'.[9] A separate supplement to the report added some details, including the advice of the Director of Military Operations (Charles Callwell) given in September 1914 that he did not favour any attack on the Dardanelles from the sea.

Hamilton had used his time when not directly involved with the Commission in preparing his own diary of his time at Gallipoli for possible publication. Jean was certainly reading it in September

1916. Since his time in the South African war of 1899–1902, Hamilton had been conscious of the need to keep a full diary for the benefit of posterity (and one's good reputation). During every day of the campaign, often while he was shaving, he had dictated entries to Staff Sergeant-Major Stuart, who typed them up and preserved numerous contemporary documents to add detail to the narrative. Hamilton added a good deal of information in the way of official cables to expand the narrative and make clear the difficulties under which he laboured. He was quite sure the facts would speak for themselves. (In his 1956 study of the campaign, Alan Moorehead clearly misunderstood the nature of this diary and imagined Ian Hamilton writing thousands of carefully crafted words each night as the battles raged outside his tent. Hamilton's secretary, Mrs Shield, pointed out that it was really 'a memoir in diary form' based entirely on typed and handwritten notes taken at the time and later dictated to her for publication.)[10]

The Commission resumed its sittings on 4 January 1917 and concentrated on the operational aspects of the campaign. No less than 170 witnesses were called before the sixty-eight meetings that concluded on 5 September. This became a real battle between the proven enemies of the campaign and the officers who had conducted it. Nicholson led the critics, often asking leading questions of witnesses and encouraging quite junior officers to comment on larger questions of military policy. His animosity was so extreme that he damaged his own case. We have absolute proof that the 'Hamilton-haters' planned secret meetings to co-ordinate their evidence to do him the greatest harm; this proof comes from one who was invited to join the cabal but refused.

Hamilton was told of a luncheon party attended by Brigadier-General Woodward (Adjutant-General, MEF), Brigadier-General Elliott (a former Director of Works, MEF) and Brigadier-General Winter (QMG, MEF) and a Captain W. Maxwell, a press censor at GHQ. Woodward admired Hamilton but had become the leading critic of Braithwaite and was also keen to shift blame for the problems besetting the medical arrangements; Elliott had been dismissed from his post for inefficiency; Maxwell was also keen to blame Braithwaite for staff problems. Woodward led the discussion to get a co-ordinated story to 'do down' the General Staff. It was

General Winter who dissented from the whole scheme, insisting that his poor health left him unable to remember details or be of any use to the group, and he withdrew himself from the luncheon. He subsequently told Hamilton of the plot.[11]

It can therefore come as no surprise that a great deal of time was spent by Hamilton in organizing the evidence to be presented to the Commission by the sympathetic witnesses. He saw to it that his people were briefed about the nature of the questioning to date and what aspects of the evidence needed to be accentuated. It can generally be said that the criticism tended to come from people of little military experience or with a pronounced personal axe to grind. The more positive view of the campaign came from those officers, admittedly defending their personal reputations, who had struggled with the actual difficulties of the fighting on the peninsula and all that was necessary to support it. Passions were certainly inflamed. At one stage Braithwaite was privately referring to Captain Maxwell as 'a dirty little dog' and 'a blighter'; strong words indeed from one Edwardian gentleman about another.[12] His critics were 'snarling dogs who are yapping at my heels'.

Towards the end of 1916 a mass of written evidence was collected from government departments and key participants. Braithwaite was able to pass on to Hamilton two bits of gossip: firstly, that most of the Dardanelles Commissioners were heartily sick of their task and thought that it should have been left until after the war was over; secondly, that the evidence had been seen by the commissioners working on the Mesopotamia enquiry, who had expressed their admiration for the direct and open submissions from the soldier witnesses, comparing it favourably with that submitted by politicians.

By and large the soldiers involved in the campaign from the start, or as reinforcements before August, had a very positive and consistent message to tell. The gunners spoke of the desperate shortages they coped with, of guns, shells and spare parts. Brigadier-General Simpson-Baikie (CRA 29th Division) explained that every major attack used up the entire stock of artillery ammunition on the peninsula; that the Territorial divisions brought out old and quite useless guns with them; that there were not enough aeroplanes and trench mortars to conduct operations properly. Lieutenant-

Colonel Forman, RHA, who commanded one of 29th Division's artillery brigades, described the narrow failure of the early battles because of inadequate artillery preparation and how they gradually lost the artillery battle to the numerically superior Turkish guns.

The infantry commanders had no complaints about the supply of food and ammunition, or even of medical provision given the peculiarly difficult conditions under which they fought. In their general remarks about some of the highly critical evidence made of the medical arrangements, these tough professional soldiers pointed out that the criticism usually came from people with little or no military experience who were, naturally, distressed on seeing the suffering of wounded men. The most consistent point they made was the lack of support at crucial moments. Time and again they saw the results of hard fighting slip away as their formations wilted for the want of reinforcement. Lieutenant-Colonel Fawcus of the 1st/7th Manchesters (42nd Division) realized soon after he landed on 7 May that if his division had just been a few days earlier they could have made a decisive contribution to the battle for Krithia and Achi Baba.

> Whenever reinforcements arrived, the psychological moment for their use had always passed. Had the 42nd Division been landed in April, instead of May, and had the 52nd Division arrived in May instead of June, and finally had the new armies of August arrived early in July, I candidly believe that we should have gained brilliant victories on Gallipoli, and that the campaign would have been most successful.[13]

The New Zealand brigadier, Russell, wrote, 'To sum up it appears to me that adequate forces for the work involved were never supplied till too late.'[14] Lieutenant-Colonel Street, who served on the staff of 29th Division and VIII Corps, also said that a fresh, well-trained brigade would have won the day on 28 April; a new division would have broken the Turkish lines on 4 June. He was addressing the London authorities responsible for the inception and running of the campaign when he summed up:

> I cannot say less than that the impression created at the time and confirmed by reflection afterwards is that at no time was

the magnitude of the task fully appreciated or adequate means for carrying it out provided. Even the results achieved were obtained only by stretching to the utmost the forces and resources available on the spot at the time.[15]

In an ironic twist, given the ill-informed remarks made in Keith Murdoch's letter, the excellent Lieutenant-General Altham recorded his impressions of the Suvla fiasco and wrote: 'One cannot but feel if a man of the type of Smith-Dorrien, with two or three young and energetic Divisional Commanders, had been there the whole coup would have been pulled off.'[16] This type of fighting general was needed. Hamilton had asked for Bruce Hamilton and been told that he was too old for active service, though he was not much older than Stopford. Even the controversial Hunter-Weston, who had been invalided home, would have brought more sanguine energy to the Suvla operations.

The Suvla generals, of course, had convinced themselves that they were facing the most powerful Turkish defences, requiring massive artillery support to overcome them. They were undone by the evidence of splendid warriors such as Colonel Allanson of the Gurkha Rifles, who told the Commission, 'Victory was slipping from our grasp, and all in my neighbourhood for want of dash, and at Suvla from want of appreciation of how little there was in front of them.'[17] They also went on at very great length about the lack of water once they had landed. Nicholson was to make this one of the main planks of his attack on the handling of the operation, together with the blatantly unrepentant evidence of Sir Frederick Stopford, who argued simultaneously that he had personally inspired much of the Suvla plan and that he was kept in the dark about it by the General Staff.

Walter Braithwaite was interviewed at great length, second only to Ian Hamilton himself, by the Commission. In a masterly performance he clearly and patiently explained over and over again the work of the General Staff of the MEF. Nicholson's aggressive questioning backfired as it brought Pickford in to mollify some of his badgering of witnesses. Nicholson came back again and again to three particular themes: the remoteness of GHQ from the front-line troops, the suffering of the wounded in April 1915 and the provision of water at Suvla in August.

Braithwaite reminded the Commission that, when soldiers complain that they never see staff officers at the front, 'that is a thing which is said about every GHQ in every army in the world in every campaign. It is said in France at this minute'.[18] (Braithwaite was commanding an infantry division in France at the time where, it should be stressed, he proved to be a fine trainer and commander of men. He commanded IX Corps when it spectacularly 'broke the Hindenburg Line' in a day in September 1918. When Lord Kitchener had asked the question in 1915 Braithwaite got one of his staff officers to draw up a complete schedule of every visit made from GHQ to the various fronts on the peninsula. It showed that staff officers visited both Helles and Anzac, and later Suvla, every single day, and that Hamilton personally visited them at least once a week. When Major-General Cox peevishly said he never saw a General Staff officer in his trenches all the time he was at Gallipoli, he was made to look rather foolish by the production of a staff report that lavished praise on the excellence of his trenches after just such a visit. Braithwaite patiently explained that this was no reflection on the general; he could, quite simply, have been absent elsewhere at the time of the visit. He also reminded them that GHQ had allocated a liaison officer to IX Corps who had been deliberately left behind; he subsequently landed at Anzac and walked over to Suvla, further giving the lie to the difficulties IX Corps was supposed to be facing.

Woodward had complained to the Commission that Braithwaite had both arrogated to his General Staff the organizing of the medical arrangements for the April landings, and that he subsequently isolated the administrative staff from the Commander and the General Staff. Braithwaite was genuinely astonished to hear these complaints when he returned to Britain. He had been a close personal friend of Woodward (he encouraged him to accept the job of Deputy Adjutant-General) and felt himself to be a staff officer known for his ability to make things run smoothly. In a pointed barb at his chief tormentor he said, 'Otherwise why did Lord Nicholson select me as Commandant of the Staff College [at Quetta, India], who must be a man who makes things go smoothly?'[19]

Braithwaite had to explain, again, how quickly the first staff – just seven operations and six intelligence officers – had to leave for the eastern Mediterranean and how, in just thirty-four days, they had to leave Mudros, reorganize and plan everything at Alexandria and return to Mudros before making the assault. The arrangements for the immediate evacuation of the wounded were made by the General Staff with the help of the divisional medical officers, the men most involved at the sharp end. But when the AG and his staff, including the Director of Medical Services, arrived at Alexandria, they were given the task of completing the work, already begun long ago by Sir John Maxwell's staff, of preparing the hospital ships and the base hospitals to receive the wounded. For Woodward to complain about this part of the work is to complain about his own work and that of his subordinates. Certainly the evacuation of the wounded was a terrible problem on 25 April and subsequent days because of the unexpectedly high numbers coming in over several days beyond the predictably bloody landing itself, which problem was aggravated by the loss of boats and crews during the attack. The system was overwhelmed in the short term but was improved as soon as was humanly possible.

To say that Braithwaite denied access to Hamilton is also a mystery. Braithwaite was able to prove that the chief staff officers met together every single day, besides the formal weekly meetings. Woodward did try to raise matters with Hamilton that were outside his immediate sphere of responsibility and incurred some displeasure, but Braithwaite actually went out of his way to restore the good relations between them. Again we are left feeling that some of these criticisms were being made to divert blame for some other shortcomings.

When it came to the staff work at Suvla, Braithwaite again withstood a sustained attack by Nicholson designed to blame Hamilton and his GHQ for the failure. It was proved that GHQ and its specialist officers had made the most elaborate arrangements for the carrying of water to the Suvla Bay area, and a special engineering ship, the *Prah*, was equipped with everything needed to establish water tanks, pumps and pipelines ashore. The Royal Navy witnesses insisted that they had everything in place, apart from the loss of three special water lighters to breakdown, and that they would have done whatever was asked of them. Nothing was! When Braithwaite visited Stopford at IX Corps headquarters he heard complaints that nobody knew what had become of the *Prah*. Braithwaite sardonically informed the Commission that he could see the ship with his own eyes sitting in Suvla Bay waiting to be told what to do next.[20]

Hamilton was quizzed about the lengthy submissions of Mr Ashmead-Bartlett, who had implied that he frequently gave the Commander-in-Chief good advice that was not followed as it should have been. He was able to prove that many of the journalist's assertions about their conversations were demonstrably false, and that large areas of his critique about the staff and operations were based on hearsay, coloured by this self-styled expert's obsession with the need to land at Bulair to the exclusion of every other possible landing place.

Hamilton's spirits were sustained during these trying days by the publication in August 1917 of a book in Switzerland by a German journalist who had defected there out of disgust at his country's policy in the Near East. *Two Years of War in Constantinople* by Herr Stuermer gave proof from 'the other side of the hill' of just how close the Allies had come not once, but twice, to winning at Gallipoli, bearing out the independent testimony of the American ambassador to which reference has already been made. He confirmed that the Turkish and German defences on 18 March 1915 were very close to breaking point when the attack was called off, and that they would never had survived a renewal of the attack next day. He also stressed the level of panic in Constantinople during the August offensive, when once again the archives and bullion reserves were moved out of the city to the safety of Asia Minor and the population expected a British victory at any moment.[21] After the war Hamilton was told that it was Kemal Ataturk's own chief of staff who had sent the warning message to the capital, so sure were they that 'the British were through'. The general who was 'always nearly succeeding' must have taken comfort from the evidence of his erstwhile enemy.

The Final Report of the Dardanelles Commission was dated 4 December 1917. It cut to the heart of the problem in the opening paragraphs of its General Conclusions.

We think that, when it was decided to undertake an important military expedition to the Gallipoli Peninsula, sufficient consideration was not given to the measures necessary to carry out such an expedition with success . . . We think that the difficulties of the operations were much underestimated. At the outset all decisions were taken and all provisions based on the assumption that, if a landing were effected, the resistance would be slight and the advance rapid. We can see no sufficient ground for this assumption . . . We think that the position which, in fact, existed after the first attacks in April and the early days of May should have been regarded from the outset as possible and the requisite means of meeting it considered . . . We are of opinion that, with the resources then available, success in the Dardanelles, if possible was only possible upon condition that the Government concentrated their efforts upon the enterprise and limited their expenditure of men and material in the Western theatre of war. This condition was never fulfilled.[22]

If Hamilton was open to criticism that he failed to see that the power of the early Turkish resistance spelled disaster for the expedition, it was pointed out that the military authorities at home shared this view and that Hamilton's call for reinforcement in May went unanswered in London for six weeks. The overall plans for the August offensive were criticized as unpractical but it was accepted that they had the full support of the long-serving commander of that sector (Birdwood) and that the failure to press home the attack at Suvla had more to do with poor leadership than with excessive demands on the new troops employed.

As regards Sir Ian Hamilton it is inevitable that the capabilities of a commander in war should be judged by the results he achieves, even though, if these results are disappointing, his failure may be due to causes for which he is only partially responsible . . . We recognise Sir Ian Hamilton's personal gallantry and energy, his sanguine disposition, and his determination to win at all costs. We recognise also that the task entrusted to him was one of extreme difficulty, the more so as the authorities at home at first misconceived the nature and duration of the operations, and afterwards were slow to realise that to drive the Turks out of their entrenchments and occupy the heights commanding the Straits was a formidable and hazardous enterprise which demanded a concentration of force and effort. It must further be borne in mind that Lord Kitchener, whom Sir Ian Hamilton appears to have regarded as a Commander-in-Chief rather than as a Secretary of State, pressed upon him the paramount importance, if it were by any means possible, of carrying out the task assigned to him. Though from time to time Sir Ian Hamilton represented the need of drafts, reinforcements, guns and munitions, which the Government found it impossible to supply, he was nevertheless always ready to renew the struggle with the resources at his disposal, and to the last was confident of success. For this it would be hard to blame him; but viewing the Expedition in the light of events it would, in our opinion, have been well had he examined the situation as disclosed by the first landings in a more critical spirit, impartially weighed the probabilities of success and failure, having regard to the resources in men and material which could be placed at his disposal, and submitted to the Secretary of State for War a comprehensive statement of the arguments for and against a continuance of the operations.[23]

If this was the worst criticism that could be made of Hamilton, that, burdened as he was with Kitchener's admonition to see the thing through once it had begun, he did not foresee the future and advise an immediate abandonment of the whole enterprise, then he had little to fear from the publication of the report.

Stopford's IX Corps came in for heavy criticism. It was recalled that Hammersley's health (it was actually his mental health) 'had in the past been such that it was dangerous to select him for a divisional command in the field, although he seemed to have recovered'.[24] Despite this the War Office had sent him out to Hamilton with a good report of his abilities. His senior brigade commander, Sitwell, was also criticized for insufficient energy and decision. Stopford himself got off quite lightly. He failed to keep abreast of developments ashore and should have intervened more effectively to get his troops moving. He was, however, defended against some of the points Hamilton made against him.

The report went on to refute the worst calumny (made, of

course, by Nicholson), that Hamilton had persisted with costly frontal attacks by using the bodies of his soldiers as a substitute for a shortage of artillery shells; it was recognized that the shortage of guns, ammunition and replacement of casualties were inadequate to the task but were all far greater than the War Office originally intended. Over the vexed question of the water supply to Suvla it was accepted that IX Corps's staff work was woefully inadequate, and the Commission went to the unusual step of naming the individual administrative staff officer deemed 'primarily responsible for the lack of due consideration'.[25] It was also accepted that the problems of medical provision stemmed entirely from the shallowness of the lodgement on the peninsula, denying the possibility of establishing proper hospitals ashore, and requiring all major casualties to be continually evacuated to base hospitals in Egypt and elsewhere.

Nicholson made one last, and rather shameful, effort to make the report more critical of Hamilton. Having volunteered to give it a final polish before it went to the printers, he inserted a damning censure of Hamilton for not having gone ashore immediately at Suvla to get things moving there. This point had never been discussed before the Commission and, mercifully, Grimwood Mears checked the final draft and discovered the unauthorized passage. He showed it to all the commissioners and every member demanded that the offending piece be struck out. In August 1923 Hamilton was to receive a letter from the daughter of Mr Justice Pickford that sheds some light on these inner workings of the Commission and must have been a further comfort to him:

> I don't know whether I ought to tell you but he always thought that you had been subjected to very unfair criticism over the Dardanelles, and he would not allow some of the other Commissioners to make comments, which they were totally unable to support with evidence.[26]

This was a valuable report, going a long way to exonerate the servicemen who fought the campaign from blame for its failure, and reminding all who read it that the roots of failure lay in its inception and in the inability of the government to decide to give either the Western Front or the Dardanelles the priority claim on

Britain's desperately scarce resources in 1915. The personal disaster for Hamilton lay precisely in this last point. Because its own shortcomings were so exposed, the government made sure that the report was never published until 1919, denying him any chance of being usefully re-employed in a military capacity.

Hamilton had many supporters in the army anxious to see him back in action but Lord Derby, the Secretary of State for War in 1918, made it clear that a public statement in his favour would be required from the Prime Minister before he could be reappointed as C-in-C Home Forces, his old job which had just come vacant again. The idea of Lloyd George making what would really be a public apology to him for the years he had been kept kicking his heels was more than anyone could hope for.

He kept a close eye on the developments of the war and developed his own trenchant critique of the attritional battles on the Western Front. He was an early advocate of the 'bite and hold' tactics, rather than the search for the big breakthrough that so often proved so costly in its failure. Based on his experience of destroying Turkish counter-attacks at Gallipoli, he suggested seizing some small but vital piece of ground with the deliberate aim of inviting the enemy to shed his blood prodigiously in trying to retake it. This was very like the tactics Plumer used in his successful battles in Flanders in September and October 1917. Writing to Churchill in July 1917 he said, 'My view throughout has been that no General should attack his enemy where he is strongest. He holds him where he is strongest and attacks him where he is weakest.'[27] He was a strong advocate of transferring British forces to Italy, where he had predicted the Caporetto disaster, and where he could see the chance for a blow against the over-extended enemy. He did offer himself for the task but only tentatively: 'I'm for it if you like, but that's by the way'.[28] In August 1918, when Japanese and American troops landed at Vladivostock to do battle with the Bolshevik revolutionaries, he again offered himself for a command there, based on his unrivalled knowledge of the Japanese army.[29] Being left unemployed in wartime was a sore trial.

During the great crisis on the Western Front engendered by the German offensive that opened on 21 March 1918, Hamilton was one of those few observers who saw immediately how the Germans had laid themselves open to a decisive defeat by leaving their formidable defences and staking all on the attack. In a letter to 'Oc' Asquith, the son of the former Prime Minister who had served at Gallipoli in the Royal Naval Division and was about to be married, Hamilton put it on record on 26 March – one of the most critical days of the battle – that he thanked God for delivering the German army into our hands. He wrote to a friend at the *Daily Mirror* describing his astonishment at the behaviour of the German General Staff, saying that, 'Till now I have had an immense respect for the technical ability of these men; at last events have released me from that burden.'[30]

While following with his usual sanguine interest the events of the war, he was also turning his mind to the forthcoming peace and while the war was still in progress he was already taking up a position that would make him one of the severest critics of the Versailles settlement and, indeed, of war itself as means for settling international disputes.

When Lord Milner succeeded Derby as Secretary of State for War he let it be known that he thought Hamilton had been ill used by the government and deserved better. He went so far as to offer Hamilton the Northern Command in Britain, but Sir Ian was now prepared to accept that such important active commands should really go to younger generals and he declined. Instead, he accepted the pre-retirement sinecure of Lieutenant of the Tower of London, and in this way he saw out his fifty years of army service.

13

Post-war Life,

1918–1947

For several years after the war, Hamilton was busier than he had ever been. He was greatly in demand for dedicating memorials to the fallen, during which he developed his ideas on the nature of the peace and the future. He was instrumental in the setting up of the British Legion and would develop strong links with the old enemy, Germany. He would produce many important books and develop still further his military ideas. And he would campaign long and hard for the Gallipoli expedition and the men who fought in it to get the recognition it and they deserved, not least to ensure that all who served in the campaign would get the 1914–15 Star as a campaign medal.

During 1917 and 1918 he had written a little book called *The Millennium*, actually published by Edward Arnold in 1919, but with its preface dated 11 November 1918. In it he developed his argument that great wars invariably led to bad peace settlements. He begged the British to set a better example:

> Now comes the tug of peace. If Britain is to maintain her pride of place throughout the most interesting half dozen pages of the histories of the future, her envoys must handle their problems without passion: she must show at the Peace Conference before the whole expectant globe that she has the broadest mind and the least rancorous heart of any of the Allies.[1]

He poured scorn on capitalist combines, likening them to vampires battening on the people for their own selfish ends. He appealed to Christian conscience:

> The Peace Conference will be sitting about two thousand years after the birth of Christ, a period during which no trace of

Christ's footsteps can be discovered in the dust of dead diplomacy and statecraft. Between Zero Hour AD and 1918, no Christian Government has ever, for one moment, modelled the conduct of their State upon that of the Christian ideal.[2]

He placed great faith in the projected League of Nations and called upon the world to 'Kill conscription and break the teeth of war!'[3]

Just as, while the war in South Africa was still in progress, he argued for the complete harmonization of the old enemy into the British Empire, now he argued for a generous peace towards the Germans and their acceptance into the League of Nations. We have to remember that Ian Hamilton was that old style of professional soldier who fought his enemy with might and main but with no particular animosity. He always warned against 'hate propaganda' in war because of the appalling long-term consequences it engendered, beginning with vindictive peace settlements and setting up new causes for future wars. In October 1918, opening a new YMCA hostel in Walthamstow, London, he reminded his audience that they were gathered to honour the memory of soldiers who fought, not for conquest, but to defend their homes and way of life and to end 'this frenzied orgy of hate'. He hoped the spirit of the YMCA would triumph over those who saw in the coming peace 'merely an opening for Capital, for combines, for boycotts and for concessions'.[4]

The Versailles conference, for him, was every bit as bad as he had feared. He was a popular general in the country and was in very great demand to give speeches opening the hundreds of war memorials that were springing up in every city, town and village. He later admitted that this wearying round of emotionally disturbing public engagements did more than anything else to turn him against war as an instrument of state policy but in the meantime he used these occasions to push along his message for a generous peace.

In April 1920 he told his audience, honouring the memory of those fallen who had been raised in Dr Barnardo's homes, 'Still we await the mutual agreement between victors and vanquished which alone is worthy of the name of peace.'[5] In August, after arguing that defeating the enemy was only one half of the battle, he clearly

upset part of his audience by urging, 'You have to turn against
your own old self; your own war propaganda; knock it out and
forget it. I don't say that the survivors are to shake hands with
those who have done to them and to the world so cruel a wrong:
that would be asking too much. But I say it is up to us to try now
and do what Kitchener did to the Boers – set our enemies going
again in a generous, large-handed way.'[6] Here he was clearly
interrupted by heckling because he has to say, 'Perhaps you do not
agree but anyway...' before going on to end his speech with the
warning that 'Asia is coming on and Asiatic Socialism and there's
no other way out of it for Europe west of the Vistula but reconciliation or ruin'. He was making a double warning here – against the
threat posed by the Bolshevist regime in Russia and his long-held
belief that Japan would one day pose a danger, either militarily or
economically. Because he thought in such a strategic and long-term
way about most things he could see the need for Europe to put
aside its old hostility and rebuild itself to face new dangers.

In October 1920 he said, 'One beautiful gesture might have lifted
this civilisation onto a higher plane and given it a fresh lease of life
– the gesture, familiar to every public schoolboy in England, of the
victor holding out his hand.'[7] In an article for the Central Press
Agency on the unveiling of the Cenotaph in London in November
of that year his theme was 'Material victories are often spiritual
defeats'.[8] Two years later his lonely, wearying campaign was still in
progress. In June 1922 at the unveiling of the war memorial in
Spalding, Lincolnshire, he said, 'Peace or war are the results of a
frame of mind. Don't be too hard on your enemies. Don't grind
them down now that they're beaten. Then I believe you will be
acting up to the ideals for which the brave men we commemorate
laid down their lives.'[9] He was giving warnings that would have
saved the world from the horrors of Hitler's Third Reich if they
had been heeded. On another occasion in 1922, and with the
behaviour of the French towards the Germans in mind, he said:

It is from the contempt and harshness of the Victor that the
spirit of revenge is bred in the defeated as surely as dirt breeds
disease. Never mind the League of Nations but try to do
something practical yourselves ... try the clean slate; try mag-

nanimity; it's not too late yet ... These boys of yours did not
die for Reparations; nor for Mesopotamia; nor even for Jerusa-
lem. They had hoped, God bless them, to kill war.[10]

His concern for social peace in Europe and the wider world was
central to his activities in the United Kingdom on behalf of the
demobilized servicemen and women. In October 1918, Hamilton
had been appointed by the Army Council to be chairman of a con-
sultative committee on the disposal of the huge profits (amounting
to several millions of pounds) made by the expeditionary forces'
canteen funds. His committee represented all the fighting services,
including the Dominions. Now he was anxious to use the committee as a means of drawing together the already burgeoning –
and splintering – ex-servicemen's organizations. His committee
proposed the creation of an 'Empire Services League', backed by all
three service ministries and funded by the Army Council. The
proposal was flatly refused by the War Office in February 1919,
ostensibly because it wanted the money disposed of quickly and
directly by the servicemen themselves. There is, however, a strong
suspicion that the government of the day did not want a single
organization with a potential membership of many millions
embracing all the ex-servicemen's organizations: it could have
wielded extraordinary political power.

Instead a new committee headed by Sir Julian Byng proceeded
to spend the 'United Services Fund' like water, meeting requests for
funds to build ex-servicemen's clubs and the like. Hamilton was
greatly disappointed that his old friend, Winston Churchill, now
the Secretary of State for War, had failed to take the opportunity to
'wipe out these small Primrose, Radical, Socialist and Bolshevist
federations and to bring them into one big League',[11] of a non-
political nature, which could have acted as a stabilizing factor in a
country going through a rather turbulent period in its domestic
politics. Indeed this antagonism between the small groups did lead
to disorderly clashes, culminating in the burning down of Leicester
Town Hall. The government belatedly realized things were getting
out of hand and recalled Lord Haig from South Africa, to begin a
two year tour of the country arguing for a unified ex-servicemen's
organization. The founding of the British Legion in June 1921 is just

one more testament to the visionary foresight of Sir Ian Hamilton, though he gave all the credit to Haig, whose authority was vital to the success of the venture.

Underlying all this concern for the ex-servicemen was a very real fear amongst the British ruling class, greatly exaggerated though it may have been, of the spread of Bolshevism. In his usual combative but educated way, Hamilton sought to engage the Social Democratic Federation (soon to become a founding component of the Communist Party of Great Britain) in debate through the pages of its journal, *Justice*. Having read denunciations of the capitalist exploitation of labour, Hamilton complained that by employing ex-servicemen on his newly acquired farm at Lullenden in Sussex (purchased from his friend, Winston Churchill), far from exploiting their labour for profit, he was actually losing money rather heavily. The SDF explained in a charming and good-natured riposte that Sir Ian was not a capitalist at all but a decent philanthropist, incapable of solving the problems of society by his altruism! Hamilton developed a great interest in the raising of a herd of Belted Galloway cattle at Lullenden. Prize-winning descendants of this herd of 'Belties' are still farmed by Hamiltons (themselves the descendants of Ian's brother, Vereker) in Scotland to this day.

In the midst of his work unveiling war memorials and addressing Old Comrades' Associations, Hamilton worked hard to build the British Legion and to win over non-Legion organizations to it, repeatedly telling the story of how his recommendations were ignored and two years wasted. His theme was the promotion of social peace and, again, he spoke a great deal of good sense in the process. At a dinner of the Glasgow and Lanarkshire London Association in November 1919, he told his audience:

We ... seem less inclined to rejoice together over the victory than to come to blows over the division of the spoils! ... when war was declared we all stood shoulder to shoulder. There was no sort of enquiry whether a man was a reckless anarchist or a stiff-necked Tory.... I don't suggest a peace between Capital and Labour – I like fighting – but, in the name of common sense, let's scrape together something worth fighting over before we strike one another dead.[12]

He called for a one-year armistice in industrial relations, 'till we get our trade back from America.... When we took off our coats to fight we pawned them with the U.S.A.!' He wanted Capital and Labour to unite and wage war on the bureaucracy of central government.

Hamilton's schemes for alleviating distress during the post-war slump were eminently sensible. He took up the idea, abroad in 1922, for the digging of a Forth–Clyde Canal. How better to use 50,000 men so newly trained in the digging of great trenches? The spending of £24,000,000 of public money would take 50,000 off the 'dole', create 80,000 ancillary jobs and transform the great central industrial belt of Scotland, giving a chance to plan and build lovely, healthy garden cities along the canal. It was this kind of thinking on the grand scale in social affairs that made Hamilton an attractive figure and possible ally to Ramsay MacDonald's Labour Party.

In 1923 Hamilton published a series of lectures addressed to the British Legion in the form of the book, *The Friends of England*. He discussed his dealings with many nations through his work as a military observer before 1914. Regretting the loss of Russia, a natural ally of the British in maintaining a balance of power in Europe, through revolution, he concluded that our best friends now should be the Germans. It expanded the ideas of his 1918–19 book, *The Millennium*, about the economic stupidity of reparations and the need for a generous peace. He called on ex-servicemen everywhere to unite in the search for peace. He was not impressed with the way France seemed to dominate the new League of Nations with the sole intent of enforcing in the harshest way the Versailles settlement. He confessed that he couldn't see the logic of sacking coal miners in Wales because we were making German miners give their coal away as reparations to fulfil the terms of Versailles. He gave full vent to his detestation of the hate propaganda used by the press and politicians in wartime, and contrasted it with the easy-going attitude of the British troops sent to occupy Germany after the war. The British Legion should set the example for unselfish gesture towards Germany.

He personally grasped the nettle and began a series of visits and exchanges with Germany, which invariably drew a great deal of publicity, leading to a fairly notorious incident in 1938. Hamilton had extensive connections with the old German Army before the war and spoke the language fluently.

In April 1922, Hamilton's old Gallipoli comrade, Alex Godley, was the new GOC, British Forces in Germany and he invited his former chief out for a visit. Hamilton took the opportunity to interview Erich von Ludendorff, and was able to report back to his colleagues (like Sir Henry Rawlinson, C-in-C, India) important information on the failures of German strategy in March 1918, and the impact on Ludendorff of the collapse of Bulgaria in late September. It wasn't long before Ludendorff and his young aides were ranting about the Bolshevik threat to Europe and how it would take the German army to subdue Russia and make it part of a European bulwark against America. Hamilton had a certain sympathy with these ideas, as he most certainly did with the German complaint that France was threatening to use black Senegalese troops to enforce the Versailles Treaty in the Saar region.

He returned to England to tell the British Legion that 'the outstanding feature of German post-war life' was the German Legion, a gathering of hundreds of regimental associations; a coming together of veterans, which, unlike in Britain, had been encouraged by the state, which was additional to the 2.5 million members of the Veterans' Associations.[13] He admired them as a bulwark against Bolshevism. That they might be a bulwark of a more sinister kind did not concern him just then. He publicly called for the British Legion to shake hands with the war veterans of Germany, and he was unanimously re-elected as President of the Metropolitan Area of the Legion by all its 224 delegates at the time. In 1928 he responded favourably to a suggestion that ceremonies at the Cenotaph should honour the war dead of both sides, but he seemed to be getting a little too far ahead of the members in this respect for, when he was canvassed about the setting up of an Anglo-German Society in February 1929, he replied that he would have to take British Legion advice before agreeing. 'A little caution is desirable,' he commented as he recalled that once in 1924 his area committee had asked for his resignation over his too-friendly attitude to Germany.

The publication in Germany in January 1929 of Erich Maria Remarque's *All Quiet on the Western Front* (soon translated into

English in March of that year) led to an interesting exchange of letters between Hamilton and the author, via Remarque's publisher, Putnam, recorded in Desmond McCarthy's journal *Life and Letters*.[14] Putnam, very shrewdly, sent an advance copy of the book to Sir Ian (which, in itself, tells us something of how highly he was regarded in the literary world in his day). Hamilton said he was glad someone had found a good translator 'clever enough to pick up Remarque's bomb and fling it across the Channel. We here just needed this bit of wakening up.' He saw it as a tale of a generation effectively lost to human progress through its suffering in the war. Having once been disposed to combat such inferences and conclusions he wrote, 'Now, sorrowfully, I must admit, there is a great deal of truth in them.' The terrible demands of attritional warfare had produced a 'lost' generation. How else could the flower of British youth have formed such a high proportion of the country's down-and-outs? Still the soldier rebelled at the full rigour of Remarque's message. 'This German goes too far . . . Even in the last and most accursed of all wars – the war "on the Western Front" . . . was there not the superb leading of forlorn hopes; the vague triumphs, vague but real, of dying for a cause?' Above all Hamilton praised those who came through the war with the courage to fight to make the world 'a better place for themselves and everyone else, including their ex-enemies'.

McCarthy and other critics praised Sir Ian's letter because it alone brought the author Remarque out of his self-imposed purdah. In an effusive, six-page letter Remarque, expressed his deep gratitude to 'Sir Hamilton' (sic) for his 'beautiful and understanding letter' and spoke of his 'admiration that my work had been so clearly, accurately and absolutely understood . . . You can well imagine that I was very uncertain what the effect of my book would be outside Germany and whether I have succeeded in making myself generally understood.' Hamilton had clearly related to the book as a tale of youth suffering in common from their confrontation with death in what they saw, each in their own way, as their duty. Both writers could appreciate the quiet heroism of the ordinary soldier. Hamilton perceived that Remarque was not preaching resignation but was sending out 'a clarion call to face up to the difficulties caused by the war and begin to build for the future'.

In his reply to this letter Hamilton once again spoke with enormous compassion for the unemployed in Britain. 'When they went to war they were the flower, not the dregs, of our people.' During those vital years between the ages of eighteen and twenty-two, when they should have been mastering their trade, they were manning the trenches, which made them especially vulnerable when recession struck in the post-war era. For him, Remarque's book showed exactly how his young heroes were not only robbed of their education but of the energy and regenerative power to see them through their early struggles as citizens. He explained that his work in the British Legion was to get the veterans to band together to influence their own government, to help one another and to strive for some high ideal, the highest being peace. He finished by urging Remarque to write another book exposing the enormity of modern war. This old soldier knew only too well how seductive an appeal the military life could have. 'For great and terrible is the counter-power of the romance and beauty of war, to which you wisely make no reference in your book.' He reminds the author of the thrill of watching an entire German Army Corps move past at the parade march, flags flying and drums crashing. 'These are the legends and illusions you have got to transfix very quickly with your pen.'

In the midst of all this activity, Hamilton kept up his own study of military history and modern military practice. In May 1920 his two-volume *Gallipoli Diary* was published. It was based on the daily diary he kept during the campaign, written up as we have already seen, in 1916 with a considerable addition of official documents, in much the same way as Sir Douglas Haig 'filled out' his own diary, to reveal the true difficulties he was labouring under. Mrs Shield described the contents as being 'chiselled, polished and re-polished' between 1916 and 1920. He reminded his readers that, ever since the South African war, he had determined to keep an accurate record of his campaigns, just in case posterity should call him to account. All the later additions were of documents either in the public domain via the Dardanelles Commission or were reprinted with official permission. He used footnotes to draw the reader's attention to facts that were not known to him at the time but had a bearing upon the narrative. It was in a long footnote in Volume Two that he explained a hiatus in his diary during the most critical days of the August offensive. During this gap in his daily record he accepted a report of IX Corps giving an account of activity on the 8 August, which asked him to give credit to Hammersley and his troops for their efforts 'against strenuous opposition and great difficulty'. With no other news to guide him, Hamilton took this at face value and sent a congratulatory message to Stopford, which he found flung back in his face at the Dardanelles Commission as an excuse for the subsequent lack of activity at Suvla. It was the alarming message from Aspinall and Hankey that finally alerted him to the dismal failure there.

Hamilton felt he owed it to the soldiers, sailors and airmen of the campaign to place his diary before the public. He certainly did not intend to 'leave my diary to be flung at posterity from behind the cover of my coffin. In case anyone wishes to challenge anything I have said, I must be above ground to give him satisfaction'.[15] It was widely reviewed and generally well received. Even those critics who were strong advocates of the main effort being made against the Germans on the Western Front admitted that Hamilton had written a masterly and practical exposition of the Easterners' case. It did reopen the rift with Sir John Maxwell, who wrote to the papers about Hamilton's obsession with obtaining a brigade of Gurkhas from Egypt when no such brigade existed. Whether this simply exposed him to the charge of being less than fully helpful to Hamilton when he needed him most is for others to decide.

One interesting aspect of the diaries is the influence they may have had on other military writers of the time. In one remarkable passage, discussing the need to create feints around the Dardanelles to assist the actual assault landings, Hamilton spoke of the need to 'upset the equilibrium' of the enemy commander and to render him 'unable to concentrate either his mind or his troops against us'. Sea power and the mobility it offered was to be used to 'rattle the enemy however imperturbable may be his nature and whatever he knows about us'.[16] These ideas would certainly have been read and must have appealed to the young Captain Basil Liddell Hart, who was soon to leave the army and become a strong critic of the frontal assaults of the Western Front, while developing his own theory of a strategy of indirect approach to achieve victory in war. He became a friend and admirer of Sir Ian Hamilton and would often illustrate his ideas by reference to the potentialities of his campaign.

Hamilton also completely revised *The Soul and Body of an Army*, adding all his experience of the First World War to what was already a remarkably forward-looking book when its publication was overtaken by events in the summer of 1914. He thought the army was failing to absorb the lessons of the recently finished war and blamed the Official Secrets Act and the dead hand of War Office bureaucracy; he favoured complete freedom of expression in print for all serving officers. The challenges posed by the new technology of war required a new free-thinking spirit in the services. Having made a case for sound organization of the army, he deplored the destruction of the General Staff as its members rushed off to join the BEF in France at the start of the war, leaving the War Office to the tender mercies of Lord Kitchener, widely known as 'Kitchener of Khaos'.

A new chapter on numbers in war allowed Hamilton to continue his fulminations against conscription and the senseless deployment of masses of troops. Recognizing that this was now a fact of life in modern war, he insisted that numbers were only a major factor if applied to the decisive point. The new skills required were the deception of the enemy as to the real objective and the restoration of surprise in strategy and tactics. Developments in modern war had provided the means to restore fluid mobility and surprise to the battlefield and it would take forward-thinking, flexible soldiers to adapt to the new circumstances. His most important ideas were contained in two new chapters added, laying out his ideas on the higher direction of war and the organization of troops.

He gave his complete backing to the ongoing debate in the country for a single and indivisible Ministry of Defence, for a United Services General Staff and for a United Services Staff College to teach the necessary combined doctrine, and he took it all to its logical conclusion by calling for a unified national officer cadet school. His personal experience of the problems of combined services warfare during the Gallipoli campaign were the mainstay of his reforming zeal, but he had held these opinions before 1914. He also feared, with very good reason, that the new Royal Air Force would soon begin to put on 'regimental side' and seek to distance itself from the other services. He saw the basic problem of high command and the higher direction of war as common to all services, and so he placed great value in senior officers changing jobs the way ministers change portfolios. This would help to end inter-service rivalry and correct the endless, aimless drifting of national defence policy. He would do anything to save officers from the monotony and boredom of their long years in junior rank. Cross-posting within and between services was one solution. He retained his scheme to put staff officers out into a major industrial concern for six months to learn new approaches to administration. In the considerable discussion in the military journals of the day, these ideas were widely aired. More than one advocate of the idea felt them to be doomed to failure as prime ministers were not likely to give up three sets of patronage (the three service ministries) and create one enormously powerful one.

On the technical side Hamilton was a great advocate of integrating tanks into the infantry, adding a fifth heavy weapons company to each battalion. He would have retained the division as the main organizational building block of the army, keeping it small and mobile, with greatly enhanced firepower, allocating aircraft to it as 'flying artillery'. He even spoke of them as being 'air portable', which would have been a great boon in the post-war army, with its huge responsibilities for imperial policing. It is unfortunate that these reformist ideas, which would have seen large savings to the public purse, were ignored by governments that were in severe financial difficulty in the inter-war period.

It was probably on the basis of this book and his known advanced social ideas that he was approached at some stage in 1924 by Ramsay MacDonald's Labour Party as a possible candidate for the post of Secretary of State for War in a Labour government. He declined the offer because, he said, he could never accept collective cabinet responsibility in a socialist administration. Once again, as with the post of CIGS in 1914, we are left to wonder what his contribution might have been at the highest level, though in both events his tenure would have been overtaken by the tide of history.

The other book Hamilton did a lot of work on but that was not published in his lifetime was his study of military command,

which was also greatly transformed by the experience of the First
World War. As we might have guessed, he was an enemy of those
generals whose obsession for 'safety first' measures led to lost
opportunity in war and he was in favour of the fast-track promotion of bold young officers, who were willing to hazard their
reputation on the battlefield but whose constant activity seized
the initiative in every situation. These had been sadly lacking at
Gallipoli, both on 25 April and repeatedly in August 1915. He
expressed his admiration for Sir Douglas Haig's staff work and
regretted that he was not made CIGS in 1914; by implication he
was also regretting that Haig was given command on the Western
Front to pursue his relentless and costly attritional warfare there.
He admired Winston Churchill's bold strategic thinking, not least
the attempt to knock Turkey out of the war by attacking her
through the Dardanelles, but also the way he used the Royal Naval
Division on the German flank at Antwerp in 1914 and employed
Royal Navy funds to develop the tank as a weapon to tackle the
problem of trench deadlock. His point was that the commander
had to be a man capable of far-reaching and imaginative thought,
while managing a vast conglomerate of departments run by specialist experts in their field. His *beau ideal* of a commander was
Marshal Foch, who co-ordinated the great Allied offensives of 1918
with a tiny personal staff while the huge headquarters staffs got on
with running the armies.

   Hamilton's discussion of the role of Lord Kitchener at the War
Office reached a new level of criticism of his old chief and could
well be the reason he didn't bring the book to completion. While
accepting that Kitchener was just the national hero needed to
mobilize broad popular support for the war in 1914, Hamilton
ruthlessly exposed Kitchener's destruction of the good order of the
War Office and the army by his determination to run the war as
his personal fiefdom. After describing Kitchener as the 'Master of
Expedients' Hamilton went on to write, in one intensely telling
comment: 'I say it with confidence because I have, for a space, gone
as near as any human being could go to sharing his arctic loneliness.'[17] The loneliness of high command should never be far from
our thoughts when we sit in comfort and pass judgement on the
practitioners of war.

One interesting passage tells us much about Hamilton's attitude to official bureaucracy but also to the wider society in which he lived.

> We must send packing, once and for all, a good deal of that 'form' to which we adhere so slavishly in many respects. In doing that we shall help to make ourselves into that sort of army that is looking forward. For when we get rid of this 'form' which dictates to us what subjects we may discuss with one another, what sort of interests we should pursue outside our profession and so on, we shall find ourselves face to face with the real values of life. Then we shall be able to tolerate the man of independent mind, encourage him, teach him, learn from him.[18]

The official history of the military operations at Gallipoli also engaged his attention in the 1920s. While the war was still in progress he had been in correspondence with Captain Atkinson of the historical section of the CID (the future Oxford don and prolific military historian) who had already set the tone for this work.

> Had the decision been taken after the failure of the May offensive (in France) to concentrate all offensive effort at Gallipoli, your success of June 28th might have been made a strategical victory instead of only a brilliant tactical success. One does clearly get the picture of England torn between two policies for the simultaneous execution of which her forces were inadequate, and between which those in power found it impossible to decide.[19]

It was the established practice that drafts of the history were circulated to the senior officers involved for their comment, giving rise to much criticism that the need to protect reputations led to a watered-down version of events. It was in just one such draft that Hamilton saw for the first time that vital order of 6 April 1915 from Kitchener to Maxwell ordering the latter to hold all his troops available to reinforce Hamilton as needed. We can only wonder at the effect this may have had during the manpower crisis immediately after the assault landings. It is generally agreed that the official

historian, Brigadier-General C. F. Aspinall-Oglander (Hamilton's
trusted general staff officer, who had added Oglander to his name
to meet the conditions of a family bequest), has written one of the
best of the official histories, certainly in terms of literary skill, to
which the majestic and historic setting of the campaign must have
lent itself. His preface spelled out clearly the principal thrust of the
history.

> Certainly the state of Britain's military resources in January 1915
> did not admit of any new and immediate commitments in
> addition to a spring offensive in France. But strong support is
> not lacking for the view that a wiser policy at this time would
> have been to have to regard the importance of the Western
> front as latent, to cancel the spring offensive in France, and to
> order a temporary defensive attitude in that theatre while
> striking a strong and sudden blow in the Near East with the
> object of destroying Turkey, succouring Russia, and rallying
> the Balkan states to the side of the Entente.[20]

Commenting on the cramped conditions of the peninsula, the
lack of rest for the troops, the 'indescribable and revolting plague
of flies' and the resulting endemic disease, he wrote: 'It may be
doubted whether any army has operated under more demoralizing
conditions than those which faced Sir Ian Hamilton's forces at the
Dardanelles.'[21] Yet for a fraction of the losses incurred in some of
the battles of the Western Front, these forces 'destroyed the flower
of the Turkish Army, safeguarded the Suez Canal and laid the
foundation of Turkey's final defeat'.[22] In later years Hamilton
reminded many audiences that, in terms of battle casualties, the
Allies lost two on the Western front to every German and on the
Gallipoli peninsula that ratio of Allied to Turkish loss was exactly
reversed. We know from draft chapters of the manuscript that the
final version of the official history (which appeared in two volumes
in 1929 and 1932) left out or toned down many criticisms of
Hamilton's perceived excessive optimism at various stages of the
campaign.

In 1929 the Boer memoir *Commando*, by Deneys Reitz, was published to great acclaim. In 1931 Hamilton wrote *Anti-Commando*,
the story of the remarkable Sir Aubrey Woolls-Sampson of the

Imperial Light Horse, from material supplied by the Sampson family in South Africa. Once again he was anxious to see that the troops under his command were fully credited for their many excellent achievements in a war where little notice was taken of the many real successes they won while, as usual, much was made of all their reverses.

Besides all this literary activity, the unveiling of memorials and the work in creating the British Legion, Hamilton was constantly in demand as a public speaker to every kind of military and civilian organization, foreign and domestic. He also contributed many introductions to other military works, especially and obviously those relating to Gallipoli. He was not averse to contributing to books openly critical of the campaign but his message was consistent to the end: the allies were not driven from the peninsula, they left it at a time of their own choosing, and the campaign was defeated not in the Dardanelles but in London where it never received the unqualified backing it deserved.

A major speech to the Birkenhead British Legion in November 1932 is worth studying for the way it gives the main themes of his considered critique of the conduct of the campaign.

First and foremeost, I blame myself for things having gone so wrong. Not for my tactical plans or military orders. These have by now run the gauntlet of examination by experts, home and foreign, and still stand upon their legs. No; but because I so culpably neglected the ceaseless internecine war raging on the Home Front of Whitehall and Fleet Street.

Secondly, because we had no effective General Staff at the War Office to weigh impartially the values of the various war theatres and to distribute support accordingly.

Thirdly, because of the undue influence under these conditions of GHQ in France plus the Government of France and its *G[rand] Q[uartier] G[énéral]*.

Fourthly, because of an inferiority complex on the part of senior Naval Officers at home and at the front who, personally fearless though they were, began to tremble for their beloved ships as soon as they saw a fort. When Nelson saw a fort he began to tremble not for his ship but for the fort, and I wish to tell you right now that we did possess at the Dardanelles the very spit and spirit of Nelson; ... and who, had he been given the chance, would have taken the Fleet slap through the Narrows within one week of our landing. To possess a man like that; to see him; to listen to him and then not use him! ... That man, I hardly need say, was Sir Roger Keyes, a leader somewhat hasty for creepy-crawly ways of peace perhaps but for war – without a peer. There is a Latin tag which being interpreted means 'They can because they think they can.' Roger Keyes looked well at the Narrows and thought he could.

Fifthly, the Suvla Generals. I will not dilate on this point or say more than one thing which is undeniable. They were the exact opposites of Roger Keyes inasmuch as it might truthfully have been said of them, 'They can't because they think they can't.' The Turkish official account gives the following reason for our failure at Suvla in the following words: 'The force which landed at Suvla did not attack vigorously and swiftly the weak force opposed to it'. The day before yesterday I got a letter from an ex-Sergeant of the Royal Engineers of the 53rd Division who said he meant coming here tonight. I suppose therefore he is sitting amongst this audience. He has given me his opinion on Suvla Bay tactics in the following words: 'I agree the new divisions were young and inexperienced but we were full of enthusiasm and with fearless leaders we would have taken the fence.'[23]

Hamilton closed this speech by reciting some of the more insulting passages from Keith Murdoch's infamous letter of 23 September 1915.

When the British began developing Singapore as their major Far Eastern naval base, Hamilton renewed his warnings that it was too vulnerable to attack, especially from the land side. He wasn't afraid to name Japan as the likely foe. He argued for Ceylon to be developed as a more secure base.

In his duties as an official of the British Legion he was inundated with letters from old soldiers, desperately sad letters telling of difficulties besetting men who had given service to their country and were now sinking into unrelieved poverty. His sense of helplessness comes through in his replies, where he had to routinely pass these cries for help on to some other charitable authority. This wearisome and demoralizing task must have added fuel to his campaign for a new understanding with Germany. In 1934 he embraced the important medium of the cinema by introducing the film *Forgotten Men*, made by Sir John Hammerton using interviews with combatants from all services and nations to push home the message that Europe must never again turn to war to settle her differences.[24]

Hamilton's next visit to Germany was an official one to the old Field Marshal von Hindenburg, to receive back the drums of the Gordon Highlanders that had been lost in 1914. The private conversations apparently avoided all references to the Great War, but Hamilton did, of course, begin to meet the officials of the new Nazi regime, including Rudolf Hess.

We must try and dispense with the wisdom of hindsight as we hear that, in July, 1934, whilst addressing the Yorkshire West Riding British Legion, Hamilton made a glowing reference to a speech by Hess of a few days before. In it Hess is reported as issuing an appeal 'to the front line soldiers in other states – they are more fitted to rebuild the bridge of understanding'. Hamilton remarked, 'At this meeting of front line soldiers it would be a shame not to respond to the challenge.'[25] He described his meeting with Hess and assured his audience that 'Hess is a very fine young fellow and that he is far more than the mere mouthpiece of Herr Hitler. As to his appeal to the front line ex-servicemen – he is right.' He went on to reinforce his pan-European, anti-Bolshevik message by concluding:

> If we want to support the cause of peace we must separate our opinions of the actions of a Government fighting for its existence from our feelings for the Germans as a whole. There are people in London and I daresay in Leeds who are only too pleased if they see misfortunes closing in upon our ex-enemies. Alas that it should be so for in my humble opinion, the collapse of Germany would be the most deadly misfortune to Europe. The one thing that can save Civilization is sympathy between ex-enemies.[26]

Again we have to note that Hamilton, passionate speaker and writer that he was, could be very selective in his reading of history. This eulogy to Hess and his organizations of old soldiers came just a year after the purge of the SA that we know as the 'Night of the

Long Knives', when the Nazi Party showed just how brutal it could be, even towards its own members. Yet Hamilton was not alone in Britain to fail to see the danger that it posed to the very cause of peace for which he fought so hard.

Hamilton's increasingly extreme anti-war stance reached its apogee in August 1938, when he was an extraordinarily spry eighty-five years old, in a somewhat bizarre and unfortunate turn of events that had an innocent enough beginning. The Metropolitan Area Council of the British Legion had organized a visit to Germany by some forty of its members, to lay some wreaths at German war memorials as a token of peace. The party was led by Sir Ian Hamilton.

His speeches, delivered in impeccable German, took on an increasingly sentimental tone, along the lines that if the world were run by old soldiers instead of autocrats and bureaucrats there would be no more wars. A day or so later, during the Berlin phase of the trip, he was suddenly whisked off by air to Munich to lunch with that 'fine young fellow', Rudolf Hess. Within a few hours he was taking tea with Adolf Hitler at Berchtesgarden. Hitler soon realized that interpreters were unnecessary; he was said to be awe-struck at being in the presence of a man who had learned his German amongst the heroes of 1871. The two men had private talks for some ninety minutes during which Hitler seems to have conducted a 'charm offensive' on the old general. Hamilton did recognize it for what it was; he has left us very full accounts of the meeting. But he did take Germany's side very strongly against Czech 'provocations', and came away convinced that Hitler was a democratic leader who was desperate to maintain peace in Europe and who was, if anything, restraining the 'war party' in Germany.

In an interview with the *Sunday Graphic* given on his return, Hamilton repeated his assertion that the old fighters of Europe alone were capable of making and keeping the peace. 'The bogey of the fire-eating Hitler is the greatest danger to peace today. It is dangerous in its effect on us; it is dangerous in its effect on Germany. But the ex-servicemen of the two nations are helping to lay it.'[27]

His closing remarks in this interview are a good summary of how he had come to this peace-at any-price sort of stand:

> Yes, certainly, I have been a soldier all my life and have loved my profession. But for years after the war I unveiled a war memorial almost every week, and the people who were given the best seats were the widows and orphans, the mutilated, the blind and the parents who have lost their sons. It was this that brought about my change of heart and enlisted me in this new and greater campaign.[28]

Hamilton's reflections on the Great War exhibit his attitude to soldiering and war in general. He was a warrior in the old, Romantic sense of the word. He loved fighting, but bore no particular grudge or ill will to the adversary. On the contrary, he often admired 'a bonny fighter', regardless of his origins, often preferring the foe to some of the money-grubbing civilians on his own side. The other over-riding obsession in his reflections on war in general is his detestation of conscription and mass warfare. He is well known in British military history for his defence of the volunteer principle and his opposition to compulsory service. Is it because he knew just how seductive the appeal of soldiering could be that he feared to unleash it unchained upon the world? Or did he see, in a Clausewitzian way, that total war logically led to total destruction?

Either way, the First World War was, for him, the proof of every warning he had given on the subject. His conviction that mass warfare bred mass hatreds that led to more of the same meant that even before the war had ended he was campaigning for a generous peace. In this he appealed to the very highest, most altruistic aspects of our human nature; it was a noble appeal; it would have saved the world a great deal of suffering if he had been heeded. We might, quite bluntly, have been spared the horrors of Nazi fascism, the Second World War and the subsequent Communist domination of Eastern Europe. It fell on deaf ears but Hamilton is to be admired for his generous nature and far-seeing wisdom.

What is harder to accept is that his warnings, now turned to a deep-seated pacifism, failed to see that his appeals to friendship with Germany played into the hands of a dangerous and repugnant regime. Let us just remember that, as Hitler came to power in 1933, Hamilton was eighty years old and had spent nearly fifteen years unveiling monuments to the dead, giving speeches to their memory and being bombarded with letters by old servicemen begging, pleading for help as they sank into poverty in 'the land fit for heroes'. These letters are painful to read even today and there really were a very great many of them. Even a certain naivety might be forgiven him.

The Hamiltons continued to live at 1 Hyde Park Gardens, and were a continuing feature of the London social scene. Jean had fostered two babies, Harry and Rosalind. Although the Hamiltons adopted them in 1919, Ian referred to them as 'her' children and seems to have had little to do with their upbringing. He did take a special interest in educating the youth of the nation in civic virtue and was a governor of Wellington College, a very popular elected rector of Edinburgh University and a well-liked visitor and speaker at the Gordon Boys' School. He kept his association with the Gordon Highlanders, of which he was the Honorary Colonel for many years, entertaining officers and other ranks at his London home throughout the war. He spent the war years in London, refusing to 'run away from a fight', though Jean's ill health had seen her leave for Scotland. She died there early in 1941, leaving a void in Ian's life; he published a memoir to her soon after. It was perhaps a blessing that she did not live to see her adopted son, Harry Knight, killed in action while serving as an officer in the Scots Guards in North Africa later that year.

Hamilton produced two volumes of autobiography, *When I Was a Boy* in 1939 and *Listening for the Drums* in 1944. Both are disarmingly frank about his human frailties, and are full of deep insights into the society and the army in which he spent his life. He remained alert and active to the end. In June 1947, well into his ninety-fourth year, he was able to make a demanding car journey to receive the Freedom of Inverness and was officiating at a visit to the Gordon Boys' School by Lord Wavell in July. He passed away peacefully at his London home on 12 October 1947 and is buried beside his wife at Doune in his native Scotland.

Some ten years later the nation recognized his service by opening a memorial to him in St Paul's Cathedral. His old friend, Winston Churchill, paid tribute to a 'brilliant and chivalrous man' who had served his country well.

Postscript

In 1934 Hamilton had the unusual experience of assisting Basil Liddell Hart in writing his own obituary. Both men were enemies of attritional warfare as conducted on the Western Front and much was made in the article of the ability of a sea power to achieve strategic surprise in its conduct of military operations. It gave a most honest appraisal of Hamilton as a general, and of the British army in 1915. 'The secret of his continued mental activity seemed to lie in his imagination. It was certainly the quality which distinguished him from most of his professional contemporaries.' After attributing his failure to the strength of the defending enemy and the relative paucity of his own resources, Liddell Hart made this important point about the transitional nature of the army at this stage of the war.

> Another cause, however, which has received less attention lay in the defects of the military system under which he was called on to operate; the system arising from the "foreign growth" of mass armies and large staff organisations, whereby command ceased to be a direct force and became a distant spring of influence filtering down through many intermediary channels.
>
> Such a system contracted [sic] the current of personal leadership which Ian Hamilton, far more than most modern generals, was capable of generating. His troubles may largely be traced to an undesired 'remoteness' which was naturally irksome to him. If he was diffident, and in a sense dilatory, in breaking through these barriers and establishing contact with the leaders in the fighting line at the crucial time, when the opportunity of victory still existed, his reluctance to intervene may be explained by his natural kindliness. Intervention demanded a ruthlessness

from which, despite his high personal courage, he instinctively shrank.[1]

Liddell Hart thought that history, especially through Turkish and German accounts, had redeemed him. He emphasized Hamilton's efforts at reform by reminding his readers not to forget 'that he had to handle an instrument that was inadequate for modern warfare. He, almost alone, had pointed out its defects almost a dozen years before, with no result except his own injury.'

Once again the main critique of Hamilton, after accepting that his task at Gallipoli was unique and overwhelmingly difficult, comes down to questions of his personality. A man who cannot be faulted in terms of experience, intellect or personal courage, stands condemned for being 'too nice'. This is hardly a satisfactory explanation for the failure of one of the great strategic efforts of the First World War. We must constantly remind ourselves that the British Army of 1914–15 was not the formidable war-winning intrument it had become by 1917–18. The staff orthodoxy of its day acted as a severe restraint on its generals. A careful reading of the exchange of cables between Hamilton and the authorities in London shows that he was a great deal more insistent with Kitchener over the inadequate resourcing of his force than has been generally accepted. As was suggested by the opening quotation from Rayne Kruger, referring to an earlier war in which Hamilton distinguished himself, we do not need to hunt out individuals to blame, but rather see a failure of the British political and military system to cope with the demands of a mass, industrialized warfare with which it was wholly unfamiliar.

Ian Hamilton was a Highland warrior of the old school. A man who loved fighting and often said he was born two or three centuries too late! An infantryman who was always abreast of, and very often in front of, the most modern developments of his chosen profession. This study is replete with his warnings and predictions coming to pass. This soldier poet was fascinated by the Modern and repelled by it in equal measure – the very definition of a Romantic figure in history.

Notes

Preface

1. Breakwell, Glynis & Spacie, Keith, *Pressures Facing Commanders*, Strategic & Combat Studies Institute Occasional Paper No. 29, 1997

1. From Boyhood to Army Commission, 1853–73

1. See Spiers, Edward, *The Late Victorian Army 1868–1902*, Manchester University Press, 1992, Chapter 4
2. Hamilton, Gen. Sir Ian, *When I Was a Boy*, Faber, 1939, p. 23
3. Ibid, p. 27

2. Service in India (With an African Interlude), 1873–84

1. Hamilton, Gen. Sir Ian, *Listening for the Drums*, Faber, 1944, p. 23
2. Ibid, p. 60
3. Ibid, p. 120
4. Ibid, p. 136
5. Ibid, p. 149
6. Hamilton, Capt. Ian, *The Fighting of the Future*, Kegan, Paul, Trench, 1885, p. 20
7. Hamilton, *Listening for the Drums*, p. 154
8. Ibid, p. 158
9. Ibid, p. 171

3. Service in Africa, India, Burma and England, 1884–99

1. Hamilton, Gen. Sir Ian, *Listening for the Drums*, p. 175
2. Birdwood, Field Marshall Lord, *Khaki and Gown*, Ward Lock, 1941, p. 29
3. Hamilton, *Listening for the Drums*, p. 197
4. Roberts, F.M. Lord, *Forty-One Years in India*, Macmillan, 1898, p. 528
5. Hamilton, *Listening for the Drums*, p. 213
6. Hamilton, ibid, p. 160

7. Ian Hamilton to Jean Hamilton, 24 April, 1895, quoted in Hamilton, I. B. M., *The Happy Warrior*, Cassell, 1966, p. 107
8. Hamilton, *Listening for the Drums*, p. 267
9. Hamilton, ibid, pp. 241–2
10. Churchill, Randolph S., *Winston S. Churchill: Youth 1874–1900*, Heinemann, 1966, p. 384
11. Hamilton, *Listening for the Drums*, p. 247

4. War in South Africa, 1899–1902

1. Penn Symons to Hamilton, 17 October 1899, Hamilton Papers in the private collection of A. V. Hamilton
2. Hamilton, I. B. M., *The Happy Warrior*, Cassell, 1966, p. 145
3. Ibid, p. 145
4. Pakenham, Thomas, *The Boer War*, Weidenfeld & Nicolson, 1979, p. 161
5. Ibid, p. 178
6. Griffith, Kenneth, *Thank God We Kept the Flag Flying*, Hutchinson, 1974, p. 224
7. Hamilton to Spenser Wilkinson, 8 March 1900, quoted in Pakenham, op. cit., p. 369
8. Ibid, p. 370
9. Hamilton to Roberts, 10 March 1900, Hamilton Archives 2/2/5
10. Amery, L. S., *The Times History of the War in South Africa: Volume 4*, Sampson Low, 1906, p. 88
11. Churchill, Winston S., *Ian Hamilton's March*, Longman, 1900, p. 60
12. Smith-Dorrien, Gen. Sir H., *Memories of 48 Years Service*, John Murray, 1925, p. 182
13. Pakenham, op. cit., p. 451
14. See File 2/6/8 Hamilton Archives
15. Hamilton, Ian B. M., op. cit., p. 174
16. Ibid, p. 175
17. Hamilton, Gen. Sir Ian, *The Commander*, Hollis & Carter, 1957, p. vii
18. Arthur, Sir George, *Life of Lord Kitchener: Vol. 2*, Macmillan, 1920, p. 52
19. Hamilton to Roberts, 16 February 1902, Hamilton Archives 2/3/17
20. Hamilton to Churchill, 20 January 1902, Hamilton Archives 2/2/9

5. Quartermaster General and Service in Manchuria, 1904–5

1. Minutes of Evidence to the Royal Commission on the War in South Africa 1903: Vol. 1. Cmnd Paper, 1790, p. 534
2. Ibid, Vol. 2. Cmnd Paper, 1791, Answer to Question 13887
3. Ibid, pp. 107–13. The quotations up to and including the mobile steel shields are taken from this report.
4. Ian Hamilton to Jean Hamilton, 7 February 1904, Hamilton Archives 3/2/3

5. Ibid, 8 February 1904
6. Ibid, 9 February 1904
7. Ibid, 10 February 1904
8. Ibid, 15 February 1904
9. Ibid, 22 February 1904
10. Ibid, 27 February 1904
11. Ibid, 5 March 1904
12. Ian Hamilton to Churchill, 15 April 1904, Churchill, Randolph S. *Winston S. Churchill: Companion Vol. 2: Part 1 1901–1907*, Heinemann, 1969, p. 336
13. Ian Hamilton to Jean Hamilton, 4 April 1904, Hamilton Archives 3/2/3
14. Ibid, Postscript 3 to 4 April 1904
15. St John Brodrick to Ian Hamilton, 8 June 1904, Hamilton Archives 3/2/3
16. Hamilton, Lt.-Gen. Sir Ian, *A Staff Officer's Scrap Book: Volume 1*, Edward Arnold, 1905, p. 70
17. Ibid, p. 271
18. Ian Hamilton to Jean Hamilton, 25 December 1904, Hamilton Archives 3/2/3

6. Southern Command, 1905–9

1. Hamilton, Lt.-Gen. Sir Ian, *A Staff Officer's Scrap Book: Volume 1*, Edward Arnold, 1905, p. v
2. Ibid, p. 5
3. Ibid, p. 116–17
4. Ibid, p. 117
5. Ibid, p. 329
6. Ibid, p. 331
7. Hamilton to Nellie Sellar, 31 January 1907, Hamilton Archives 21/2
8. Hamilton, Lt.-Gen. Sir Ian, *A Staff Officer's Scrap Book: Volume 2*, Edward Arnold, 1907, p. 33
9. Ibid, p. 46
10. Ibid, p. 186
11. Hamilton to Leo Amery, 20 July 1909, Hamilton Archives 4/1/8
12. Hamilton to Leo Amery, 7 August 1909, Hamilton Archives 4/1/8
13. Hamilton to Nellie Sellar, 3 February 1907, Hamilton Archives 21/2
14. Hamilton to Methuen, 16 January 1908, Hamilton Archives 4/3/5
15. Hamilton to Methuen, 26 January 1908, Hamilton Archives 4/3/5
16. Hamilton to Methuen, 15 February 1908, Hamilton Archives 4/3/5
17. Hamilton to Methuen, 1 March 1908, Hamilton Archives 4/3/5
18. Brett, M. V. *The Journals and Letters of Reginald, Viscount Esher*, Nicholson & Watson 1934, Vol. 2, entry for 13 January 1908
19. Hamilton to Churchill, 16 January 1906. Churchill, Randolph S., *Winston S. Churchill Companion Vol. 2: Part 1 1901–1907*, Heinemann, 1969, p. 426

20. Hamilton to Nellie Sellar, 14 December 1906, re: Speech to Midland Volunteer Association, Hamilton Archives 21/1
21. Speech to Boys Brigade, Plymouth 6 March 1907, Hamilton Archives 21/2
22. Hamilton Archives 4/4/2 Territorial Lectures, Oxford 14 May 1908
23. Hamilton Archives 4/4/2 Territorial Lecture by Gen. Haking to a meeting of businessmen
24. Travers, Tim, *The Killing Ground*, Allen & Unwin 1987, p. 44–5, quoting from Hamilton, Gen. Sir Ian, *Compulsory Service*, John Murray, 1910, p. 121–2
25. Hamilton, Gen. Sir Ian, *A Staff Officer's Scrap Book: Volume 2*, p. 232

7. Adjutant-General and GOC, Mediterranean, 1909–14

1. Hamilton, Gen. Sir, Ian *Compulsory Service*, John Murray, 1910, p. 59
2. Hamilton to J. Strachey, 12 August 1909, Hamilton Archives 4/1/8
3. Report on Russian Manoeuvres, 1 September 1909, Hamilton Archives 4/2/6
4. Ibid
5. Hamilton, Gen. Sir Ian, *The Friends of England*, Allen & Unwin, 1923, p. 10
6. Ibid, p. 233
7. Hamilton Archives 5/3/1
8. Hamilton Archives 5/3/25 (see pages 8 & 24)
9. Sir Leslie Rundle to Miss Sellar, 12 April 1914, Hamilton Archives 21/9
10. Hamilton Archives 5/3/23
11. Hamilton Archives 5/3/27
12. Ibid
13. Ibid
14. Serle, Geoffrey, *John Monash: A Biography*, Melbourne University Press, 1982, p. 197
15. Hamilton to Seely 29 March 1914, Hamilton Archives 5/1/17
16. Sir Leslie Rundle to Miss Sellar 12 April 1914, Hamilton Archives 21/9
17. Ian Hamilton to Jean, 11 May 1914, Hamilton Papers in the private collection of A. V. Hamilton
18. See Hamilton Archives 15/1/36–7 for drafts completed in 1913 and 1914
19. Ian Hamilton to Nellie Sellar, 6 February 1912, Hamilton Archives 21/3

8. The World War Spreads, 1914–15

1. Brett, M. V., *The Journals and Letters of Reginald, Viscount Esher*, Nicholson & Watson, 1934, Vol. 3, entry for 12 August 1914
2. Hamilton to Churchill 8 March 1915, Hamilton Archives 7/1/1

9. Attack at Gallipoli, 1915

1. PRO. CAB 19/31. Cables presented as evidence to Dardanelles Commission, No. 84

2. Ibid, No. 94

3. Ibid, No. 143

4. Asquith to Venetia Stanley, 30 September 1914. Brock, Michael and Eleanor (eds), *H. H. Asquith, Letters to Venetia Stanley*, OUP, 1982 (L. 169)

5. Hamilton to Churchill, 5 March and 10 March 1915, Hamilton Archives . 7/1/1

6. *Manual of Combined Naval and Military Operations*, 2nd edition, War Office, 2 September 1913, Hamilton Archives 7/4/2

7. Hamilton to Churchill, 12 March 1915, Hamilton Archives 7/1/1

8. PRO. CAB 19/31, Cable No. 299

9. Ibid, No. 298 (sic)

10. Ibid, No. 314

11. Ibid, No. 344

12. Ibid, No. 374

13. Ibid, Nos. 414 and 421

14. Ibid, No. 465

15. Ibid, No. 539

16. Ibid, No. 553

17. Ibid, No. 569

18. Ibid, No. 599

19. Aspinall-Oglander, Brig.-Gen. C. F. *Military Operations Gallipoli: Volume 1*, Heinemann, 1929, p. 137

20. Blake, Robert, *The Private Papers of Douglas Haig 1914–1919*, Eyre and Spottiswoode 1952, p. 90

21. Callwell, Maj.-Gen. Sir C. E., *Experiences of a Dug-Out 1914–1918*, Constable, 1920, p. 99

22. See *Goose Green* by Mark Adkin (Orion 1997) for the hazards of landing with untried troops. The parallels with 1915 are numerous.

23. Aspinall-Oglander, Brig.-Gen. C. F., *Military Operations Gallipoli: Volume 1*, Heinemann, 1929, p. 268

24. Ibid, pp. 269–70

25. Callwell, op.cit., p. 99

10. Stalemate at Gallipoli, 1915

1. PRO. CAB 19/31, Cable No. 628

2. Ibid, No. 632

3. Ibid, No. 634

4. Ibid, No. 634

5. Ibid, No. 635

6. Ibid, No. 720

7. Aspinall-Oglander, Brig.-Gen. C. F., *Military Operations Gallipoli: Volume 1*, Heinemann, 1929. See Chapter XVII 'Reinforcements' for a full discussion of this problem.

8. Bean, C.E.W., *The Story of Anzac Volume 1*, Angus & Robertson, 1921, p. 605

9. PRO. CAB 19/31, Cable No. 732

10. Ibid, No. 742

11. Aspinall-Oglander, Brig.-Gen. C. F., *Military Operations Gallipoli: Volume 1*, Heinemann, 1929, p. 332

12. Ibid. p. 333

13. Hamilton, Gen. Sir Ian, *Gallipoli Diary*, Edward Arnold 1920, Vol. 1 pp. 201 and 206

14. PRO. CAB 19/31, Cable No. 768

15. Ibid, No. 774

16. Ibid, No. 791

17. Ibid, No. 810

18. Ibid, No. 836

19. Ibid, No. 811

20. Ibid, No. 823

21. Callwell, Maj.-Gen. Sir C.E., *Experiences of a Dug-Out 1914–1918*, Constable, 1920, p. 213

22. PRO. CAB 19/31, Cable No. 852

23. Ibid, No. 881

24. Ibid, No. 894

25. Ibid, No. 903

26. Ibid, No. 919

27. Ibid, No. 1044

28. Ibid, No. 1049

29. Ibid, No. 1075

30. Murray, Joseph, *Gallipoli As I Saw It*, William Kimber, 1985, p. 64

31. PRO. CAB 19/31, Cable No. 1075

32. Ibid, No. 1081

33. These cables are depressingly frequent. See Nos. 1124, 1187 and 1193 as examples.

34. Pro. CAB 19/31 No. 1180

35. Walter Braithwaite to Hunter-Weston, 16 June 1915, Hamilton Archives 7/1/21

36. PRO. CAB 19/31. Cable No. 1129A

37. Ibid, No. 1147A

38. Ibid, No. 1167

39. Ibid, No. 1179

40. Hamilton to Gerald Ellison, 10 July 1915. Hamilton Archives 7/1/17

41. PRO. CAB 19/31, Cable No. 1233

42. Ibid, No. 1250

43. Ibid, No. 1316

44. Ibid, No. 1360

45. Ibid, No. 1374

46. Ibid, No. 1494
47. Ibid, No. 1547
48. Ibid, No. 1682
49. Ibid, No. 1688
50. Ibid, No. 1697
51. Ibid, No. 1711
52. Hamilton Archives 7/4/23 (Note by Lt Gen Sir Frederick Stopford 11 July 1915)

11. Defeat at Gallipoli, 1915

1. Aspinall-Oglander, Brig.-Gen. C. F., *Military Operations: Gallipoli Volume 2*, Heinemann, 1932, p. 152
2. Ibid, p. 234
3. Ibid, p. 247
4. Ibid, p. 200
5. Ibid, p. 277
6. PRO. CAB 19/31, Cable No. 1783
7. Ibid, No. 1791
8. Ibid, No. 1802
9. Ibid, No. 1815
10. Ibid, No. 1853 for this and quote re: 54th Division.
11. Ibid, No. 1853
12. Ibid, No. 1895
13. Scott, Peter, 'Guy Dawnay and the Evacuation of Gallipoli', *The Great War 1914–1918*, Vol. 3 No. 2 February 1991
14. See the article by Nicholas Hiley, 'Enough Glory for All: Ellis Ashmead-Bartlett and Sir Ian Hamilton at the Dardanelles', *Journal of Strategic Studies*, Vol. 16 No. 2, June 1993 pp. 203–65
15. Hamilton, Gen. Sir Ian, *Gallipoli Diary*, Vol. 2, Edward Arnold, 1920, p. 236
16. PRO. CAB 19/31, Cable No. 2414A
17. Ibid, No. 2424A
18. Ibid, No. 2443
19. Brett, M. V., *The Journals and Letters of Reginald, Viscount Esher* Vol. 3, Nicholson & Watson, 1934, entry for 13 October 1915.
20. Fewster, K., *Gallipoli Correspondent*, Allen & Unwin, 1983, p. 169

12. The Dardanelles Commission, 1915–18

1. PRO. CAB 19/29, Memorandum by Gen. Sir Ian Hamilton on a letter from Mr K. A. Murdoch to the Prime Minister of the Australian Commonwealth, 26 November 1915
2. See Hamilton Archives, Files 7/3/36

3. Cooper, Duff, *Old Men Forget*, Hart-Davis, 1953, p. 56

4. Bombardier Clarke et al. to Ian Hamilton, 18 April 1916, Hamilton Archives 7/9/2

5. Lady Jean Hamilton's diary, 11 September 1916, Hamilton Archives 20/1/3

6. Hamilton, Gen. Sir Ian, *Listening for the Drums*, Faber, 1944, p. 260

7. PRO. CAB 19/1, First Report of Dardanelles Commission. paragraph 'n'

8. Ibid, paragraph 'p'

9. Ibid, p. 40

10. Mary Kay, later Mrs George Shield, became Hamilton's secretary in 1916 and remained in post until his death in 1947. She continued as literary executor of his papers and, scouring the media for all things related to Hamilton and Gallipoli, added greatly to the archives. See her devastating critique of Moorehead's *Gallipoli*, dated 26 May 1956, in Hamilton Archives 17/115.

11. Ian Hamilton to Brig. Gen. Winter, 26 September 1917, Hamilton Archives 8/1/66

12. Walter Braithwaite to Ian Hamilton, 14 March 1917, Hamilton Archives 8/1/13

13. PRO. CAB 19/29, Notes and Impressions of Gallipoli Campaign by Lt.-Col. Fawcus, 12 December 1916

14. PRO. CAB 19/30, Statement by Maj.-Gen. Russell

15. PRO. CAB 19/31, Statement by Lt.-Col. Street, RA, 17 December 1916

16. PRO. CAB 19/28, Statement by Lt.-Gen. Altham

17. Allanson to Dardanelles Commission. Reply to Question 11,759, 19 January 1917, Hamilton Archives 8/2/1

18. Braithwaite to Dardanelles Commission, Hamilton Archives 8/2/10–11. Reply to Question 13398

19. Braithwaite to Dardanelles Commission, Reply to Question 13,590, Hamilton Archives 8/2/10–11

20. Braithwaite to Dardanelles Commission, Reply to Question 13,574, Hamilton Archives 8/2/10–11

21. See Stuermer, H., *Two War Years in Constantinople: sketches of German and Young Turkish ethics and politics*, Hodder & Stoughton, 1917

22. PRO. CAB 19/1, Final Report of Dardanelles Commission, 4 December 1917, p. 86, paragraphs 1–4

23. Ibid, pp. 87–8, paragraph 9

24. Ibid, p. 87, paragraph 7

25. Ibid, p. 89, paragraph 3

26. Hamilton Archives 15/3/14

27. Hamilton to Churchill, 11 July 1917, Hamilton Archives 8/1/16

28. Hamilton to Churchill, 27 October 1917, Hamilton Archives 8/1/16

29. Hamilton to Churchill, 1 August 1918, Hamilton Archives 8/1/16

30. Hamilton to W.K. Haselden, 28 March 1918, in author's collection

13. Post-war Life, 1918–47

1. Hamilton, Gen. Sir Ian, *The Millennium*, Edward Arnold, 1919, p. 26
2. Ibid, p. 48
3. Ibid, p. 156
4. Hamilton Archives 16/1, 12 October 1918
5. Ibid, 16/15, 22 April 1920
6. Ibid, 16/18, 4 August 1920
7. Ibid, 16/19, 10 October 1920
8. Ibid, 16/20, 11 November 1920
9. Ibid, 16/43, 8 June 1922
10. Ibid, 16/50, 16 September 1922
11. Hamilton to Eddie Marsh, 28 July 1919, Hamilton Archives 13/24
12. Hamilton Archives 16/12, 5 November 1919
13. Ibid, 16/42, 1 June 1922
14. Ibid, 13/88 and Hamilton 19/27: *Life and Letters*, Vol III, No 18, November 1929
15. Hamilton, Gen. Sir Ian, *Gallipoli Diary*, Edward Arnold, 1920, p. viii
16. Ibid. See the entries in late March and early April during the planning phase of the campaign.
17. Hamilton, Gen. Sir Ian, *The Commander*, Hollis & Carter, 1957, p. 100
18. Ibid, p. 66
19. Hamilton Archives 7/9/5
20. Aspinall-Oglander, Brig. Gen. C.F., *Military Operations Gallipoli: Volume 1*, Heinemann, 1929, p. vi
21. Ibid, p. vii
22. Ibid, p. ix
23. Hamilton Archives 16/409, 25 November 1932
24. This remarkable film was reissued commercially on video cassette in 1999 by DD Video. The notes state that this is 'the only known film footage of the commander of the ill-fated Gallipoli campaign', but in the 1920s Hamilton had appeared as himself in the Gallipoli film *Tell England*.
25. Ibid, 16/462
26. Ibid.
27. Ibid.
28. Ibid.

Postscript

1. Liddell Hart Archives 1/351

Sources and Bibliography

Place of publication is London unless otherwise stated.

Manuscript Sources

Ian Hamilton Papers, Liddell Hart Centre for Military Archives, Kings' College, London

Basil Liddell Hart Papers, Liddell Hart Centre for Military Archives, KCL

Dardanelles Commission of Inquiry Papers, CAB 19, Public Record Office, Kew

Department of Documents, Imperial War Museum, London

Published Sources

Amery. L. S. (ed.), *The Times History of the War in South Africa*, 6 volumes, Sampson Low, 1900–1909

Arthur, Sir George, *Life of Lord Kitchener*, 3 volumes, Macmillan, 1920

Ashmead-Bartlett, E., *The Uncensored Dardanelles*, Hutchinson, 1928

Aspinall-Oglander, Brig.-Gen. C. F., *Military Operations Gallipoli: Volume 1*, Heinemann, 1929

——, *Military Operations Gallipoli: Volume 2*, Heinemann, 1932

——, Cecil, *Roger Keyes*, Hogarth Press, 1951

Austin, Ron, *The White Gurkhas: Australians at the Second Battle of Krithia*, McCrae, Australia 1989

Bean, C.E.W., *The Story of Anzac Volume 1*, Angus & Robertson, Australia 1921

——, *The Story of Anzac Volume 2*, Angus & Robertson, Australia 1924

Birdwood, Field Marshall Lord, *Khaki and Gown*, Ward Lock, 1941

Blake, Robert, *The Private Papers of Douglas Haig 1914–1919*, Eyre & Spottiswood, 1952

Brett, M.V. (ed.), *The Journals and Letters of Reginald, Viscount Esher*, Nicholson & Watson 1934

Brock, Michael and Eleanor (eds), *H. H. Asquith, Letters to Venetia Stanley*, OUP, Oxford, 1982

Burness, Peter, *The Nek*, Kangaroo Press, Australia, 1996

Bush, Capt. Eric, RN, *Gallipoli*, Allen & Unwin, 1975

Callwell, Col. C. E., *Tirah 1897*, Constable, 1911

——, Maj.-Gen. Sir C.E., *Experiences of a Dug-Out 1914–1918*, Constable, 1920

——, *The Dardanelles*, Constable, 1924

Cassar, G.H., *The French and the Dardanelles*, Allen & Unwin, 1971

Chatterton, E. Keble, *Dardanelles Dilemma*, Rich & Cowan, 1935

Chisholm, Ruari, *Ladysmith*, Osprey, 1979

Churchill, Randolph S., *Winston S. Churchill: Youth 1874–1900*, Heinemann, 1966

——, *Winston S. Churchill: Companion Vol. 2 Part 1 1901–1907*, Heinemann, 1969

Churchill, Winston S., *Ian Hamilton's March*, Longman, 1900

Cooper, Duff, *Old Men Forget*, Rupert Hart-Davis, 1953

Delage, Edmond, *The Tragedy of the Dardanelles*, introduction by Sir Ian Hamilton, Bodley Head, 1932

Ellison, Lt.-Gen. Sir Gerald, *The Perils of Amateur Strategy*, Longman, 1926

Evans, Michael, *Amphibious Operations: The Projection of Sea Power Ashore*, Brassey's 1990

Fewster, K., *Gallipoli Correspondent: Frontline Diary of C. Bean*, Allen & Unwin, Australia, 1983

Gilbert, Martin, *Winston S. Churchill Volume 3: 1914–1916*, Heinemann, 1971

Gillam, Maj. John, *Gallipoli Diary*, Strong Oak Press, 1989

Griffith, Kenneth. *Thank God We Kept the Flag Flying: The Siege and Relief of Ladysmith 1899–1900*, Hutchinson, 1974

Hamer, W.S., *The British Army: Civil-Military Relations 1885–1905*, OUP, 1970

Hamilton, Capt. Ian, *The Fighting of the Future*, Kegan, Paul, Trench, 1885

——, Lt.-Gen. Sir Ian, *A Staff Officer's Scrap Book Volume 1*, Edward Arnold, 1905

——, *A Staff Officer's Scrap Book Volume 2*, Edward Arnold, 1907

——, *Compulsory Service*, John Murray, 1910

——, *The Millennium*, Edward Arnold, 1919

——, *Gallipoli Diary*, 2 volumes, Edward Arnold, 1920

——, *The Soul and Body of an Army*, Edward Arnold, 1921

——, *The Friends of England*, Allen & Unwin 1923

——, *When I was a Boy*, Faber, 1939

——, *Listening for the Drums*, Faber, 1944

——, (ed. Major A. Farrar-Hockley), *The Commander*, Hollis & Carter, 1957

Hamilton, Ian B. M., *The Happy Warrior: A Life of General Sir Ian Hamilton*, Cassell, 1966

Hamilton, Vereker, *Things That Happened*, Edward Arnold, 1925

Hargrave, John, *The Suvla Bay Landings*, Macdonald, 1964

Hickie, Michael, *Gallipoli*, John Murray, 1995

Higgins, Trumbull, *Winston Churchill and the Dardanelles*, Heinemann, 1963

James, Robert Rhodes, *Gallipoli*, Batsford, 1965

Jenkins, Roy, *Asquith*, Collins, 1964

Kannengiesser, Hans, *Campaign in Gallipoli*, Hutchinson, 1926

Keyes, Admiral Sir Roger, *The Fight for Gallipoli*, Eyre & Spottiswoode, 1941

Kruger, Rayne, *Goodbye Dolly Gray:The Story of the Boer War*, Pan, 1974

Laffin, John, *Damn the Dardanelles!*, Osprey, 1980

Lee, Celia, *A Soldier's Wife: Lady Jean Hamilton 1861–1941*, Lee, 2000

Liddle, Peter, *Men of Gallipoli*, Allen Lane, 1976

—— & Cecil, Hugh, *Facing Armageddon*, Leo Cooper, 1996

Mackenzie, Compton, *Gallipoli Memories*, Cassell, 1929

Masefield, John, *Gallipoli*, Heinemann, 1916

Moorehead, Alan, *Gallipoli*, Hamish Hamilton, 1956

Moorhouse, Geoffrey, *Hell's Foundations: A Town, Its Myths and Gallipoli*, Hodder & Stoughton, 1992

Moseley, Sydney, *The Truth About the Dardanelles*, Cassell, 1916

Murray, Joseph, *Gallipoli As I Saw It*, William Kimber, 1985

North, John, *Gallipoli: The Fading Vision*, Faber, 1936

Pakenham, Thomas, *The Boer War*, Weidenfeld, & Nicolson, 1979

Pemberton, T.J., *Gallipoli Today*, introduction by Sir Ian Hamilton, Ernest Benn, 1926

Powell, Geoffrey, *Buller: A Scapegoat?*, Leo Cooper, 1994

Ransford, Oliver, *The Battle for Majuba Hill*, John Murray, 1967

Roberts, Field Marshall Lord, *Forty-One Years in India*, Macmillan, 1898

Sampson, Victor & Hamilton, Ian, *Anti-Commando*, Faber, 1931

Serle, Geoffrey, *John Monash: A Biography*, Melbourne University Press, Australia, 1982

Sixsmith, Maj. Gen. E. K. G., *British Generalship in the Twentieth Century*, Arms & Armour Press, 1970

Smith-Dorrien, Gen. Sir H., *Memories of 48 Years Service*, John Murray, 1925

Spiers, Edward, *The Late Victorian Army 1868–1902*, Manchester University Press, 1992

Steel, Nigel & Hart, Peter, *Defeat at Gallipoli*, Macmillan, 1994

Travers, Tim, *The Killing Ground*, Allen & Unwin, 1987

Vagts, Alfred, *Landing Operations*, Military Service Publishing Co., USA, 1952

Winter, Denis, *25 April 1915*, University of Queensland Press, Australia, 1994

Index

Throughout the index General Sir Ian Hamilton is referred to as 'IH'. Individuals' ranks are the most senior noted in the book. Vessels and literary works are given in italics.